Women on the Ball

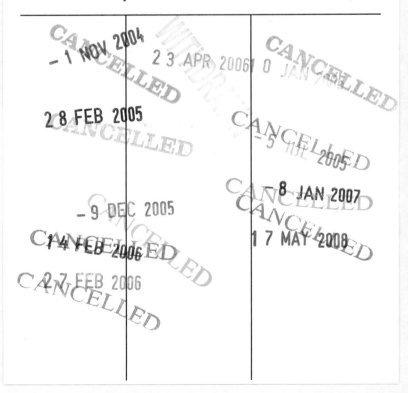

LIBRARY
Tel: 01244 375444   Ext: 3301

This book is to be returned on or before the
last date stamped below. Overdue charges
will be incurred by the late return of books.

UNIVERSITY COLLEGE
CHESTER

About the author

Sue Lopez played for Southampton Women's Football Club from 1966 to 1986. In 1971 she spent a season with the Italian club Roma, helping the team to win the national cup and to be runners-up in the semi-professional national league. She played for England from 1973 to 1979, winning 22 caps, and became one of first five women FA Preliminary Award coaches in 1974. Today she is the only practising FA Advanced Licence coach (gained in 1990). She coached at USA soccer camps in the 1980s and, in 1994, at Jan Smisek's elite women's camp and Michelle Akers' elite student camp, staffed by international coaches. She served on the Women's FA executive from January 1992 until the FA takeover in July 1993, and was manager of the Welsh women's national team for the 1995–96 season.

Sue Lopez was a Physical Education (PE) teacher in Hampshire for 16 years and a visiting lecturer at Roehampton Institute London in 1994. She gained her Masters Degree in PE at Southampton University in 1985. In 1994 she became the first woman FA Coaching Representative, organising coaching awards for Hampshire FA and, in 1995, coordinator of Southampton Football Club's girls' football coaching courses.

She has been a guest coach and speaker on several occasions: in 1992, at the Scottish Sports Council/Scottish Women's FA seminar 'Heading for the Future'; as guest speaker at the FA's inaugural Women's Football Conference at Lilleshall in Shropshire the same year; and in 1995 at the National Soccer Coaches' Association of America convention in Washington. She also represented the FA at the inaugural FIFA conference on women's football in Zurich in 1992. In 1995 she was elected to the committee of the Association of Football Coaches and Teachers as their women's football representative and in 1996 to the board of directors of the USA-based Women's Soccer Foundation.

Women on the Ball
A Guide to Women's Football

Sue Lopez

Scarlet Press

Published by Scarlet Press
5 Montague Road, London E8 2HN

British Library Cataloguing-in-Publication Data
A catalogue record for this book is available from
the British Library

ISBN   1 85727 016 9 pb
ISBN   1 85727 021 5 hb

Designed and produced for Scarlet Press by
Chase Production Services, Chadlington, OX7 3LN
Typeset from author's disk by
Stanford DTP Services, Milton Keynes
Illustrations printed by the Witney Press
Printed in the EC by J.W. Arrowsmith Ltd, Bristol

This book is dedicated to all those who supported me over two years of research and writing, especially my mother, Val and Larry. To all the early pioneer players, especially Jean Seymour, whose memories and hopes for the future were an inspiration, and to Flo Bilton, who, as an early administrator, symbolises those who worked genuinely for the love of women's football, especially on behalf of the players. Without the commitment and passion of women like these there would probably be little organised women's football in England today. My final dedication is to the new pioneers, worldwide, to whom we look to steward the game into its challenging but potentially exciting future.

Contents

Foreword

Professor Sheila Scraton
Leeds Metropolitan University

During the 1990s women's football in England has begun to receive the interest and recognition that it deserves. Over a weekend many women will be involved in the game either as spectators, playing locally in the many registered clubs, or perhaps officiating on the touchline, or as the referee. However, although women's football continues to grow and flourish it has done so only through the determination of those involved and despite the numerous barriers and constraints that have been put in its way. This book provides a comprehensive and detailed account of women's involvement in the game. It may be surprising to some readers to find that women's football has a long history and that back in 1920 a match between Dick, Kerr Ladies and St Helens attracted a crowd of 53,000 at Goodison Park with 8,000 locked out! Far from being a 'post-feminist' phenomenon, resulting from the advances made by women in the past 30 years, it is a sport that women have played here since the last century. Yet it is a sport that has 'suffered' from being traditionally defined as unsuitable for women, it has been controlled and influenced by the male sporting establishment and continues today to face problems that are associated with the cultural and social expectations about what it is to be a 'sporting female'.[1]

One of the themes running through the book is the relationship of the women's game to the male football administration. Since the end of the First World War women's football has been largely controlled and informed by the male Football Association. Unsurprisingly, the control and definition of the women's game has been founded on ideological beliefs and ideas about what it is to be a 'woman' and to be 'feminine'. Although these ideas and beliefs have shifted over time they have had a pronounced effect on women's opportunities to develop as players and to organise and play *their* game. Soon after the end of the First World War, and just as women were really establishing themselves on the football pitch, the FA banned women's teams from playing on affiliated clubs' grounds (1921) citing football as being unsuitable for women. This had the profound effect of virtually halting the growth of women's football right up until the success of the England team in the 1966 World Cup which sparked interest back into the women's game. This demonstrates the power that the men's sporting establishment had to impede women's sporting progress and to intervene just at the moment when women were seriously challenging the sanctity of the traditionally 'masculine' domain of men's football.

Since the 'renaissance' of women's football after 1966 it is possible to trace the continued power of the male football administration over the development of women's football, even throughout the period when the Women's Football Association (WFA) formally administered the game. Since 1993, a women's committee has run the game but it is dominated by the top FA administrators and county FA men, with just three representatives from the Women's Football Alliance, a forum for clubs that meets approximately three times a year. The England manager and assistant manager are male and although there is a female Women's Football Coordinator, her decisions have to be agreed by her male line-manager, the women's football committee and the full FA council committee.

In coaching there is a similar gender imbalance. Women wishing to become coaches in football have to enter a male arena with male coaches and colleagues, have to learn male coaching technical jargon and accept a particular style of coaching that may not be the same for men and women. As there are so few qualified women coaches it is difficult to provide 'women-only' courses and there is little to encourage women to remain in the game as leaders. Most women who do work as coaches do so in women-defined sports where there are no male players.[2] Consequently it is men that dominate the coaching and administration of women's football with most school teams, women's clubs and representative teams run by men, coached by men, and officiated by men.

What appears strongly from the pages of this book is that women constantly have to seek approval and support from the male establishment for the continued development of the women's game. The message that comes through is that it remains a 'man's game' and that women are allowed to play only under certain conditions. This is not to deny the tremendous advances that have been achieved by many significant and committed women in the world of women's football. However, the game continues to advance under the umbrella of the 'real' game, i.e. men's football. The reasons for this are complex and contradictory. In order to understand how and why women's football has developed the way it has, there has to be some awareness of the gendered power relations that have defined sport and the social world in which we live. Because there have been such strong and powerful messages about 'femininity', sports that have been defined as 'masculine' have continued to be seen as the domain of men. Although the stereotypes of 'femininity' and 'masculinity' have shifted over time, there remains a view that although women may now, in the 1990s, have legitimate rights of access to play football they may do so only on the terms and conditions laid down by men.

The problem of uneven gender structures and practices is not unique to women's football. As Jennifer Hargreaves points out, this issue is linked to separatism in the organisation and administration of sports. Women's sports that remain separate in their administration and organisation may control the decision-making processes and resources but often do so from a position of difference that confirms their lower status. In the long term this serves only to institutionalise gender power differences. Women's football faces difficulties in that it is a traditionally 'male-defined' sport that cannot compete for resources and control from a marginalised position. It will be in a position to control its own development only when, or if, women who are centrally involved in the game have an equal say in its administration and development. This will involve the awareness by those involved in the sport that this can only happen when the gender power relations are challenged, ideas about 'femininity' and 'acceptable' female sports are contested and women's football is accepted in its own right and does not have to compete or be 'the same as' men's football. This book is crucial in raising these issues by placing women's football today in the context of its historical development.

However, it is extremely difficult to create an 'even playing field' for women's and men's football when other areas, that remain so uneven, provide the contemporary context for its existence. One of these areas is education and the opportunities that girls and boys have to play football in school. In England, Physical Education in school traditionally has been single-sex, with girls and boys being taught separately and curriculum activities being differentiated by gender. In primary schools the philosophy for some years has been for integration in primary PE although there remain many schools that still separate the girls and boys for competitive team games. For most young people in England the school is the most influential place for motivating them into sport participation and providing them with the opportunities to play in teams. Girls have had to fight for their rights to play competitive football in primary schools, as evidenced by the case of Theresa Bennett, aged 11 years in 1978, when she took the FA to court for alleged sexual discrimination over not being allowed to play football in a local league with boys. Although she lost her case on appeal, she made national news and created an awareness both in and out of school about the anomalies of a law that discriminated against pre-pubescent girls in sport. Eventually, in 1991, the FA allowed under-11 mixed football. This demonstrates not only the historical legacy of gender differentiation in school sport but also that struggles to create both institutional and cultural change can be successful.

However, although girls now do have the right to play competitive football up to the age of 11 years, the situation in secondary schools, for those aged between 11 and 18, is quite different. Secondary-school PE has been characterised in its historical development by policies and images of difference. My own research, in the mid-1980s, into girls' PE showed that the majority of teaching remained single-sex and few schools, in the local education authority that was the focus of the research, were providing the opportunities for girls to play football.[3] The research revealed, also, the stereotyped ideas held by the women PE teachers about girls' abilities and perceived needs in the area of sport and PE. These were based on notions of 'femininity' including ideologies and images of physical ability, motherhood and sexuality. This latter finding is even more crucial than the awareness of the lack of institutional opportunity for girls to participate. In the 1990s, with the National Curriculum and more co-educational teaching in PE, if the stereotyped ideas and expectations of the teachers remain unchanged then girls will remain disadvantaged in their access to, and experience of, non-traditional sports for women. Anne Flintoff's research into PE teacher training suggests that we should not presume that these stereotyped views no longer exist.[4] Although girls increasingly are receiving more opportunities to play football in school, there remain powerful messages about appropriate girls' and boys' sports. Football is still marginalised from the more 'female-appropriate' sports such as netball, hockey and rounders. There are few school teams for girls' football and girls and boys over 11 years cannot play together in league teams.

The lack of opportunity for girls to become centrally involved in football in school between 11 and 18 years creates problems in motivating and encouraging girls and young women into football in their own time. Unlike some European countries (for example, Germany and Norway), England does not have a strong tradition of junior sport in clubs. Most competitive sport for young people is organised and controlled through the school system. Current comparative research that is investigating women's experiences of sport in England, Germany, Norway and Spain identifies a real gap in English women's football experiences between the ages of 11 and 16 years, unlike that of their German and Norwegian equivalents who, during this period, were playing regularly in well-organised club settings.[5]

Prejudice against women's sport in general, and women's football in particular, continues to be evidenced in the media coverage that it receives. There is little coverage of women's football on television or in the press. There is plenty of evidence that women's sports are marginalised and trivialised by the media and women's football is no exception.[6] The messages transmitted daily on the back pages of our press, or at the weekend on our televisions, tell us that men's sport is important. The role models in football are men, with few girls or young women even knowing the names of the women national players. Women continually are seen to be on the periphery in the sport media and if present, presented in terms of their appearance or family role rather than for their abilities as *sportswomen*. The media's construction of the debate about women's suitability to play football has been reduced to simplistic and prejudiced arguments and a fear of seeing their notions of 'femininity' and sexuality challenged. Yet this book reminds us that women's football has a long history and that 70 years ago people turned out in their thousands to watch the women's game. At that time women's football was newsworthy as a sporting event with considerable media interest. The argument that 'no one would be interested in watching a women's game' seems conveniently to forget the historical evidence.

The book is, therefore, both timely and important in raising the profile of women's football. It is important to recognise the struggles that the women's game has faced and continues to face in a sporting world founded on gender power differentials. Yet there is evidence from other countries that women can make inroads into the male establishment and thus have more influence over the development of their sport. In Ireland, Scotland and Germany there are women's committees running women's football, with Germany and Scotland having all-female representation. Norway's executive includes several women, with no distinction made between women's and men's football, except that a male will always be in charge of the senior male team. Therefore, it is seen as quite acceptable for a woman executive member to deal with the male U21 team and to travel with them to their fixtures. Many of the top nations in women's football, for example Norway (current World Champions), Germany (current European Champions) and the USA (World Champions in 1991) have given women more autonomy, created a well-funded and efficient development structure and have involved ex-players in the development of the game. These developments reflect not only the sporting culture of these countries but also broader social and cultural differences. However, all sport must be placed within the historical and cultural context in which it exists. This book gives us an insight into the English game; an understanding of the exciting opportunities that there are for the continued development of women's football and the barriers that still need to be hurdled in order for women to have *real* opportunities to participate. It is to be hoped that, in the future, football will no longer only be 'a man's game' but will be a sport that includes women, whereby their skills and abilities will allow it to be defined also as 'a woman's game'.

Preface

Football has become one of the fastest-growing sports for women around the world. This book looks at the history and structure of the women's game in England, and at the global developments that have been encouraged by the women's football championships organised by world and European governing bodies. In only a decade its popularity and success have grown dramatically in the USA, and in Sweden and Norway it is the most popular sport for girls and women. As a result, there has been a burgeoning amount of observation and opinion about the women's game. Often this commentary has been made without any sense of the game's history and has only served to marginalise, devalue and propagate an image of novelty.

This book sets out to fill some of the gaps in information about English women's football, from the early days when women played in factory teams to the 'modern era' from 1966, which saw a remarkable rebirth of the game after it had almost been extinguished by the Football Association's ban in 1921. It also looks at other issues that have an impact on the development of the game: referees, coaching, fans, initiatives in schools and community projects, and the media.

While the author acknowledges the invaluable support of many men involved in women's football, central to the book are the women who have challenged male authority, not only as players, but as referees, coaches and administrators. Although football is now an acceptable game to play, in some countries women are still unable to act as leaders and make decisions about their own sport. As participation rates grow and the need to improve standards increases, a strong case is made for using ex-players' expertise and empathy for the game – they just need to be given the opportunity and resources. This book illustrates the tremendous progress certain nations have made with respect to encouraging women in all aspects of the game, and armed with this information, others can learn from them. While I am encouraged by these developments I hope to see the day when women genuinely lead the game in England.

Sue Lopez

Acknowledgements

This history could not have been written without the help of the women who are themselves the subjects of this book. They patiently provided interviews, information and precious archive material about their football careers. I thank Gail Newsham for kindly providing invaluable information on Dick, Kerr Ladies and David Marlowe and Martin Reagan who provided source material about the Women's FA and the England team respectively. Colin Aldis and Wilf Frith were very helpful with current information, as well as the English Schools Football Association chairman, John Morton, and Paul Power of the Professional Footballers' Association (PFA). I am particularly indebted to Rainer Hennies, Thorsten Frennstedt and Joop de Graaf, who supplied international information and for whom nothing was ever too much trouble; and to the translators who helped with the German written material, Ruthie Brocklehurst, Dorte McCourt and Angela Rankin. I also thank Sonia Denoncourt, Bente Skogvang, Inger Marie Vingdal, Ruth Callard, Ann Moses and Jan Smisek, who all found time to respond to all my requests for material at short notice, and Sheila Scraton for interrupting her busy schedule to offer her invaluable contribution and support. John Williams at the Sir Norman Chester Centre for Football Research provided assistance throughout the whole project and Gill Clarke gave information and guidance regarding referees. Among many others I thank Michele Adams, Vic Akers, Debbie Bampton, David Barber, Sue Barwick, Lesley Boomer, Sue Buckett, Pat Chapman, Josie Clifford, Yvonne Cooper, Ted Copeland, Gill Coultard, Helen Croft, Steve Darby, Liz Deighan, Eileen Foreman, Keld Gantzhorn, Sylvia Gore, Pat Gregory, April Heinrichs, John Hughes, Helen Jevons, Julian Lillington, Jill Long, Maureen McGonigle, Niamh O'Donoghue, Sheila Parker, Brian Parrish, Hannelore Ratzeburg, Kelly Simmons, Marieanne Spacey, Chris Unwin, Lou Waller, Anita White, the editor of *FIFA News*, the Hants FA, the FA's Public Affairs Department and all the women who participated in the referees' questionnaire. Finally, I thank Avis Lewallen and Alex Fenner at Scarlet Press for their guidance and support.

1 Invading the pitch

Men's football was officially recognised in 1863 by the Football Association (FA), the governing body of English football, and in 1888 the first professional league was established with 12 teams. By the 1900s football was becoming a popular spectator sport with crowds of approximately 100,000 attending the Cup Finals at Crystal Palace, Manchester United's Old Trafford ground, and Chelsea's Stamford Bridge. The first final at Wembley, in 1923, attracted around 200,000 spectators, although no official gate was recorded.[1]

It is not known precisely how many women were following or playing the sport at this time but Jennifer Hargreaves, in her book *Sporting Females*, says: 'There was no question that sports were the natural domain of men and that to be good at them was to be essentially masculine. Whereas men were identified with culture, and with their roles at work and in other spheres outside the home, women were symbolically aligned to nature and to their reproductive roles and positions as wives and mothers in the home.'[2] Many women would agree with Hargreaves' analysis with regard to women and sport at this time and some would say things have not changed significantly between then and now. Early organised sports and physical education for females were 'marked by their insular, separatist nature, developing mostly in the private spheres of schools, colleges and clubs ... it was easy to define them as qualitatively different, in tune with conventional ideas about "femininity" and "masculinity"'.[3] Hargreaves describes the idealised male sporting body – strong, aggressive and muscular – as the popular symbol of masculinity against which women, characterised as relatively powerless and inferior, have been measured. Middle-class educational establishments, such as Roedean, under autonomous pioneering headmistresses, were where the traditional Victorian male public school games, such as cricket, tennis and field hockey could be adopted by girls. The pioneering women's colleges, such as Girton (Cambridge) and Somerville and Newnham (Oxford), produced hockey players who were to go on and start the All England Women's Hockey Association in 1895 (this remained as a separate association until a vote was taken in 1996 to join the men's association – officially recognised on 1 June 1997). At this time too, women could play tennis at Wimbledon but they were still excluded from the modern Olympics of 1896.

In elementary schools, however, working-class girls and boys had few sports facilities. Netball for girls and football for boys were only gradually introduced with the main aim of their attaining basic fitness for health and, in particular, military conscription for the boys. Undoubtedly, the separatist nature of schools, colleges and clubs helped women's sport develop, but 'in order to survive, organised female sports tended to accommodate the traditional biological assumptions rather than openly challenge them'.[4] The fact that both netball and hockey have remained the accepted games for girls to play, with football being vehemently eschewed by schools until very recently, illustrates this point.

It is, therefore, all the more remarkable that in this social setting the first recorded organised game of women's football took place. This was on 23 March 1895, at Crouch End in London, between a team from the north of England and one from the south. The match was organised by a woman player called Nettie Honeyball, who later became the first secretary of the English Ladies' Football Team. The team from the north won comfortably 7–1 but the Manchester *Guardian*'s account of this pioneering fixture focused less on the actual game than on the players' attire – a feature of newspaper reporting that continues even to the present day. Not long after the Crouch End game, another match was played in Newcastle, reputedly attracting a crowd of more than 8,000.[5]

In 1902 the council of the FA issued a warning to its member clubs not to play matches against ladies' teams. Football was considered to be an unsuitable game for women; it offended middle-class propriety and gave concern to some of the medical profession, who felt it would damage female reproductive organs. Football was predominantly a working-class game for men – controlled by middle-class men at the FA. Today, football is England's major national winter sport, alternating with cricket in the summer, and English sport remains one of the most distinctly male of all social institutions.

Dick, Kerr Ladies

A huge growth in women's football took place during the time of the First World War when women were called upon to fill the void in the factories left by men who had gone to fight. The women not only took over the male roles in the workplace but spontaneously took over the traditional male pastimes, such as football.

The most well-known women's football team formed during this period was Dick, Kerr Ladies. The team was named after W.B. Dick and John Kerr's engineering works in Preston, that made tramway and railway equipment. The factory began producing ammunition during the war and female employees filled the depleted workforce. Gail Newsham has recorded the history of the team in her book, *In a League of their own!* and her work provides much of the information there is known about Dick, Kerr Ladies.[6]

Initially, the women working in the factory joined the apprentices in kicking a ball about, during tea and lunch breaks, in the works' yard. The women eventually challenged the men to a proper match. Their right-half, Alice Barlow, explained: 'I suppose the women were "kicking up!" Before, we had to have the men's things ready before they went off to football on Saturday afternoons and we had to stay at home and get their tea ready for when they came back. Women had had enough!'[7] Grace Sibbert worked at the Dick, Kerr factory while her husband was fighting in France. She organised the first proper match and in recognition of her achievements was presented with the match ball afterwards. A draughtsman at the firm, Alfred Frankland, then offered to organise and train the newly-formed women's team. Other factory teams began to appear, especially in the north-west of England, including another Preston team from the Arundel Coulthard Foundry. They challenged Dick, Kerr Ladies to a charity match, played at the professional league ground of Preston North End, Deepdale. For no fee, on Christmas Day 1917, in front of a crowd of 10,000, they raised in excess of £600 for wounded soldiers at the Moor Park military hospital.[8]

Undoubtedly, the initial appeal for the spectators was the novelty of seeing women play football and, at first, the crowds were inclined to be amused. Gradually, however, people started to respect the women's skill and enthusiasm. With the dearth of men's football, and increasing need to raise money for charity to help families and soldiers, it wasn't long before Dick, Kerr Ladies' matches became one of the most popular spectator attractions of the time. Working together for the common war effort gave men, and for the first time, many women, the opportunity to meet people from different social backgrounds. This provided an important stimulus for the organisational impetus necessary for the establishment of the new factory football teams. No one objected to the women's teams because of the 'patriotic nature' of their fundraising activities. Some were even mixed-sex matches and others were performed in novelty costumes, thus negating accusations that women might be taking their sporting involvement 'too seriously'. However the women playing in Dick, Kerr Ladies were deadly serious. They had the support of the company, who were gaining added publicity, and their regular matches played at Preston North End's ground were welcomed, as the owners gained the extra hire charges and refreshment sales. Soon other women wanted to emulate the Dick, Kerr Ladies. By the end of the 1917–18 season, the famous women, who proudly wore Dick, Kerr Ladies' black-and-white strip, had played four charity matches against local teams at Deepdale: Coulthards, Lancaster, Barrow and Bolton.[9] An article in the Lancashire *Daily Post*, in August 1918, stated that the balance sheet, submitted by Alfred Frankland, recorded a sum of £804 raised that season, which, minus amusement tax and expenses, meant £553 went to charity.

After the war ended many semi-professional men players found work back at Dick, Kerr and Co. and some helped in training the women's team. Often, famous male players and celebrities 'kicked off' and refereed the women's games. Although the war was over, the men had returned to take back the factory jobs and professional football had resumed, there was still a demand for Dick, Kerr Ladies to play benefit matches to help hospitals and bereaved families. The team went from strength to strength, with Alfred Frankland signing up talented players from all around the north-west, finding them work at the factory and lodgings with one of the girls in the team. In 1919 they played Newcastle Ladies at Deepdale. The return match at Newcastle's professional ground, St James' Park, attracted 35,000 spectators.[10] Writers John Williams and Jackie Woodhouse record that in 1920, the team, in effect, became the unofficial England women's national team, astutely adopting a small Union Jack on their playing strip.[11] They travelled throughout Lancashire, Cheshire and Yorkshire playing friendly matches for charity almost every Saturday (they turned down 120 invitations to play that year). In one match they overwhelmed a team representing Scotland by an aggregate of 22–0. The highlight of the year was playing a French XI selected from the few teams that had started playing in Paris. They played four matches against the French at various grounds, Deepdale, Stockport, Hyde Road in Manchester and Chelsea's Stamford Bridge, winning three and drawing one. Alfred Frankland and 16 players then went to Paris for a return game, where the crowd was an estimated 22,000.[12] Despite the 1–1 draw in Paris, they arrived back in Preston to a large and rapturous reception, with Dick, Kerr's factory band marching in front of the team's bus, as they made their way to a celebratory dinner at the firm's canteen. Not long after, two of the French team joined Dick, Kerr Ladies and played their first match against Coventry Ladies at the professional ground of Birmingham City. Another famous game was on Boxing Day, 1920, when at Everton's Goodison Park, Dick, Kerr Ladies beat St Helens 4–0 in front of a crowd of 53,000 with an estimated 10,000 to 14,000 locked outside![13] In the same year, the firm of Dick, Kerr's purchased a new ground called Ashton Park. This was an 83-acre site for the use of employees, with leisure facilities including cricket and football pitches, tennis courts and a nine-hole golf course. Although many of their matches had been played away or at Deepdale (which attracted a larger gate) Dick, Kerr Ladies now had the benefit of training and playing on their own pitch.

In 1921 the team were booked for an average of two games a week all over Great Britain and played 67 matches with a total of over 900,000 spectators.[14] Newsham makes the point that compared with modern-day professional footballers (who play approximately 42 league games but don't have to work full-time in a factory as well), Dick, Kerr Ladies' players were truly remarkable.[15] The women received expenses for loss of work, travel and refreshments, but nothing else. By this time the team had a number of women who worked as nurses, or in other demanding jobs, as well as those who still worked in the factory. Frequently, they had to return long distances from away matches and go straight back to the rigours of factory life or working long shifts at the hospital. Newsham quotes the example of a star player, Joan Whalley, who worked as a bus conductress. On one occasion Joan finished her work shift in the early hours of the morning on the day the team were to depart for a trip around Britain. She got to bed at 1.00 am and had to be up at 5.00 am.

She overslept and arrived 20 minutes late, to find that Alfred Frankland – ever a stickler for time-keeping – and the team, had left without her.[16]

It was in this year they also played at another professional men's ground, Anfield, home of Liverpool. Here they played a Great Britain team containing the best players from London, Barrow-in-Furness, St Helens, as well as Ireland, Scotland and Wales. In front of a crowd of 25,000 (with gate receipts totalling £1,500), they won 9–1.[17]

An unsuitable game for women

By 1921 there were around 150 women's teams in England, mostly in the north and the Midlands.[18] However, there was growing resentment towards women's football within the male football establishment. Large crowds were attracted to the women's games, often bigger than those attending the men's matches. Newsham believes that the women's games were proving more popular than those of male amateur teams and comments that there was 'too much support for women's football and the boys didn't like it'.[19] Rather than attack women's football by questioning their ability to play, accusations of 'financial mismanagement' were engineered. A smear campaign was built upon rumours that too much money was being 'absorbed' in expenses. Newsham quotes the FA's unanimous resolution passed on 5 December 1921:

> Complaints having been made as to football being played by women, the council feel impelled to express their strong opinion that the game of football is quite unsuitable for females and ought not to be encouraged. Complaints have also been made as to the conditions under which some of these matches have been arranged and played, and the appropriation of receipts to other than charitable objects. The council are further of the opinion that an excessive proportion of the receipts are absorbed in expenses and an inadequate percentage devoted to charitable objects. For these reasons the council request clubs belonging to the association to refuse the use of their grounds for such matches.[20]

Dick, Kerr Ladies' players were astounded. They had had nothing to do with the money, other than receive very basic and justifiable expenses. Why didn't the FA take up the matter of misappropriation of funds with Alfred Frankland and the treasurer, rather than penalise the Dick, Kerr Ladies and all other women footballers? Despite protestations from Alfred Frankland, the FA would not change their minds – not for another 50 years. Newsham aptly comments that 'the chauvinists, the medical "experts" and the anti-women's football lobby had won – their threatened male bastion was now safe'.[21] Alfred Frankland died in 1957, at the age of 75, after a 40-year association with Dick, Kerr Ladies. During this time, the team had played 748 games, won 702, drawn 33, lost only 13, and had raised in the region of £150,000 for charity. When Kath Latham became manager after Frankland's death, all that his son, Ronald, handed over was one old scrapbook – incredibly, all the records and correspondence had mysteriously been destroyed. Gail Newsham asks, 'Wouldn't you think that if someone was credited as being the "Father of Women's Football", and was responsible for raising £150,000 for charity, his family would be so proud of his achievement they would want the world to know about it?'[22] The only other reference Newsham makes to Alfred Frankland in this context was when there was 'trouble' at the Dick, Kerr factory in 1926. What the 'trouble' was has never been confirmed, but Frankland was told that the company no longer wanted its name associated with the team and stopped them from playing at Ashton Park. The team had to change its name (officially to Preston – but this was hardly ever used). Newsham says, 'One can only speculate as to whether Alfred Frankland's intentions and involvement in women's football were as pure and as honourable as he would have us believe.' She elaborates only by relating some of the doubts expressed by older players, especially one, who recalls opponents as saying that Dick, Kerr Ladies were 'too expensive to play against'. Dick, Kerr's players didn't understand, they thought opponents were charged only expenses actually incurred and nothing more.[23]

Falling foul of the FA

On 10 December 1921, 25 women's football clubs, out of approximately 150, met in Blackburn and formed the first English Ladies' Football Association (ELFA). At a second meeting, support improved, with 60 clubs in attendance.[24] Women's interest in football was still growing; it was particularly strong in the north and the Midlands, and clubs were beginning to emerge in the south-east and in Southampton and Plymouth in the south-west. The new ELFA issued statements illustrating its determination that: 'there will be no exploiting of the teams in the interest of the man, or the firm, who manages them'.[25] This reflected the apparent 'inevitability' of male control in a world – and a sport – in which male sanction for the activities of women remained, for most, simply a routine fact of life. However, the ELFA lacked the necessary organisational base, support, and sufficient numbers, especially in the south of England, to manage successfully the transition from staging frequent but ad hoc charity matches to an autonomous regional league structure.[26] Although a majority of teams continued playing friendly or charity matches, the FA ban on using affiliated pitches was having its desired effect. Dick, Kerr Ladies were famous enough to be able to continue but for the new developing teams it was difficult to find grounds that were not used by FA-affiliated clubs, or referees who were not associated with affiliated football. Even the professional players, who had previously helped train the women or refereed matches, had to be careful of associating with the women's teams, lest they themselves fell foul of the FA. Over the next four decades there were several incidences of referees, trainers and clubs being suspended for being involved in women's football. The legendary Preston and England international, Tom Finney, explained how it was after the ban:

> I remember being invited to referee at several of their [Dick, Kerr Ladies'] matches and being presented to the girls. There wasn't much women's football in those days and to actually see them play was quite remarkable. Some of them were very good players and they always had big crowds. I knew the FA did not look very kindly upon them and it was thought that we professional players should not encourage them. I personally couldn't see that they were doing any harm, especially when they were helping so many people by raising such a lot of money for charity.[27]

However, by 1922 charitable causes were dwindling and women's football matches, even if they could overcome the imposed restrictions, were less in demand.

In September of that year, Dick, Kerr Ladies accepted an invitation from the United States Football Association (USFA) to play in the USA and Canada. Although there was great interest in women's soccer in colleges, there weren't sufficient numbers to organise a team for them to play against and all nine matches were played against men. The average attendance for men's soccer games in the US was around 4,000, but the Dick, Kerr Ladies' exhibition matches attracted an attendance of between 8,000 to 10,000. Before the final match, to illustrate their fitness, four of Dick, Kerr's team took on America's Olympic women's team in a 4 x 100m relay – and won. One of the four was Lily Parr, who was to become a star player of the team, and a footballer who, many said, would have reached international level – had she been a man. By the end of her career Lily had scored over 1,000 goals.[28]

Decline of Dick, Kerr Ladies

Dick, Kerr Ladies continued to play successfully, both nationally and internationally, throughout the next two decades. In 1937, a team from Edinburgh challenged them for the title of European champions (having heard of their triumph over a Belgium team in 1934), but the Dick, Kerr's team won convincingly 5–1. At a celebratory dinner in Preston, attended by many local dignitaries, the local MP for Preston complimented the team on their success and all their charity work, and said: 'he had heard how tough they were but now he could see for himself, that although they played a man's game, they hadn't lost any of their femininity!'[29]

Little football was played during the Second World War. Dick, Kerr Ladies re-advertised for players and continued to play matches soon after war had finished, but the impact they had made in the 1920s and 1930s was never to be recaptured. There is evidence of a match played between Dick, Kerr Ladies and a team from Weymouth in 1946. The programme from that match suggests that many other teams existed in the south-west: Steane and Co. from Bournemouth, Vickers from Trowbridge, and teams from Westbury and Faversham. Local press reports, in Southampton and Portsmouth, reveal that there were also factory teams in that area. One Portsmouth team had played charity matches as early as the First World War, at the men's professional ground, Fratton Park. After the Second World War, a Portsmouth newspaper recorded a reunion of Portsmouth women who had played during the 1920s. This report shows that, although the women's matches had made approximately £3,000 to help the war effort, some of them endured the disapproval of friends and relatives and the team disbanded because a Portsmouth clergyman disapproved. Despite the evidence of existing teams, women's football still revolved around festivals and fundraising; it remained out of the public eye and localised. By 1947, there were only 17 teams left in the country.[30]

A new team formed in 1949, Manchester Corinthians, were to assume Dick, Kerr Ladies' mantle and become the most successful team of the new decade. Jean Seymour, who played for Manchester Corinthians in the 1950s, kept a record of all their matches, including games against Shaw Inn from Barnsley whom they played 18 times in five years. This lack of opposition reflected the struggle women had, throughout the country, in organising and maintaining teams and overcoming the FA ban. In 1950, a match between Chelmsford and Maldon Ladies at Chelmsford Park drew a crowd of 4,000, but only because the Essex FA's warning to its member clubs against staging the match had brought extra publicity.[31]

More research would probably reveal a far greater number of women's teams playing during the earlier part of this century, although their ephemeral nature makes this research difficult. D.J. Williamson alludes to the fact that it was one thing for women to accommodate the occasional charity or 'just for fun' type of game, but it was harder for them to make a serious commitment given the constraints imposed on the game by the FA: 'To take the game so seriously, as to struggle for players and pitches week in week out, took an immense amount of dedication and hard work. On top of all this, the older girls in particular were beginning to turn their attention elsewhere; careers and motherhood being just two things that had great importance in the early years.'[32]

The Dick, Kerr Ladies had given women's football a great start, but in truth the FA ban had squashed the life out of the game. They were also finding it difficult to attract new players. When Kath Latham took over as manager in 1957, she began signing up players, such as Sheila Parker (née Porter) and Joan Briggs, who used to travel from London. Despite acquiring talented players such as these, they began losing to the up and coming 'younger' teams and eventually, in 1965, through lack of players, the team finished altogether. Dick, Kerr Ladies' final record was: played 828, won 758, drawn 46, lost 24. They had scored 3,500 goals. If they could have survived one more year, they might have been revitalised by the rebirth of the women's game which occurred after the 1966 England men's World Cup victory at Wembley. It would have been their fiftieth anniversary in 1967.

2 Post-war players and clubs

This chapter looks at the most successful post-war clubs in England and provides information based on interviews with some of the key players and newspaper cuttings from that era.

The players

Jean Seymour's (née Gollin, b. 1930) involvement in women's football spans 50 years. She started playing for Dick, Kerr Ladies in 1946 when she was 16 and she went on to play for Manchester Corinthians in the early 1950s. She spent much of her time travelling around the world playing with the Corinthians, including matches when the team represented England in various international tournaments. She then moved to the south of England, where she became involved in the rebirth of the women's game, playing for Portsmouth and then for the first Southampton team, in 1966. Not only did one of her sons play for Southampton FC, but both Jean and her daughter, Janice, also played for another Southampton team, Patstone United. Jean continued as player/coach in the Portsmouth area until moving to Milton Keynes. She is now involved in voluntary development work in women's football.

Yvonne Cooper (née Hamer, b. 1935) started her career with Dick, Kerr Ladies, a team she heard about when she was 15. She contacted Alfred Frankland and he paid for her, and her mother, to make the trip from Crewe to Preston. She said, "When he asked me what position I played, I told him anywhere, but I especially liked scoring goals. He gave me a set of kit and boots to try on – I felt like a million dollars with that kit on!" She played centre-forward in her first game two weeks later, against Manchester Corinthians – and scored six goals. Yvonne remembers these early days with Dick, Kerr Ladies as exciting: "They were great

years – we stayed in first class hotels and toured all over England."
Yvonne went on to become one of the founder members of
Fodens in 1956 – a team she stayed with for 15 years.

Sylvia Gore (b. 1946) came from Prescot in Lancashire. She
played for Manchester Corinthians and also travelled with the team
around the world. She started playing for Fodens in 1967 and was
part of the team when they were at the height of their success,
winning the Butlin's Cup in 1969 and 1970. She scored the
opening goal in the first official England match against Scotland
in 1972, and played for Fodens in the Women's Football
Association (WFA) 1974 Cup Final. She was manager of the Welsh
women's football team in the mid-1980s, when it was not
recognised by the FA of Wales and had no funds. In 1991 she won
the North West Amateur Sports 'Personality of the Year' award,
for her voluntary work in girls' football development for the
local authority in Knowsley (Liverpool). She now works voluntarily
for Liverpool FA, as their county coaching representative (women
and girls), and as assistant manager of the Liverpool women's team.
Despite all these efforts, and with her knowledge and expertise,
Sylvia laments the fact that she is unable to obtain paid work in
women's football development.

Sheila Parker (née Porter, b. 1947) is another great player who
had links with the famous northern clubs. She played for Dick,
Kerr Ladies in the early 1960s up until they finished in 1965. She
then went on to play for Fodens, St Helen's and Preston North End
and captained the first official England team in 1972. She retired
from playing in the early 1980s and is now a Class II referee in
the Lancashire area.

Eileen Foreman (b. 1954) became synonymous with the team
from the little west country town of Warminster, Wiltshire,
managed by her father, and for whom she played from 1972 to
1981. She played in the first official England match against
Scotland and for Warminster, when they lost to Southampton, in
the 1975 WFA Cup Final. She spent her last seasons with
Southampton (1981–83), before retiring at the age of 29, somewhat
disillusioned with the lack of development of the women's game,
and she has not been involved since.

Apart from a few months with another local team and a season
in the Italian national league (1971–72), I played for Southampton
for 20 years, from when it was first formed in 1966 (when I was
21) up until it folded in 1986. During that time, Jean Seymour and

Eileen Foreman were club colleagues at Southampton and Eileen, Sheila Parker and Sylvia Gore were England colleagues.

Although we all developed our football skills isolated from other women, there are similarities in how we became involved in the game. The following examples illustrate some of the ingenuity and determination that I and many other women had to show, just to have a ball at our feet.

Kicking in the back yard

All the women learnt their football kicking a ball about in informal games with boys in their area or with their fathers, who helped and encouraged them. Jean Seymour remembers joining in with the local boys when she was six years old – and being better than they were – as did Yvonne Cooper, who started playing at age seven. Sheila Parker played football at the local recreation ground with older boys, who she felt made her better, because they were stronger and more skilful. Sylvia Gore started kicking a ball about with her father at the age of four and later, at primary school, her headmistress allowed her to join the school team. Eileen Foreman also recalls playing football with the local boys and watching her father play for Warminster Town. I remember when I was ten playing with two neighbourhood boys and my cousin during the summer holidays, and we played endless two or one against one 'matches' in a nearby field.

The influence of parents was a crucial factor in encouraging, and perhaps more importantly, not stopping these girls from participating in what in the post-war days of the late 1940s and early 1950s was considered by many to be a very unfeminine activity. Jean talks fondly of her early childhood days in Manchester when her parents encouraged her in all sports:

> My parents were the most influential people in my football development. They were sporty themselves and hard working ... they didn't drink or smoke, apart from the occasional shandy. They didn't go into pubs. They were into cycling. My Dad used to cycle with the Cyclists' Touring Club with Reg Harris, who was then world champion. Dad could make anything – he'd get an old frame and make a bike up for us and we'd go out Sunday cycling. Every morning before we went to school we had a round of

boxing with him – me, my sister and brother, in the kitchen, while Mum was getting breakfast. My sister liked sport but didn't get into it so much as me. She played a few games for the Dick, Kerr's team and played against me a couple of times. My brother was more into cycling and weight lifting and boxing, and he carried on with that in the army. At school I only played netball – there was nothing else ... everything was separate. We did our cookery and they did their woodwork. Girls weren't allowed to do anything the boys did. Fortunately, nobody minded us playing in the streets afterwards, so long as we were visible to our mothers. There were few cars around, and there was no drugs or smoking then, so we just enjoyed our football.

Sylvia had no brothers or sisters, but her parents were very supportive. Her father, Jack Gore, used to play centre-half for British Insulated Calendar Cables in Prescot, as did her uncle, Larry Nash, and they both encouraged her football skills. A local newspaper reported:

> When she was eleven, Sylvia could tackle and shoot as well as the boys at her school, but the headteacher would not let her turn out for the school. At fourteen she was able to join Manchester Corinthians and went on to play for them in charity matches in Italy, Portugal and South America. She had scored 50 goals in her first season with them. Her mother is quoted as saying that 'Sylvia is a wonderful footballer. Everybody thinks so, including the boys.'[1]

It was also Eileen's father who strongly influenced her involvement in football:

> I started playing when I was five or six with local lads. None of the girls were interested, so it was just me playing with them in the evenings and weekends on a playing field near an estate where all the local lads played. My interest came from my father – he was the only one who played football in the family. He didn't encourage me to play as such, but it must have been handed down. He played a good local standard for a long time as left-winger for Warminster Town. I watched him quite often and the teams that they played against.

At school, Eileen asked the teachers if the girls could play football with the boys, but it just wasn't allowed: "It was school policy – girls played netball and hockey and the boys played football. I played netball, hockey, badminton and did athletics for the school and county, but I still loved football the most, even though I never played an organised game until I was 13 or 14."

Sheila didn't receive actual encouragement, but was not dissuaded from playing, although neither parents ever saw her play. She, too, was the only girl playing football with the local boys in Standish, Lancashire:

> Mum never watched, she never saw me play, but she did buy me my first football kit when I was seven years old – blue-and-white, with blue-and-white socks – I looked like a convict! And I had some football boots – I do wish I'd held on to them – you used to have to use dubbin to polish the toes and the footballs had laces in then and were real heavy in the wet. When I came in all muddy from the recreation ground I used to try and get the gear off without Mum seeing it and try and hide it! My brother played but he wasn't as good as me or as interested. Dad was a good goalkeeper ... he didn't encourage me, but he didn't stop me.

Sheila remembers she was the only girl at school interested in football: "We had to play rounders at Notre Dame juniors and netball at the senior school. I used to kick the netball around until the teacher came!"

My mother's interest in football stemmed from watching the local village team. After the Munich air disaster, in 1956, in which most of the Manchester United team were killed, she started to support them and became a particular admirer of Bobby Charlton, one of the few survivors. We lived in Marchwood, near Southampton, and my first recollections of football were of my mother taking me with her every Saturday to watch the local match. I was even dressed up in their green colours when they won the final of the Hampshire Cup in 1951. When I was ten, we moved house and I found an old pair of football boots in the garden shed. I polished them up and wore them, despite them being the wrong size and without studs. I became obsessed with the game and spent most of my leisure time playing football with neighbourhood boys. If the boys weren't around, I'd practise rebounding a tennis ball against the house wall. I also rigged up a goal, made from hazel sticks, at the top of the garden and spent hours shooting penalties or running up the path and shooting from the 'edge of the penalty box', trying not to slip in my studless boots. Sometimes garden plants would get damaged and this would provide my mother with the opportunity to ask me when I was going to take up a more feminine activity. She would be particularly annoyed when people asked me what I was going to do when I grew up. I always replied 'be a footballer'.

At school the only games on offer were netball and hockey. I enjoyed hockey because it was similar to football tactically, but lamented the rigid barrier between sporting and recreational activities considered appropriate for boys and girls. On reflection the 'street' football played by girls was the kind of ball practice that provided the great male players, like Bobby Charlton, with their outstanding individual skills. Today, learning by small-sided games is recognised as far more preferable to prematurely playing 11-a-side football, as so many boys still do. In some ways, although they were denied proper coaching the early women footballers had the advantage of this kind of skill practice. I didn't even know that women's football existed and remember being the only girl at school interested in the game. My grandfather introduced me to the professional men's game in the 1950s, when he occasionally took me to watch Southampton FC. I also followed Wolverhampton's great European Cup campaigns and England internationals Billy Wright and Peter Broadbent were the first players I idolised (this was until I saw Pele score in Brazil's 1958 World Cup victory over Sweden).

Eventually, when I was 21, I had the chance to play for a women's team at Southampton Common and I bought a proper pair of boots. My mother had accepted my desire to play football and used to watch some of the games at the common. By the time I had achieved some success, especially in Italy, she was very supportive and said she wished she had come out to Rome to see me play.

The clubs

In the north-west of England, in the post-war years, it was easier than in the south for women to find organised women's football teams in which to play. Dick, Kerr Ladies reassembled soon after the war and Jean Seymour remembers seeing, in May 1946, an advertisement in a local Manchester paper requesting new players to attend a trial:

> I asked my Mum to take me down to Preston. It was about an hour by train from Chorlton-cum-Hardy. They had two teams of trialists and I got noticed because I headed a goal – which was photographed and appeared in the *Daily Sketch*. I was also really fast and had good ball control, and was happy to play anywhere, even in goal, which I did in later years.

Jean recalls Alfred Frankland, as well as many of the early players. Her comments about Alfred Frankland illustrate that she did not suspect any of the financial problems that had caused the FA to ban women from using affiliated pitches:

> Alfred, Margaret Thornborough and Nancy Thompson were very helpful when I joined. Margaret was like an assistant manager to Alfred and Nancy was the captain and they took me under their wing. They were in their late twenties and early thirties and were both nurses at a mental hospital. Joan Whalley and Lily Parr were two of their most famous players then. Lily was about six feet tall and played on the left wing and had terrific ball control. She was fast too, and was a prolific goalscorer – until I came along! There were seven nurses in the team then. There was great team spirit and enthusiasm. Alfred and the other men who helped organise things were great – they did it for the girls, not for themselves. After the war, the men's game had resumed and some of the professional players helped us out, even though they shouldn't have had anything to do with us, being that they were affiliated and we weren't. Margaret Thornborough's brother, Elie, played for Preston and through him we met the legendary England forward, Tom Finney, and he used to come out with Elie and give us some tips, especially to Joan Whalley, our outside-right. Tom Finney's house was opposite the park we sometimes played in. We'd train once a week with Margaret and Nancy in charge. They didn't do a lot of technical stuff, but the girls seemed to have learnt their skills, like me I suppose, by kicking around with the lads. Other professional players helped by refereeing our charity matches. When we played Bolton Ladies in August 1947,

in aid of church funds, the Mayoress of Burnley kicked off and Burnley's Alan Brown and Harry Potts were the officials.

One of Jean's earliest games was against Weymouth, Dorset, played at Weymouth Recreation Ground on 12 June 1946, in aid of the Mayor's Welcome Home Fund. Jean scored five goals in Dick, Kerr Ladies' 11–2 victory. The crowd of 7,000 was recorded in Preston's *Daily Post* as being the biggest attendance for any sporting occasion in Weymouth. Jean recalls the game by saying:

> It was the first time I had been away from home, and I remember sitting at the window of the train, looking at all the factories and all the other different things along the line to Weymouth. When I saw the pitch, it was fantastic. I'll never forget it, it was like playing on a bowling green. There were thousands there. Weymouth were a company team who Dick, Kerr's had played back in the twenties, so there was a bit of rivalry from that time.

The Dorset FA, however, had recorded their opposition to women's football. After the match, Alfred Frankland told a local paper that when some of the Lancashire FA had opposed them in the past, he had obtained the opinions of 21 doctors, who declared that they considered football to be of benefit to the general health of a woman. He also pointed out that many of the players were nurses themselves and while the FA were at pains to criticise football as being 'unsuitable for women', they weren't concerned that these same women had served their country in the forces, and in nursing, during the difficulties and horrors of a world war.[2]

A newspaper cutting from the North Cheshire *Herald and Hyde*, in June 1946, records another match, where Dick, Kerr Ladies beat a Lancaster Counties' Ladies team 7–4 at ICI's ground at Hyde. It not only recounts Jean's continued goalscoring, but illustrates the high esteem in which the team was then held. Prior to the match they were taken by the Hyde British Legion organisers to tour the Ashton Brothers & Company's mill, before having a civic reception in the mayor's parlour. They were then accompanied by the deputy mayoress to the ground, where she kicked off the game. Such was the superiority of the Dick, Kerr's team in this match, they were 6–0 up by half time, that they let Jean play for the opposition in the second half. She went on to score the Lancashire side's four goals! The paper also reported that the 'girls can display grace as well as ability in playing football', and that the 'outstanding feature of the game was the pace and enthusiasm with which the ladies played'. Civic receptions were a notable feature at most of the charity matches that Dick, Kerr Ladies played. By 1947 they had attended over 150, including those held by the lord mayors of London, Manchester, Liverpool, Sheffield, Glasgow and Belfast.[3]

When Jean was 18, she went into the army as a physical training instructor and continued to enjoy playing sport:

> I was in the army for about five years, stationed at Guildford and then Bulford, on Salisbury Plain. It was terrible there, but there was plenty of sport. I could go to the gym, play basketball and table tennis and kick a ball around, which was good, because I was able to get back to play games for Dick, Kerr's.

Manchester Corinthians

Dick, Kerr Ladies dominated women's football until Percy Ashley from Didsbury, Manchester, formed the Manchester Corinthians in 1949. They were formed partly to provide a team in which his football-mad daughter, Doris, could play. The team in its inaugural year consisted of typists, clerks, machinists and schoolgirls. The average age of the players was only 16½ and Percy called them 'Corinthians' in recognition of the best Corinthian amateur ideals. They ran into trouble with the FA immediately, when trying to find pitches to stage matches on. Consequently, their first games were played on any available ground, including rugby pitches, cricket grounds and even greyhound tracks. Often there were no changing facilities or running water to wash with. Despite the difficulty of finding suitable grounds, the team did have their own physiotherapist and accident fund.

Jean Seymour recalls her early days with the Corinthians:

> They'd started up while I was still in the army. I came home on leave to Rochester, in Kent, where my parents then lived, but I went up to Manchester and went to see a Corinthians' match. I found that my old work-mate, Doris Ashley, was running the team with her Dad. He ran it from his house and the pitch was across the road at Didsbury. We used to go there and change and walk across the road. There were a couple of buckets of water outside

the house for us to wash off the mud after the game. Percy was brilliant. I got involved with them and fortunately, my Mum and Dad moved back up to Manchester, so I didn't have to travel so much.

Like Dick, Kerr Ladies, the Corinthians played for charity, and travelled over 1,000 miles around Britain in their first year. One match against their reserve team, the Nomads (whom they later played in exhibition matches around the world), attracted 2,500 spectators at the Radcliffe cricket ground. Other well-supported matches were to follow and by June 1953, they had played 101 games, won 88, drawn 4, lost 9, scored 593 goals and raised £14,000 for charity. Doris Ashley became known as 'Dynamite Doris' in recognition of her goalscoring feats (over the first four years she scored 502), and Percy likened her to two of the great male international players of the time, Raich Carter and Peter Doherty. However, he was always at pains to stress that the girls in both teams, the Corinthians and the Nomads, were not tomboys. An article from Jean's scrapbook quotes him as saying he liked teaching women football because: 'they are more willing to learn than boys, and don't get big-headed when they reach high standards'.

By now, many well-known local men players and officials could see no reason not to support women's football and were only too willing to assist the Corinthians. Another newspaper report from Jean's scrapbook records how the women received much support. After a match at Preston Street, Gorton, in which they defeated a Northern Ladies XI 15–0, the officials were quoted as congratulating the girls for their excellent play and sporting behaviour, particularly in 'playing to the whistle'. Jean was as impressed with the off-the-field back-up as with the actual football:

> We'd usually get around three to four thousand people watching us. The manager was brilliant – he used to have one of those silent motor bikes and go around putting up posters on lamp-posts and trees advertising the games, all for charity, and folk would come from miles away to watch. Usually we played on rugby grounds, Widnes, Wigan, all those sorts of places. After the game we'd dress up – no baggy jeans and scruffy shirts, like you see today – we put on dresses and skirts and looked like ladies. We were treated well, like VIPs – going to civic receptions, all expenses

paid ... it seems to have gone downhill today, when you think about it!

The Corinthians' most famous association was with Manchester City's German-born goalkeeper, Bert Trautman. Trautman first met the team in 1951, when he presented them with the Festival of Britain Trophy. In 1957 he escorted them to Berlin for a European tournament, and acted as their interpreter. The Corinthians defeated Germany 4–0 in the final of the tournament, in front of a crowd of 30,000.

The Corinthians started playing at a time when the effects of the 1921 ban had significantly reduced the number of clubs in existence. The lack of competition, coupled with the problems of finding non-affiliated grounds to play on, prompted the Corinthians to seek playing opportunities abroad. Over the next ten years, the two teams played exhibition and charity matches in a variety of countries, worldwide, often organised by the International Red Cross, who would pay their hotel and living expenses. Their destinations (proudly listed on their club's letterhead) included: Germany twice in 1957, a tour of Portugal 1957–58, Madeira in 1958, Holland in 1959, South America and Ireland in 1960, Italy in 1961, Morocco and North Africa in 1966. In a letter to a local Manchester newspaper, in the late 1950s, Doris Ashley reproaches the Cheshire Ladies' team for being 'put out by the fact that the FA do not look with favour on ladies' football'. She added that she had put up with the problem for nearly twenty years, but it had not deterred Manchester Corinthians; it had led to them going abroad as much as possible to play. She also proudly reports that her club had, since 1949, played 287 matches, won 256, travelled over 60,000 miles and raised over £70,000 for charity.[4]

Jean Seymour recalls playing for the Corinthians during their tour of Portugal and the exhibition matches, held in Lisbon's national stadium, where they beat the Nomads in all three games played. She also has fond memories of a six-week trip to Tunisia, after which she returned so tanned that her twin daughters didn't recognise her: "They came to the door and said that Mum wasn't in – I said, I am your Mum!" Jean speaks warmly of Percy Ashley and the excellent organisation of the trips:

> Percy did all the paperwork and everything. His house was like an office and a treasure trove of trophies and pendants. There's a special Red Cross Diploma for all the money

we'd raised for them. He told any charity organisation that we'd play for just our travel expenses. We always had a lady welfare officer when we went abroad and if we needed medical attention we would see someone locally. We'd train at 7 am to avoid the heat if we were in a hot country. I didn't believe in too much running around – we'd do short bursts of fitness, twisting and turning, plus some stamina training. We used to run as a club round the field each day. We used to go down to the street markets and see all the locals dressed up in kaftans and whatever. But there were never any hassles, not even in South America, except from the crawling things in the bed. Most of the hotels were nice. We didn't stay in one place very long – we were one or two nights in the same place then we were off, so we hardly unpacked our bags. Sometimes we had to wash our clothes, like the locals, in the river. It was great ... I believe in do as the Romans do and don't be stand-offish.

The South American tour lasted 12 weeks and included matches at Curacao, Aruba, Columbia, Paramaribo, Dutch Guiana and Georgetown. They then went on to Trinidad and Jamaica, where they played on the cricket test grounds, before returning via New York. The whole trip had raised over £1,500 for charity. Not surprisingly, as they were away from home so long, only three of the team were married, including Jean, who by 1958 had four children. Sylvia Gore was also playing for the Corinthians during this time and remembers the trips with affection, "It was incredible playing in those great stadiums. In one of them, in South America, 80,000 people watched us play. Although we were getting good crowds in England, it was so nice to play on proper football pitches, rather than on the rugby and recreation pitches we had at home."

Manchester Corinthians' decline

Jean Seymour's association with Manchester Corinthians ended when she moved to Portsmouth in 1960 and she became involved with the new Southampton women's team that started in 1966. Sylvia Gore moved, in 1967, to a team in Cheshire, called Fodens, that had started in 1956. Both teams were to vie for the Corinthians' mantle throughout the 1970s. The euphoria created by the England men's World Cup victory in 1966 gave a fillip to the whole nation, regardless of their interest in football, and the women's game enjoyed a boom in both participation and spectators. But by the end of the 1960s and early 1970s, the Corinthians, despite their international status, were in decline. Percy Ashley was reaching old age and almost certainly finding it difficult to continue with all the organisation required to maintain a successful club. Doris Ashley was nearing the end of her playing career and by 1969, Gladys Aikin was in charge. They won the 1968 and 1969 Deal International Tournament, but in 1970, were put out of the competition by the previous year's runner's-up, the Hooverettes. Gladys Aikin's 'rules', however, were an indication of the pride and high standards which the girls who signed to play for the Corinthians or Nomads were still expected to maintain. They were told that tie-ups, for keeping up their socks, must not be elastic nor rubber bands. The club kit had to be taken home to be washed and ironed and returned to the club the following Sunday. Bad language was not tolerated and no girl under the age of 18 was allowed to smoke while in the club, unless parental consent was given. Trousers were not to be worn to away matches: 'we are called Corinthian Ladies and we will dress like ladies'. Finally, they were reminded of the club's good reputation built up over the years and therefore players 'must behave in a manner that will only bring credit to the club name'. Despite their reputation and discipline, however, they were still losing to the new up and coming teams.

The Southampton women's team last played the Corinthians in two exhibition matches at the Empire Pool, Wembley, in April 1970. Some of the final references to the Corinthians' existence came through one of their players, Jean Wilson, who attended the first England team trials in July 1972. There is also a match programme indicating that they beat Fodens, 3–2, in a testimonial game at Buxton FC's ground, in October of that year. The final reference is another match programme from May 1973, which records the Corinthians beating the Nomads 4–1, at Horwich, but apart from Jean Wilson and Gladys Aikin's daughter, Carol, the names on the team sheets are unrecognisable from their halcyon days. Presumably the team finished around 1973 or 1974.

Fodens

Fodens began at a lorry manufacturing firm in Sandbach and, initially, most of the team was made up of factory workers.

According to Yvonne Cooper, Fodens started when they were challenged by Manchester Corinthians to form a team to play against them for a celebratory cause in 1956. Yvonne had started playing with Dick, Kerr Ladies but her football career was interrupted by her marriage:

> I was 23 when I was married and my husband made me choose between football or him, so I chose him. But about ten months after my baby son was born I started playing for Fodens. I had a friend who played for another lorry firm called E.R.F., just down the road from Fodens, and she asked me to play for them. We won the game 6–1 and after that Ray Atkinson, who ran Fodens, came to my house and asked me to play for his team.

Fodens began in the same vein as Dick, Kerr Ladies and Manchester Corinthians, playing charity matches, mostly in the north of England and in Northern Ireland. Yvonne recalls:

> Fodens supplied the bus in which we travelled and had their own works' ground, or we used school or rugby pitches. We also raised money with jumble sales and dances. Apart from the trips to Belgium and Holland, the most memorable match was when we became the first English team anyone could recall to beat Manchester Corinthians. We also played a charity match against Coronation Street personalities and I suppose our best achievement was later winning the Butlin's Cup ... and of course becoming the first team to beat Southampton in the national WFA Mitre Cup in 1974. We also beat Southampton 4–1, in a friendly match at the Southampton Sports Centre in 1968, and I played in defence, but when they came up to us for a charity match, I played in goal and Southampton won 3–2!

I was playing for Southampton at this time and I remember how strong the Fodens players were, compared to other teams we had met so far. Most of all, I was impressed with the speed and skill of certain players, such as their left-winger, Lesley Caldwell, and their two forwards, Joan Tench and Joan Briggs. Joan Briggs was a PE teacher from London and had played some games for Dick, Kerr Ladies and Manchester Corinthians. She later played for the East Midlands Gas Board team, EMGALS. Yvonne Cooper sadly recalls Joan Tench's premature death, in her early thirties, from cancer, and the infamously contrived *Daily Mirror* photo of her jumping to head a ball, while her shorts supposedly 'fell down':

> Joan was one of the longest-serving members of the club ... she played nearly 200 games in nine years. She'd scored many vital goals, including the only one scored in the Butlin's Cup Final at Greenock, against Westthorn United. She was captain, but when we started doing so well, she couldn't cope with the public speaking demands and gave up the captaincy. It was a pity about that photo. I don't know how they talked her into doing it because she was a very shy girl about the limelight. It was a sad loss when she died.

Fodens were a strong, determined and hard-working team and had some of the best forwards in the game, including Lesley Caldwell and Sylvia Gore. By 1974, the team had acquired two new young and talented forwards, 16-year-old Pat Firth and 17-year-old Jeannie Allott. Pat had a tremendous shot and was an excellent header of the ball, and Jeannie was a phenomenally fast, strong, tricky left-winger. In Sheila Parker they had one of the best defenders in women's football. I was fortunate to play with Jeannie, Pat and Sheila in the early England teams and always appreciated having them on my side. Sylvia Gore remembers the great 1974 Fodens' team and their cup victory over Southampton:

> It was the first time Southampton had ever lost in a cup game in the three seasons the national cup had been in existence. We were determined to beat them. We weren't frightened of them – even though they had six international players on their side, compared to our four. It was close though, but I think we deserved our 2–1 win.

Warminster

Warminster was another famous club to emerge in the early 1970s. It was built around a great forward player, Eileen Foreman, and managed by her father, Reg, much as Percy and Doris Ashley had been the cornerstones in the development of Manchester Corinthians. Eileen Foreman remembers in 1969 responding to an advert in the local paper for women players for a team in

Weymouth. The Weymouth team was run by a woman called Pat
Dunn, who was a qualified FA referee (Pat Dunn had also become
the first WFA chair and was well known for her lively campaigns
against the FA because they would not allow females to referee
affiliated football). In order to play proper organised matches,
Eileen travelled from Warminster to Weymouth for six weeks, until
an official at Warminster Town men's club, Bill Everitt, offered to
help set up their own women's team. Eileen recalls Bill Everitt's
assistance with gratitude:

> He was a really nice old chap who was for women's football.
> He did all the organisation. We advertised for players in the
> local paper and he got some of the men's old kit. Bill
> trained us at first with a few basic ideas. It was great playing
> at Warminster Town's ground – it felt like Wembley to me
> after the park at Weymouth. It seemed huge, and all official
> and nice.

The team was unique in having the advantage of a close link
with the local men's club. They used Warminster Town's pitch,
advertised their matches in the men's Saturday programme and
had the goodwill of the club's officials. Eileen's father became the
first manager and the team went from strength to strength in the
Western League, with early success as champions. They remained
self-supporting, gaining sponsorship for playing kit, tracksuits and
travel expenses from a coffee company, and they received
supportive local media coverage. The team drew good crowds and
soon the supporters, as well as the team, became feared by
opponents all over the country, especially for national WFA Cup
games. Eileen remembers what a boost the vociferous spectators
were for the team:

> Cup games at Warminster were something special. The
> crowd would get right behind us. You could tell the women
> were better supported than the men by all the cars parked
> down the hill on a Sunday – far more than on a Saturday.
> I think we've still got the record attendance at the ground,
> more than for any man's game. Everyone heard about us
> and wanted to be involved with the club.

Although Eileen is grateful for all the support from her father,
she also explains how difficult it was being the manager's daughter,
as well as the only international player in the side:

He put in lots of hours training with me on my own and he attended lots of committee meetings, which sometimes weren't very pleasant due to all the politics. He got very involved with it and sometimes it led to clashes between us. I always wanted to play for a club where I didn't have my father as manager. I sometimes felt some of the players thought I got priority treatment, although I don't think I did. Some of the players didn't want to do anything for the club – just play. I wondered if they really appreciated all the behind-the-scenes work by people like my father.

The club dominated the Western League Championship and League Cup for many years and, in 1975, reached the final of the national WFA Mitre Cup played at Dunstable Town FC. Here they played three-time winners, Southampton, who were determined to win back the cup they had lost to Fodens the previous year. Southampton were 3–0 up in the first 20 minutes but Eileen, roared on by the supporters, hit back with two goals. She nearly scored another, but Southampton finally captured the cup with a fourth goal. Eileen says:

> Some of our players would be so intimidated when we played Southampton. They had a deservedly fine reputation and our defence tended to freeze when their England players like Lynda Hale, Pat Davies, Pat Chapman and Sue Lopez got the ball. But I always thought we could unsettle their defence and we were so close to clawing back to 3–3, and then anything could have happened – especially with our supporters cheering us on – we had three coachloads with us that day. It was a great day. I'll never forget it – but I was obviously not meant to win a cup medal!

Eileen got her wish to play for another team when Warminster folded in 1981 and she joined Southampton for two seasons:

> It was totally different playing with the girls of Southampton because there were so many internationals of such a high standard and I had to fit into their way of playing, whereas I'd been used to doing my own thing at Warminster. I needed a lot more self-discipline, but it was enjoyable all the same.

However, by this time, Southampton was also in decline and did not reach another cup final. Eileen's career was prematurely ended and she expresses some regrets about not being able to be involved in football any more:

> I miss playing even now. That feeling when you have a ball at your feet. Those were happy times, but really and truly even now, I feel I could go out and kick a ball, yet I've not kicked one for about ten years. I could have put an awful lot back into the game with coaching. I used to bring ideas back from England training to use at Warminster but I think you have to be very committed. Warminster finished and I had to travel a distance to find a team to coach. If I could turn the clock back, one thing I would have loved is to have had coaching at an early age and learnt the skills properly and how to read the game and how to play confidently on the ball. You can have natural talent, and most of the England team had that, but they lacked the confidence on the ball that only comes when you're completely confident in your skills. I think I could have done a lot more on the field if I'd had top-class coaching locally, instead of a few bits we learnt at international gatherings.

The next chapter looks in more detail at the success of the other great team of the 1970s, Southampton. Southampton played a key role in the development of women's football between 1966 and 1986 and emerged in a different way to the previous clubs. However, there are similarities between all the teams in that they could begin, and be sustained, only through the hard work and enthusiasm of dedicated individuals, people who would give up their time to organise, manage, coach and promote the women's game. All the clubs' games were initially 'legitimised' by being played for charity. There was great camaraderie among the women, but it wasn't just a social event, there was a willingness to shoulder individual responsibility for fitness and a collective desire to work hard for the team's benefit. They were prepared to travel long distances, not only to play their opponents, but in order to find a team for whom they could play. They had to overcome prejudice, often pay money from their own pockets, and endure the constant battle of finding suitable pitches to play on.

Players from earlier times may wonder what they might have achieved if the development structures and opportunities that exist today had been put in place in the 1920s – instead of a ban. Most new players can't imagine what it was like trying to find a women's team to play for; or to be dismissed to a recreation ground or rugby pitch in order to play a match. According to Jean Seymour, these differences do not detract from the fact that women have the ability to play football:

> Apart from girls like Gill Coultard (Doncaster Belles) and Marieanne Spacey (Arsenal), [England stars for over ten years, both of whom played for England in the 1995 World Cup], I don't think today's players are any more skilful than Dick, Kerr's and Manchester Corinthians' star players. Certainly, I'd put Southampton on a par with Dick, Kerr's players and some of the Southampton team were the best I've ever seen. Because there's more competition today, they're probably fitter, but then you see, Dick, Kerr's team had an Olympic sprinter in Nellie Halstead, and I could almost beat her!

Despite today's greater acceptance of the women's game, many women ex-players are still excluded from it. In men's football and other sports, it's normal to provide ex-players with real opportunities to stay involved with the game in some way. Many women players have a genuine desire to use their experience and expertise, but there is a lack of encouragement for women to get involved on a coaching or administrative level. Jean Seymour says, "Over the years, too many people who really have no interest in women's football have used it for their own gain." She admitted that sometimes players had been guilty of just wanting to play and ignored the organisational side, but added, "There's not many men who would want to play and coach or administrate as well, but when they finish playing, they can." She felt that since the WFA was formed there were a lot of ex-players who knew the game 'inside out', who could have trained as coaches, physios, referees and administrators. In particular, Jean spoke of her frustrations of liaising with a local authority sports development official. His department had the finances to support local girls' football but he used Jean's knowledge on how to do it. She said she didn't mind but, "I was only a volunteer and he was getting paid to do it and made all the decisions. He could then take the credit for developing the girls' game and when it suited, leave us to fend for ourselves." Some ex-players, like Eileen Foreman, became tired of the 'politics' and many others, steeped in the tradition of the women's game, are disappointed at the lack of opportunity to be involved after playing and see it as a waste of their knowledge and talent.

Another example comes via a male community development officer of a men's professional club. He told me that, at his club, the volunteer coaching post of the women's team now attracts a budget and has become a paid role and that a man has replaced the volunteer woman. The community officer added that he rated the woman coach more highly and, since the man's appointment, the team had enjoyed little success. It always seems easier for men to get jobs in women's football than the other way round. Ex-players feel that the women's game is generally different and that women's needs are frequently ignored by male coaches and male and female administrators, who have little or no experience of the game. The FA's strategy document, 'Women and Football', sets out one of its development objectives for future action as 'increasing the number of women involved in coaching and coach education and to encourage and assist them to reach higher levels'.[5] Twenty-six years on, since the ending of the FA ban, there is a vital need for this objective to be effectively actioned. All the women ex-players, with a wealth of talent and experience in women's football, have already waited too long.

3 Southampton – from local league to Italy

The England victory in the 1966 World Cup proved to be the catalyst for a dramatic renaissance in the women's game and this time the upsurge of interest would be sustained. For a group of women football players in Southampton, it was to be the beginning of a long and successful career.

The Cunard shipping line had helped Southampton to become a well-known passenger port and it was the Cunard company that led the way in the development of women's football teams in the area. The secretary of Cunard's social club (the Queen Mary Social and Athletic Club), Hank Coombes, responded to the women office workers' interest in football by challenging other Southampton offices to provide teams for friendly and charity matches. In the summer of 1966, the new Cunard team, made up of the company's clerks, typists and teleprinter operators, played their first match in aid of the Youth Crusade charity. Appropriately enough, they played against another team with nautical connections, the Girls' Nautical Training Corps (GNTC). Coombes was careful to justify the match to the local *Southern Evening Echo* by saying, 'Our main reason for the match is for the cause of charity; our splendid ship has always been in the fore in this respect, and there is plenty of life in the old girl yet.'[1] The *Echo* continued its support, of what was to most people a novel sport for women, by photographing the Cunard team with the professional men's team, Southampton Saints, outside the local cinema, where both teams had enjoyed watching a film that celebrated the England World Cup win. The caption read: 'England's World Cup triumph in July created enormous interest in soccer, not least among women. So it was not surprising to find one of the top women's soccer teams in Southampton with the Saints to see *Goal! World Cup 1966*!'[2]

Another office team to emerge was a group of women who worked at Southern Gas, and who took their name from their company's magazine, *Flame*. The team was run by captain Carol Lovegrove and a 17-year-old employee, Eileen Clarke. The girls started training in July 1966 and obtained a £30 donation from the Southern Gas Sports and Social Club for their kit. The colours were white shirts and pale blue shorts, representing the company's blue 'flame'. Their first match was also against GNTC, which they drew. Carol's brother, Colin, was an ex-player and he helped to organise and run the team. He later took charge of another office team called Royex, from the Royal Exchange Assurance office, for whom I had started playing (I didn't work for the company but I had written to the *Echo* asking for team contacts and Royex had given me a trial). Other teams were to follow: Sunny Saints, from the Sun Alliance Insurance company; a village team, North Baddesley; and a garage team, Sparshatts. The women in the teams worked mostly in offices and had learned team play from traditional female sports such as hockey and netball. They had also picked up ideas by watching men's football games live on TV. Office colleagues, boyfriends, husbands, brothers and spectators were soon offering them tips and supporting them. All seven teams, Cunard, Flame United, Royex, Sunny Saints, GNTC, North Baddesley and Sparshatts, were to form the first Southampton League.

The League was known officially, in the beginning, as the South Hants Ladies' Football Association (Southampton and District) League. It was governed by a management committee and one member from each club. The chair was Roy Barrett, who also managed the Sunny Saints, the president was Chris Cox, of Patstone and Cox sports outfitters, and the first secretary was Ted Miles. One of the prime movers in starting and maintaining the League was Harry Holt, whose daughter Sandra worked and played for Cunard before moving to Sunny Saints. Harry Holt took over as secretary in the early stages and did a huge amount of organisation. He arranged the fixtures list, booked the pitches, found referees, ensured that all the volunteers met regularly and worked endlessly at fundraising.

The costs for each club were: entry to the association, 10 shillings (50p) per club, players' registration, 7 shillings (35p) and affiliation fee, 3 shillings (15p). Players could be transferred, up until midnight on 31 January, for a fee of 2 shillings and sixpence (12$\frac{1}{2}$p). The cost of hiring one of the Southampton Common pitches was £1.2.6d (£1.22½p). The Rules of the Association make quaint reading because, although they stated that matches would be played according to the FA's rules, there were exceptions for women players:

The four-step goalkeeper's rule did not apply – goalkeepers could take more than four steps before releasing the ball into play.

Obstruction was at the referee's discretion.

The offside rule was to be clearly explained to every team and strictly enforced.

Handball was at the referee's discretion – handball resulting from a person protecting her body would not be penalised.

A substitute was allowed for injury at any time, at the discretion of the referee.

Any swearing, arguing, or rough play was not tolerated by the referee and was liable to serious consequences.

The first League games were played on Sunday, 20 September 1966, at Southampton Common. The common, situated about a mile north of the city, consisted of open land and woods, a lake and three football pitches with goals but no nets. There were wooden changing huts, a toilet, and an outside cold water tap for rinsing off dirty boots and filling up the 'trainer's bucket'. On a sunny Sunday afternoon it attracted strollers and dog walkers and the lake, surrounded by numerous oak trees and bushes, looked tranquil and attractive. On a cold, wet, winter's day, the single attraction for football players was that there were three pitches to play on. Our only major complaint, however, came when we were assigned to the pitch nearest the lake, because then someone would have to wade into the freezing water to collect the ball when it was hit out of play. As we didn't know any different, we just accepted the pitches and poor facilities.

Daryll Holloway was one of the players who had the knack of kicking the ball into the lake. She worked at Cunard and learnt her football from her father, Norman. Norman soon became very interested in women's football and trained and ran a Post Office team, where he worked, in the second year of the league. He was typical of the many fathers who got involved to help their daughters. He had been a scout for Sheffield Wednesday and was the first man I and many others encountered who actually taught us more than basic skills and tactics. His greatest achievement in women's football was to be the first manager of the team to win the WFA Cup, with Southampton in 1971. He smoked incessantly, enjoyed a drink and worried a great deal, which altogether did not help his health. It was a loss to both women's and men's football when he died of a heart attack while refereeing in the mid-1980s. It says everything about Norman that he had only gone to watch a men's match, but had stood in for an absent referee so that the teams could play.

The formation of the Southampton League was well publicised in the local press and company magazines. However, the *Echo* began to adopt a more flippant attitude in its reports. In an article about Flame United, the paper concentrated on the girls' appearances, rather than on their football achievements, and in discussing minor injuries said, 'They have bruises and grazes just like the Saints players, Tony Knapp and Terry Paine, but the difference being that they are only five feet tall, weigh around eight stone and are called Carol and Eileen.' The report continued: 'They are as feminine as their names suggest ... I had expected some tough looking Tamara Presses [alluding to the then Soviet discus thrower, renowned for her masculine appearance] to arrive for the interview!' Finally, the article couldn't resist the pun on passes, concluding: 'The girls have been taught to kick, tackle and make passes (you know what I mean) and the only complaint from Carol and Eileen was that they didn't care for the "press ups"!'[3]

The women were still thrilled to see their names in the press, however patronising the reports may have been. Many had represented school, and some even the county, at netball, hockey and other sports, but playing football was special. We didn't mind the stony pitches and the most basic of changing facilities. The most important thing was that we could have a serious, organised game for the first time in our lives, with referees, managers, proper kit and boots and media recognition of our feats. There was always a 'buzz' around the common on those afternoons when the top teams in the League met. Cunard and Flame United had the more flamboyant players and managers and received most of the publicity, especially Cunard, whose manager/coach, Dave Case, played for the Hampshire League team, Sholing. Dave was the first manager in the area to defy the FA ban on affiliated players having anything to do with women's football. FA secretary Fred Tyler instructed him to end his association with the Cunard team, otherwise he would have to stop playing for Sholing. Dave promptly put someone else in his place as the official manager but continued coaching Cunard – and playing for Sholing. Until this incident, none of us had any idea about the FA ban and its implications, and certainly no one knew about Dick, Kerr Ladies or Manchester Corinthians or their achievements.

The first Southampton League ended in a thrilling climax. Flame United finally pipped Cunard when they beat them 1–0, with one game still to play. Flame gained 18 points and Cunard finished their programme with only 17. Cunard beat Sunny Saints 3–1 in the Cup Final and also won the League six-a-side tournament. My team, Royex, finished fifth, but I had the consolation of being the League's top scorer with 24 goals. Second top goalscorer was Flame United's Ann Hooper, who was an extremely fast sprinter. Her hard shots were legendary and only the bravest would attempt to head her crosses or free-kicks. Ann had attended an all girls' school called Weston Park (now Chamberlayne Park) which, although not allowing girls to play organised football at school, produced many excellent women players. Besides Ann, there were four other Southampton players from the school, Jill Long and Barbara Birkett (who played together in the first WFA Cup Final), Jill Osman (who was also an outstanding netball player) and future England goalkeeper, Sue Buckett.

The first season had gone well, with football played in true amateur spirit, and credit was due to the excellent organisation by all the volunteers, including the referees, who worked free of charge. The only general complaint concerned the lack of nets on the goals. The League winners, Flame United, were particularly annoyed that they had been refused a 'goal' that they were convinced passed through the posts. The referee had been equally convinced it went the 'wrong side' and had given a goal-kick. It would be unthinkable to play a game at any level today without nets. The matter of treatment of injuries had also been somewhat overlooked. The first League secretary, Ted Miles, had sent a warning letter at the beginning of the season to all the clubs and referees about injuries, but incredibly, instead of instructing them to ensure they had first-aid kits and someone with training, the letter merely warned players to be more careful as 'over eagerness in all forms of sport could well lead to them receiving serious injury'. It went on to warn players that the committee would 'take the severest of action against offenders'. When I was badly concussed in one match, no one seemed to know how to advise or treat me, nor did anyone seek medical advice; when I saw a doctor myself, he suggested that I should 'take up fishing instead of football'. It wasn't until years later that I discovered how serious concussion could be. My experience at the common illustrates the risks we all took in those days with the deficient medical knowledge regarding injuries.

The end-of-season presentation evening and dance, efficiently organised by Harry Holt, was a very formal occasion and local businessmen, who had supported the League, provided and presented the trophies. It gave the players, managers, volunteer helpers, parents and friends an opportunity to reflect on a very successful start to women's football in Southampton.

The birth of the Southampton team

Early in the first 1966–67 season, it became apparent that there were some women who wanted to take football more seriously, and some who were happy to continue playing on a friendly, recreational basis. The League managers and officials also agreed that if the standard of football was to improve, the better players would need to aspire to a higher level and gain selection into one representative team. It was decided that a committee, consisting of Roy Barrett, Dave Case and Colin Lovegrove, should select the top players from the League clubs to form a new Southampton team. A challenge match was arranged for the first appointed team, against a club from Portsmouth called Paulsgrove Ladies (later known as Portsmouth) and for whom Jean Seymour, now aged 37, had started playing. The match was to be played on Sunday, 11 December 1966, at the Sholing FC ground. In her letter accepting the challenge, Jean obviously recalled the problems Dick, Kerr Ladies and Manchester Corinthians had experienced when they tried to obtain the use of FA-affiliated pitches. She queried whether the Southampton officials had gained permission to use the Sholing pitch for the game. Manager Dave Case had booked the pitch but, true to form, was prevented from using it by the Hants FA. At short notice the Southampton officials managed to gain the use of the Southampton Sports Centre pitch, but if Jean had not alerted them there could have been a last-minute cancellation. Consequently the match, signalling the beginning of the great Southampton team and the dawning of the new modern era of women's football, had a rather ignominious start. It was played on a small, stony, muddy pitch, in lashing rain, and was watched by a few regular League match supporters, parents and friends. It was played, in the time-honoured tradition, for charity: the Cervical Cancer Research Fund. The line-up for the first Southampton team's match was: goalkeeper, Lynn Attwood (Cunard); full-backs, Val Jenkins (GNTC) and Jenny Martin; half-back line, Jane Martin (Cunard), Joan Cronin (Royex) and Jill Long (Flame United and captain); forwards, outside-right, Sandra Holt (Sunny Saints), inside-right, Ann Hooper (Flame United), centre-forward, Val Chalk (Cunard), inside-left Sue Lopez (Royex) and outside-left Joy Lovell (GNTC). The team proudly wore the Southampton FC Saints' colours of red and white stripes.

It didn't matter to us that we were not playing on a Hants League ground – we were just thrilled to be playing for the city and it was not surprising that we played well. The forward line, that had already scored 56 goals between them in the League, scored five goals during the match, and Ann Hooper scored a hat-trick. The defence kept a clean sheet and Southampton won 5–0. Captain Jill Long remembers the day vividly:

> Bobby Moore was my hero and I never thought when I saw him lead out England in the World Cup Final at Wembley that I'd lead out a team on to a football pitch – and I was so proud it was my city team. We wore the Saints kit too and won. My Mum and Dad watched. Dad had taught me and my brother all we knew about football and it was great to have the chance to put it all into practice in such an important game. Despite the awful conditions, it was one of the greatest days of my life!

The 1967–68 season

In the second season, Flame United obtained sponsorship from Charlie Malizia, a Southampton bookmaker, and became known as Inter-Malizia. My team Royex also changed their name to Real FC. We had a brand-new strip of maroon and pale blue stripes, rather similar to Barcelona, but our name was more suggestive of the other great Spanish side, Real Madrid, whose star players, di Stefano and Puskas, I admired. I had convinced the team that Real would sound better than Royex and would stand for Royal Exchange Assurance Ladies, if anyone still cared, as only one or two of the original office employees now remained. We had acquired Daryll Holloway (ex-Cunard), who had become a terrifying tackler, and a very reliable goalkeeper called Doreen Bridle, who had learnt her sport in the army.

The season also saw a few club additions, Tottonians, St Francis, Seven Seas Athletic, Post Office and Minicab Maidens. North Baddesley had withdrawn, and the Cunard team, as they had been known, disbanded. League president Chris Cox and Dave Case formed a new team, consisting of some of the best Cunard players, called Patstone Utd. Apart from the talented players signed to Patstone Utd, they were a young team and most of the top women footballers were contained in the better clubs, Real, Inter-Malizia and Sunny Saints. These teams dominated the League. Real FC eventually swept the board by becoming League leaders, winners of the six-a-side tournament and joint Cup-holders with Inter-Malizia.

The next big match for the new representative Southampton team was against Ipswich, on Saturday, 7 October 1967. It was played at the Royal Victoria Hospital grounds at Netley and, as the pitch was owned by the Royal Army Medical Corps, there was no fear of FA intervention. The opposition was crushed 9–0, and I scored my first hat-trick. Jean Seymour was now playing for Southampton, having signed for Patstone Utd. Sue Buckett (Inter-Malizia) and Barbara Birkett (Tottonians) made their debut appearances in the match, as did two new young players, centre-forward Pat Davies and outside-right, Lynda Hale. Both Pat and Lynda had been discovered by Dave Case and were now also playing for Patstone. Despite her diminutive height, Pat Davies was one of the best strikers in women's football, with a shot that earned her the name 'Thunder'. She had an incredible ability to jump higher than players much taller than herself and superbly head the ball once she reached it. Lynda had an amazing right foot that enabled her to power her way past defenders, and had, perhaps, the hardest shot of any woman. As well as this fearsome duo, playing for Southampton was Patstone's Maureen Bailey, a solid and constructive midfield player, who later married Dave Case.

On Sunday, 17 December 1967, Southampton took on Coventry, a representative side selected from the seven clubs that formed the new Warwickshire League that had started in September. They had previously beaten Hereford 18–0, but lost to Fodens 5–1. Southampton won 9–1. Another newcomer to the squad in this match was Minicab Maidens' Dot Cassell. Dot was an outstanding player and despite being small in height, had audacious ball control.

With a record of played 3, won 3, and 23 goals scored, with one against, it was no surprise that the team and the organising committee next set their sights on the famous Fodens side, who were reputed to be the strongest women's team in the country.

The first match against Fodens took place on Sunday, 31 March 1968 at the Southampton Sports Centre and was played in aid of the Mayor's Appeal Fund. I remember that we were very confident we would continue our successful run of victories, despite losing the services of Lynda Hale, Pat Davies and Maureen Bailey. Dave Case had decided to 'go it alone' with Patstone Utd and had withdrawn them from the League in order to play friendly matches around the country. However, many of us had second thoughts when we saw the Fodens team warming up. They seemed bigger, stronger and more mature than our players. Fodens' Lesley Caldwell seemed to mesmerise Southampton's defence. Full-backs Daryll Holloway and Barbara Birkett worked hard, but they could not stop Lesley or their other star player Joan Tench. I equalised a goal from Joan Briggs but, just before half-time, Joan Tench scored another. In the second half our lack of fitness was telling and Fodens scored another two goals to win 4–1. We were overwhelmed by Fodens' power, strength and fitness and it seemed we needed to step up another gear if we were to compete with the best.

The Southampton team steams ahead

The 1968–69 season saw the Southampton League split into two divisions with Real FC, Inter-Malizia, Sunny Saints, Tottonians, Minicab Maidens and Seven Seas Athletic in the First Division and the rest in the new Second Division. Real FC won the League again and shared the Cup with Tottonians after a 2–2 draw.

The Southampton team continued playing representative matches with easy wins, over an improved Coventry team 5–3, Maidenhead 6–1, 14–0, and Swindon 12–0, 14–0. The Southampton manager, Colin Lovegrove (who took over from Dave Case), reported to the League's management committee that some of the Swindon's men's team had watched the Swindon away match and had commented on how well the Southampton women had played. The highlight of the season was a return match against Fodens, on Saturday 10 May 1969, played at a local school in Sandbach, Cheshire, in aid of building the school's swimming pool. As well as the players who had tormented us in the first match, they now had Sheila Parker, the ex-Dick, Kerr Ladies' player and future England captain, in their defence. However, we were well prepared and determined to erase the embarrassment of the previous 4–1 defeat. The most significant difference to our team was the inclusion of Jill Osman from Inter-Malizia. She was not always available for matches due to her teacher training commitments, and her enthusiasm to win inspired us all. After a thrilling match, with two goals from Inter-Malizia's Angie Mills and one from me, we finally conquered Fodens, 3–2.

In June, Southampton returned to Coventry to play the Midlands Ladies' Football League representative team, but the game ended in an anti-climatic 0–0 draw. The League contained the Leicester club, EMGALS, who were later to organise successful summer tournaments that proved valuable pre-season practice for most of the top teams in the country.

A pleasant diversion in the summer of 1969 was the visit of Rapid Jihlava from Czechoslovakia. The Southampton team arranged to play them at the Nursling Recreation Ground in Southampton, on the evening of 18 July. Over 100 people turned up to watch Southampton's first encounter with foreign opposition, which ended in a 4–1 win for us. It was a notable game for Sue Buckett and me, as I scored my hundredth goal since I had started playing, and it was the first time Sue Buckett played in goal for us. Also, attending the match as guest of honour, was the great Southampton and Wales centre-forward Ron Davis. He often used to watch the Sunday-afternoon games at Southampton Common, where he would offer words of advice and never refuse a request for an autograph. Like some of the old professional players in the past, who helped Dick, Kerr Ladies or Manchester Corinthians, he always showed respect and support for the women's game.

By now, the women in the Southampton team had aspirations to become the best team in the country, and we could not wait for our next challenge. In addition, our fame was beginning to spread: apart from the usual match coverage in the local paper, *Goal* magazine printed a feature article on the team.

The Deal International Tournament

The Deal Tournament was organised by Arthur Hobbs, who worked as a carpenter at the Deal Council offices in Kent. Arthur

Hobbs had a genuine passion for women's football and was determined to develop the game to a higher level by introducing a prestigious tournament. He had planned for the inaugural competition, in 1967, to be played on the Charles Sports Ground, home of Deal Town FC. At the beginning all the teams involved were local, made up from various workplaces, youth organisations, and staff from St Augustine's Hospital, Canterbury. The money raised was to go to the Mayor of Deal's Appeal Fund for Deal Town FC. However, Kent County FA insisted that the FA's ban on women's football meant that women's teams could not use the pitch, even for charity purposes. The chair and a committee member of the club resigned. The local *East Kent Mercury* newspaper stated:

> Promoters of the tournament were staggered by the ruling which forbids the club accepting the proceeds, despite the fact that last season two ladies' teams played on the ground. The two resignees talked to the newspaper about the pettiness of the Kent County FA. The County FA said that they had to abide by the ruling preventing the County FA having anything to do with unaffiliated football. They said they had not known about the two ladies' matches played on the ground during the previous season.

Arthur Hobbs eventually found the Betteshanger Colliery Welfare Sports Ground in Deal to hold his tournament and the proceeds of the competition went to the British Empire Cancer Campaign for Research. Frustrated by events of this sort, Arthur Hobbs became even more determined for women to have equal access to the country's national game and to overcome the ban on women's football in England.

In the 1968 tournament, 32 teams entered, including Manchester Corinthians who went on to win. The Corinthians' participation heralded the beginning of a more serious competition, and in the 1969 tournament there were 52 entries, including Southampton, for the first time, and three foreign teams – Start Praha and Slavia Kaplice from Czechoslovakia, and the Austrian Ladies' Football Union from Vienna. Cambuslang Hooverettes, the Scottish champions from Glasgow, also entered. Manchester Corinthians won again – beating Southampton 2–1 in the quarter-finals – and Deal Hockey Club in the final. The trophy was presented by the local Member of Parliament, David

Ennals, who later went on to support Arthur Hobbs in forming the WFA.

Southampton returned to the tournament in 1970 and met Hooverettes in the final. Hooverettes' midfield 'General', Paddy McGroarty (who later moved to the London team, QPR) and I had to take 'sudden-death' penalties, when the score was 0–0 after normal time. I missed the first, then Sue Buckett made an incredible save. I scored the second time but Paddy missed. It was Southampton's first major trophy.

The Butlin's Cup

In 1969 the Deal Tournament was to have a rival national competition, jointly organised by ITV, the *Daily Mirror* and Butlin's Holiday Camps. The idea originated from a challenge laid down by TV personality Hughie Green on the *It's a Knockout* programme. In the autumn, a knock-out cup competition was staged in England to find a winning team to take on the winners of a parallel Scottish competition.

The Southampton team entered the competition, but found that some of the opposition they encountered lacked the seriousness and ability to play at the top level. In the early rounds Southampton beat a Cornish team called Dobwalls 21–0 and a team from the London area called Beacham Belles 13–0. The competition did, however, attract national media attention – I scored ten goals in the Beacham Belles match and this was featured in the *Daily Mirror*. After our easy wins in the early rounds, Southampton met Fodens in the semi-final at the Butlin's camp in Minehead, Somerset. In front of several hundred holiday makers, Fodens drove through our defence to win 5–1. Although I had scored the only goal, I was as disappointed as the rest of the team. Again, we all had to concede that our opponents had been fitter, stronger and sharper.

The first Italian tournament

As there was no official England team, Harry Batt, the manager of the Chiltern Valley women's club, was invited by the Federation of Independent European Female Football (FIEFF), to take an English XI to the Italian Tournament in Turin in November 1969. In the absence of the Union of European Football Associations (UEFA), organising women's football, FIEFF, set up by Italian businessmen, had taken on the role and done much to popularise the sport throughout the world. They organised European and world competitions and supplied the teams with equipment, kit and all-expenses-paid travel and accommodation.[4]

The four-nation tournament was between the hosts Italy, Denmark, France and England. Harry Batt took his own players but supplemented the team with five Southampton players: goalkeeper Sue Buckett, defenders Jill Long and Barbara Birkett, forwards Dot Cassell and myself. For some unknown reason, Harry Batt failed to select players from the top teams, Fodens and Manchester Corinthians. From our point of view, with just two or three players, such as Sheila Parker, Joan Tench and Lesley Caldwell, we would have achieved better results and received some positive publicity.

We travelled to Italy by train and ferry, where we spent most of the time sewing Union Jacks on to our tracksuits in an attempt to 'patch' on some sense of unity and identity. We arrived in Turin late in the day and travelled up into the mountain area of Aosta by coach. We shared the hotel accommodation with the Danish team, represented by the club side Femina and, in conversation with these players, we began to discover how advanced women's football was in Europe; how it was widely played and how it had been allowed to flourish. Our first match was against Femina; we narrowly lost 4–3. It was unfortunate because we could have equalised with a penalty right at the end. We went on to beat France easily in the play-off for third and fourth place. Italy finally beat Denmark 3–1 in the final.

Despite not being as successful as we had hoped, it was a thrill to play foreign opponents on some of the best pitches in Italy. All the grounds were excellent and were the same ones used by the professional men's teams. The crowds of 10,000 plus were beyond anything we had experienced. We felt elated to have been part of such an exciting tournament, after the small-scale events in England, and it was remarkable to find everything taken more seriously. It was how we imagined the professional male players were treated, with nice hotels, beautiful venues and respect, especially from the press. I personally enjoyed the lively atmosphere, the enthusiasm and friendliness of Italian women's football.

Southampton players leave the League

With the establishment of major national and international competitions and tournaments, the women in the Southampton team felt that the Southampton League was not competitive enough and seemed rather parochial. Some women were content to play recreational football on Sunday afternoons, but others, having also experienced the quality of play abroad, aspired to a higher level. We realised we would have to make commitments and sacrifices in order to play a more 'professional' and competitive game, and that we needed to concentrate our efforts on playing for the representative Southampton team and leave our League clubs. The opportunity arose after the WFA was formed, as in 1971, the first chair, Pat Dunn, and other officials, complained about the unfairness of the Southampton League 'feeding' into a representative team. The Southampton club was found guilty by the WFA of 'misrepresentation' as they were not registered as a League club but had been playing as such in the tournaments and the WFA Cup, and we were fined £20. The Southampton team separated and joined the larger Home Counties League. The original Southampton League continued, changing its name to the Wessex League, but with the better and more dedicated players and managers gone, it lasted only a few seasons. In retrospect, £20 was a small sacrifice for such a great return.

4 Giallorosse – the Italian affair

During the Italian tournament, in November 1969, my goal-scoring had been noticed by some of the Italian club managers. Before our departure from Italy I was invited by the Real Torino manager, Mr Ramboudi, to be his guest for a few days and train with the team, with a view to signing for them. I could not believe I was being offered a contract to play full-time football. I was sad to see my team-mates leave for England, but I was in the company of a Danish player, Birgit Nilsen, and a Czechoslovakian player, Maria Scevikova, who had also been approached. I had an enjoyable few days in Turin and played a friendly match before returning home to what was to be months of indecision. Later, another Italian club, Roma, also expressed an interest in me and although I had no doubts I wanted to play in Italy, the decision to leave was complicated.

I continued to play for Southampton, to whom I felt great loyalty. By winning the Deal Tournament in 1970, we were now confirmed as the top team in the country. The FA ban had been lifted and the WFA had been formed. I had become involved as an administrator for the new WFA organisation and it was an exciting time for English women's football. The WFA had also decided to set up an official international team and were threatening to ban players who jeopardised their amateur status by playing professionally. However, as the WFA were too preoccupied with banning Harry Batt for his illicit England XI trips, and players associated with him, I thought my leaving for Italy would not cause too much concern. After attending initial WFA meetings, I realised there would still be a long way to go before things really improved.

After much deliberation I chose to play for Roma and left for Rome on 15 May 1971, a week after Southampton had won the inaugural WFA Cup competition. Leaving my secretarial job was the easiest task – nothing could ever beat playing football full-time.

Southampton player Dot Cassell had also received offers, but was still undecided, so I arrived in Italy on my own.

Roma

The Italian League season ran from April until November, when the men's teams were not using the pitches. Roma was founded by a woman, Mira Bellei, who was a physical education lecturer, and the team had been playing since 1967. Their first match was against Napoli; it ended in a 2–2 draw. The first League Championship had started in the spring of 1968, organised by the Federazione Italiana Calcio Femminile (FICF) based in Viareggio. There were four teams in the northern division and five in the southern. The two top teams from each division played the runners-up in the other League. Genova beat Roma in the final 1–0 in 1968, but Roma won the championship in 1969. There were ten teams in the 1969 championship, Genova, Real Torino, Cagliari, Ambrosiana, Fiorentina, Piacenza, Napoli, Lazio, Roma and Milano. Players from these teams made up the Italian team that the England XI had played in the 1969 tournament. In 1970, another federation was formed, the Federazione Femminile Italiana Gioco Calcio (FFIGC), which oversaw a League of 14 teams and was based in Rome. FICF moved its headquarters to Turin. Roma came fourth in the League that year, behind Genova, Piacenza and Gommagomma from Milan. Roma's Stefania Medri had scored nearly all the goals during the season and they were desperate to find another goalscoring forward.

Living and playing in Italy

I had received a lot of publicity about my transfer from the local and national press and had even represented women's football at the *Daily Express*'s 'Sportsman of the Year' award, a few months prior to leaving. However, my home in Italy was not the luxurious apartment in Rome that the newspapers had suggested but a small first-floor flat about ten minutes' walk from the sea at Ostia Lido, outside Rome. I shared with Gibus, an English-speaking French girl, who captained Roma's Second XI, called Lazio. The previous year, Roma had played against Reims in exhibition matches in Indonesia, Thailand and the USA. After the tour, Gibus, a Reims player, had transferred. Gibus was a very kind and sensitive person and she helped me to get to know the players and personalities connected with Roma and Lazio. Another foreign player was Monika Karner from Austria, who lived with Mira and Franco Bellei. Mira managed the Roma team and Franco ran Lazio. Our trainer was a man called Guglielmo Tamilia.

The first chance to prove myself came in my debut match on Sunday, 23 May 1971 in the Ina Casa stadium in Rome. The ground held about 10,000 people but on this occasion only six or seven hundred turned up. The pitch was made of dusty shale. The trainer, Tamilia, announced the line-up – I was to be substitute, so that I would have a chance to watch the team play. We were playing last year's League runners-up, Piacenza. Both teams had eight points from four games, with Roma placed at the top of the League with a slightly better goal average. Piacenza's international players, Luciana Meles, Maura Fabbri, Stefania Bandini and Rosa Rocca, gave the side a confident air, whereas nerves inhibited the Roma team, especially when, after just 12 minutes, star player Stefania Medri was substituted because of an injury. The weakened 'Gaillorosse' ('Red and Yellows' as Roma were nicknamed), not surprisingly, were struggling and by half-time were 2–0 down. After his initial anger, Tamilia calmly started to reorganise the team. I could hardly contain my excitement when he announced that I would be starting the second half in place of Elena Dell'Uomo, who had also been injured. The crowd roared us on and we made some determined attacks, but the opposition defended well. I finally made a breakthrough in the last few minutes of the game and unleashed a hard shot past the stranded goalkeeper, but it was too late to start a rally. It was disappointing to see in the *Corriere dello Sport* that the League table showed Piacenza installed at the top with ten points. Football journalist Gianni Bezzi quite rightly claimed, 'First round to Piacenza'. On the other hand, I was not only amazed to see the excellent coverage of our game, from Italy's major national sporting daily, but a whole page devoted to women's football.

Later in the season, *Sunday Times* football journalist Brian Glanville met me in Rome on his way back from an England v. Greece match in Athens. Brian was fascinated by Rome and spoke impeccable Italian. I was interested to hear his football anecdotes and his 'inside' information about Italian women's football, which he gained from Gianni Bezzi. He informed me that two foreign players with Fiorentina were supposedly earning £40 a week. I told him that I hoped that gossip of that nature would not get back to the WFA in England or they would ban me – I only received living and travelling expenses. He was convinced that the women's game would always struggle in England because of the intransigence and indifference of the football establishment. The 'macho' professional side of the game, like the media, felt that football was a man's game and should not be played by women. Brian, it seemed, was a convert to women's football – in Italy – once back home, he reverted to the typical reporting he so adamantly criticised.

I found the Italian players, fans and media, enthusiastic and encouraging. It was like playing a Cup Final every week and I never tired of seeing Monday's *Corriere dello Sport*, carrying all the match reports. It was a pleasure not to be embarrassed or angry at having to deal with the negative reactions to women playing football. It was accepted and admired. I continued to enjoy the technically superior type of play that I found in the National League. Apart from the three bottom clubs, all the teams provided keenly contested matches and most teams had some extremely talented players. I now had a regular place in the team and our next games were against Trastevere, Genoa and Autoroma. I scored both the goals in the Autoroma match and was awarded the headline, 'Two splendid goals from Lopez' in the *Corriero dello Sport*. Later in the week, Gianni Bezzi flatteringly discussed in the paper the possible revival of Roma since my arrival.

Also playing in the Autoroma match was ex-Hooverettes player Joan Clements, who was having a trial with Roma. Joan struggled in the intense afternoon heat and she found that her tough tackling was not as acceptable as it was in Britain. She was booked for a mistimed tackle that would not have, in England, raised an eyebrow. The Italian referees were much stricter and far less patronising. In England most women didn't learn how to tackle properly, and the referees were far too lenient; they didn't seem to understand that a dangerous tackle could be made by a woman as well as a man.

Roma's success continued with victories against Audax 4–0, Bologna 4–0 and Lubiam 2–0, and in August we beat Fiorentina, Messina and Napoli. By now I had developed better team play with my colleagues, especially Stefania Medri, and at the age of 26 was playing at my peak. The warm climate, absence of bureaucratic distractions, and respect from all concerned, proved to be the most perfect way to play football.

Dot Cassell had finally decided to come to Italy, but to play for a bottom-of-the-League team, Trastevere. Despite the team's problems, Dot too began enjoying the Italian way of life and football. She had learnt French at school and therefore found Italian easy to pick up and in fact she became more 'Italian' every time I saw her, smoking, socialising and using the occasional expletive, to the amusement of her team-mates. Joan Clements was not so happy and had decided to return home. Later, the talented Rose Reilly, who played for Stewarton and Thistle, came to play for Milan in 1973 and stayed. It seemed that I had opened up the floodgates for other disillusioned British women players, who were willing to risk being banned in their search for challenging football.

My close friends in the team were the captain, Lucia Gridelli, an English-speaking player called Elena, who often interpreted for me, and Patrizia de Grandis. Lucia spent most of her spare time looking after an invalid mother and therefore did not work and rarely joined in with the team on social occasions. Elena worked at a pizzeria and provided the team with free pizzas whenever we went there. Patrizia de Grandis was as grand and as good-looking as her name suggests, but like Lucia was tied to a very mundane life away from football. She worked as a wigmaker from 8 am until 6 pm in the evening and lived with her parents and their two youngest children. Her family invited me to stay with them, rather than in the apartment in Ostia, which I accepted, since Gibus had returned home to Reims after an argument with Franco Bellei. Mrs de Grandis was a splendid cook and kept her family in rigorous order. By the time I moved in with them, my Italian had improved and I could make simple conversation and pick up words from the television. Apart from the occasional agitated shouts from Mrs de Grandis when her family did not comply with her household regime, it was a happy family and I was glad to stay. Occasionally, I would be reminded of the problems I had left at home. Norman Holloway, now the Southampton manager, would write with all the news and in one letter informed me that Southampton's success as a club was in jeopardy. Many clubs were keen to 'knock us off our pedestal'.

The USA trip

In early September I went on a trip with Roma to play a number of exhibition matches in the USA. Prior to the tour, Mira and

Franco Bellei had asked the team to suggest suitable opponents to take with us. I suggested that the Southampton team would make a good match. It was to be Southampton's first foreign tour. The trip was paid for by sponsors known to the Belleis in the USA who, I assumed, were keen to promote women's football. I never knew exactly how the money was found to pay for our national League matches, ground hire, training facilities and foreign trips. The foreign trips were possible, maybe, because the games attracted large crowds and brought in sufficient revenue. Crowd attendance in Italy could also be several hundred, or thousands, for a big match, but even this could not have paid for our nationwide travel. Obviously there must have been rich benefactors or businessmen who recognised the potential profitability of the sport. The main thing for players was that we paid nothing to play football. We occasionally received more than generous expenses, and sometimes gifts, such as inscribed gold bracelets for winning the Italian League Cup. The all-expenses-paid transatlantic trip was going to be altogether different from what the Southampton team had experienced so far.

In New York we stayed in a hotel in the centre of Manhattan, just off Times Square, and both teams trained in nearby Central Park. Unfortunately, Dave Case, who was now the trainer for Southampton, ignored the team's jet lag and exhausted some of the players. Dave Case and Norman Holloway took an instant dislike to the Italians and complained about them, and the trip, at every opportunity. Norman constantly told me that he believed the Mafia had financed the trip and I should beware of being associated with Roma. I felt he was just trying to warn me away from playing in Italy and entice me back to England. Although the Southampton officials displayed a hostile attitude, the players in the two teams mixed very well, despite the language barrier. After just a few days Southampton's problems were compounded when Dave Case went into hospital with pneumonia, where he had to stay for several weeks. The other official with the Southampton team was Pat Gregory, the WFA assistant secretary, who came along as the WFA's representative. This was the first trip that the new governing body had sanctioned and after all the altercations over Harry Batt's unofficial trips, they were determined to see for themselves that all was well. Once Pat could see that the Italians were not trying to lure the entire Southampton team to Italy and that there was no evidence of Mafia involvement, she began to enjoy the tour as much as the players.

The matches were held in specially adapted baseball and American football pitches in the Italian quarters of New York, Philadelphia and Boston. The pitches were, consequently, quite rough where they had been marked for the American sports, but the matches proved to be splendid entertainment for the spectators. Roma's superior experience of a competitive national league gave them a sharper edge and the best that Southampton could achieve was one 4–4 draw out of four games. Roma won 3–1, 3–2 and in the final game overwhelmed them 6–3. The last game was played on 16 September in Boston, where I maintained my goal-a-game record and Stephania Medri scored a hat-trick. For all the players it had been a memorable and exciting experience, and my only regret was my pulled hamstring in the second match.

A few of the English-speaking Italian players kept in touch with the Southampton team after they had returned home and inevitably, there was some discussion about players transferring. Norman Holloway was particularly upset when Lynda Hale went to Rome afterwards to see one of the players. Although she was not seriously considering a transfer, he suspected otherwise and took the matter up with the WFA. In a letter dated 23 October, Norman told me that the WFA was looking into the 'poaching by Italian clubs' and that Sir Stanley Rous, the English president of the world governing body of football, the Fédération Internationale de Football Association (FIFA), was investigating an unofficial Women's World Cup in Mexico (which had included an England XI organised by Harry Batt). Despite my repeated claims that I only received expenses, he said that people were convinced I was a professional because they had read it in the papers. He was concerned that I should be able to prove my amateur status when I returned and told me that it was up to the player to prove it. The WFA's association with any professional player could jeopardise grant allocations from the Sports Council. He also informed me that Southampton's WFA Cup-winning squad player, Louise Cross, had received a three-month suspension for going to Mexico and Italy with Harry Batt. I wondered how many more cigarettes Norman was smoking a day, as a result of these frustrations. Unfortunately, the debate over players going abroad did not serve to provoke action from those with power to change things. What was needed in England was the positive development in the structure of a national team and a national league, not the threat of bans.

Runners-up in the League

Within four days of the final match in the USA, Roma returned to the climax of the season with three crucial League matches and the final stages of the Coppa Italia Cup. We flew to Genoa and played the first of our League games against the Genovese side at Rapallo. The team continued to play as well as they had done in America and won 2–0. Piacenza drew with Juventus, but were still top of the table, with 35 points from 19 games. Roma were second with 30 points from 18 games. As we played, and drew, against both Piacenza and Cagliari, it looked as if the League Championship was slipping away from us and so we concentrated our efforts on winning the Coppa Italia Cup.

One of my best matches in Italy was a Cup game against Napoli, on 28 November. We played on a large ground in Naples that the men's team sometimes used and it had one of the most perfect pitches. In the dressing room we all felt very excited, but nervous; we desperately wanted to win and progress into the quarter-finals. Tamilia had decided on a new formation because two of the regular forwards were unavailable. I was given a midfield role with Monica Karner, but it didn't work and we immediately went 1–0 down. In the second half, I was put back into my familiar forward position but my injured hamstring began to hurt. After just nine minutes we were awarded a penalty which I was urged to take and I managed to place in the right-hand corner of the net. In the twenty-third minute I was brought down in the penalty area and we were awarded another shot. The atmosphere was incredible and the partisan Neapolitan crowd were hissing and shouting as I went up to score our second goal. With only a few minutes left, I completed my hat-trick, which was just as well, as Napoli scored a second goal almost on the final whistle. The next day I had treatment on my leg and resigned myself to a week out of training. When I turned to the football page of *Corriere dello Sport*, there was an action picture of myself with a headline that read 'Lopez lets fly at Napoli with three goals'.

A trip to Thailand

Just when I was beginning to make plans to be home for Christmas, the Roma team had an offer of a tour of Thailand, leaving just before New Year's Eve. As I didn't really enjoy the traditional English Christmas and New Year celebrations, I couldn't think of anything better than visiting Bangkok and playing football. Roma had been to Bangkok the previous year and their matches had been so popular that the Thai organisers wanted them back.

We departed from Rome via Bombay, on 28 December. As soon as we stepped off the plane we were garlanded with flowers by our Thai welcoming party and photographed and interviewed by the press. We trained the next day at the National Stadium Complex, observed by curious football fans and photographers, and we helped promote the tour by visiting two Thai newspaper offices and a children's hospital.

Due to the lack of women's teams in Thailand, we played against an U18 boys' team and an ex-international men's XI. The first match, against the boys' team, was played under floodlights at the National Stadium, in front of a crowd of approximately 60,000. The boys were extremely fit and it was a struggle to keep up. I missed a penalty in the sixty-ninth minute, but we were cheered on by the crowd, who got very excited whenever we managed to get into the opposition's half of the pitch. The boys proved to be a much stronger side and we finally went down 8–1. We met the ex-international men's team the next day and regained some of our honour in a 3–3 draw. The men's team were less fit and slower and we were able to play a more orthodox attacking game with fewer defensive duties. It was a memorable trip and we were treated like VIPs wherever we went.

Cup consolation

In the first week of the New Year, after the Thailand trip, Roma began preparing for the Cup Final. We had played and won against Bologna in the semi-finals, 1–0, and were now to meet Fiorentina. Piacenza had won the League and Roma were runners-up. We were determined not to be runners-up in the Coppa Italia as well. The final match was played in Rome on 9 January 1972. Neither team played with confidence as both were anxious not to concede the often decisive first goal. In the fifteenth minute of the second half I received the ball on the halfway line and proceeded goalwards past two defenders. With a pass to Monika Karner, who slotted the ball past the goalkeeper, we went into the lead. Roma managed to hold on to their advantage and eventually captured the Cup 1–0. I was proud to have been part of Roma's success.

I was very happy during my time in Italy, having achieved more than I ever dreamed of, including travel, amazing football

experiences and long-term friends. Until the 1971 recommendation by UEFA, that governing bodies take control of the game,
there were no other national leagues for women and nowhere in
the world where women could play football and have everything
provided.

I returned to England with the intention of going back to Italy
for the 1972 season, but three things changed my mind. First, I
got caught up with the Southampton team's attempts to retain
the WFA Cup. Second, (and most importantly), the opportunity
arose to be in the first official England team. Third, the ever-present
threat of a ban on players who went abroad, even semi-
professionally, (as it was now called, if you received only expenses),
would mean I could jeopardise the chance of ever playing for
England. I chose to stay but, unluckily, after learning how to avoid
concussions, and having rehabilitated my hamstring, I fractured
my ankle in a friendly match against a men's XI. I was not fit
enough to attend the first England trials and had to wait another
year for the next selection opportunity.

5 Women's Football Association, 1969–1993

This chapter highlights the key events in the history of the WFA and gives a broad outline of the part the association played in establishing the game in England during its 24 years in existence. The complete history of the WFA has been written by David Marlowe, one of the association's longest-serving administrators, and offers a more comprehensive insight into the association's development.[1] David Marlowe became vice-chairman of the association in 1971 and was involved, right up until the FA takeover in 1993, when he helped with the transition. He was chair for five continuous years and, in 1977, he became an honorary life member. Until 1991, he took on the role for which he is best known, that of rules coordinator. One of the first tasks he undertook was to rewrite the WFA constitution, which led him to say, "I suppose when I rewrote the constitution, I sealed my own fate and became the WFA 'godfather of administration' for the next 24 years."[2] In 1982 he did the legal work involved in making the WFA a limited company and became the first company secretary. He resigned in 1984 because he said, "I would not accept the accounts and I knew that if I did I would become legally liable for any ensuing problems that could arise."[3] Perhaps David knew more than the rest, but certainly his words had serious implications.

If David Marlowe was the 'godfather of administration' then Arthur Hobbs was the 'father of women's football'. Arthur Hobbs was the person most instrumental in starting the WFA. He ran the successful Deal International Tournament, and he knew that if the women's game was to grow, it needed a governing body, which could provide a development structure, and which could lobby the FA to rescind the ban. He could not have anticipated the huge financial implications concomitant with running the association, especially when the game started to expand more quickly than resources could manage. The main intention was to make up for 48 years of stagnation. From the foreign teams who had participated in the Deal Tournament, or – like Rapid Jihlava – who had toured England, it was apparent that women's football was developing much faster elsewhere in the world. Arthur's ambition was for English women's football to be at the forefront. Perhaps it was as well that he did not live to see the association descend into the political infighting that finally led to its ignominious end in 1993. He might have appreciated the irony, but probably would not have appreciated the fact, that the WFA had to turn to the FA to rescue women's football from its problems, a move which subsequently allowed the FA to take over lock, stock and financial barrel.

The lifting of the ban

At the conclusion of the Deal International Tournament on 6 July 1969, Arthur Hobbs declared the formation of a new Ladies' Football Association of Great Britain. The prospect of a new organisation that would raise the status of the women's game gained a lot of media interest. On 1 November 1969, representatives of 44 women's clubs attended an inaugural meeting at Caxton Hall, in London. Key people attending were: Arthur Hobbs (honorary secretary), Gladys Aikin (membership secretary) of Manchester Corinthians, Patricia Gregory (assistant secretary) representing the White Ribbon club and the South-East England League, and Mrs Pat Dunn (chair). Other representatives included: Flo Bilton, from Hull, June Jaycocks, from Brighton and myself (minute secretary), from Southampton. Olive Newsom, of the Central Council for Physical Recreation, assisted in preparing the first constitution and other formal matters. It is Olive who deserves the thanks for quickly eradicating the clumsy and archaic title of 'ladies', by saying, 'Ladies play golf – women do athletics and football!' So, with the launch of the new organisation, under the name of the Women's Football Association, the problems facing women's football in Great Britain, we hoped, would finally be addressed.

Although Arthur Hobbs had invited the FA secretary, Denis Follows, to the meeting, neither he nor any other FA representative attended. The FA Council were considering a recommendation to its members that women's teams should be permitted to affiliate to a county association which would, therefore, rescind the ban. The first mention of this appears in a newspaper article in the *Daily Express*, 2 December 1969, headlined: 'FA say O.K. to the girls'.[4] Arthur continued to liaise with the FA and in January 1970, received a letter from Denis Follows saying:

> I am writing to inform you that the whole question of women's football was considered by the Council of the Football Association at its meeting on Monday last, and it was decided as follows:
>
> 1. That the Council's Resolution of 1921 be rescinded.
> 2. That women's football teams may be allowed to use grounds under the jurisdiction of the Football Association and registered referees may be permitted to officiate at matches between women's teams.
> 3. That the appropriate Rules of the Football Association be amended accordingly.[5]

For Arthur Hobbs it was marvellous news but, unfortunately, the FA were very slow in putting the recommendation into practice. The first years of the WFA's existence, therefore, proved to be more problematical than the founder members had imagined.

At the first WFA annual general meeting on 6 June 1970, there were representatives from seven leagues – South-East England, Kent, Midlands, West Mercia, Sussex, Northampton, Southampton – plus representatives from Scottish teams, and Kevin Gaynor from the Irish FA (representing the unaffiliated Irish teams). Since the inaugural meeting the WFA had received £151, mostly from £2 affiliations. Most of the meeting was taken up with a discussion on whether affiliated teams should play non-affiliated teams. Arthur Hobbs prophetically said, 'It has taken 49 years to get the FA on our side, so why go against their practice for the sake of £2, the cost of affiliation?' Arthur's political acumen was soon tested at the next WFA meeting in August. He had been advised (he was unable to declare by whom, but commonsense told us) that Mrs Dunn's continuance as chair of the WFA was detrimental to the association and was impeding its progress and costing it money. As a qualified referee, Pat Dunn had clashed with the FA in the past over not being allowed to referee affiliated football. Arthur had asked her to resign before the meeting, but Pat was reluctant to do so. It was felt, according to Arthur, that she reflected a bad image to prospective sponsors, who were willing to help the

WFA financially, but who did not want to deal with a chair who 'upset the FA'.[6] Pat eventually resigned, and Mr Pat Gwynne, who was vice-chair, took over as chair.

It was not a good start, and in just over one year, there were signals that it would be a slow process before women could enjoy the benefits of properly organised football. There was the ever-pressing need to obtain funding and the need for qualified coaches and officials. It emerged at a WFA meeting, on 12 December 1970, that the FA had responded to Arthur's request for help, in organising and funding coaching courses, by telling him that they could not finance what was in effect 'unaffiliated' football. The FA suggested that the WFA try and arrange courses through local authority education departments, 'under the guise of physical education courses'. This would satisfy the FA's requirements, at no cost to them, or the WFA. [7] After some delay, the WFA arranged for Joan Briggs of Fodens (who worked as a PE instructor in London) to run a course of instruction for players who aspired to coach, and this was overseen by Walter Winterbottom, the FA's director of coaching. There was also a need for an international team. At the same meeting in December, there was mention of letters from FIEFF requesting closer cooperation with the WFA and suggesting an international competition. The WFA turned down the suggestion of a competition because 'it was too short notice'.[8]

Also on the agenda was a letter from the BBC expressing regret that they had not been able to televise the two women's five-a-side exhibition matches at the Empire Pool, Wembley, in April 1970, because 'they could not get the all-clear from the FA'.[9] The matches between two of the top clubs, Southampton and Manchester Corinthians, had been staged as a means of 'legitimising' the women's game, and were played before the men's tournament final in front of 8,000 spectators. The event was backed by the Central Council for Physical Recreation, sanctioned by the FA, and sponsored by two newspapers, the *Daily Express* and the London *Evening Standard*. It was unfortunate that such a high-profile exhibition of women's football did not receive the media attention it deserved.

In May 1971, the WFA launched their first national knock-out competition, sponsored by the Yorkshire-based sportswear manufacturers, Mitre Sports, officially known as the WFA Mitre Cup, and in 1972 the first official England international team was formed. While both these initiatives raised the status of women's football, they were reactive not proactive decisions. The Cup superseded the commercially-driven Butlin's Cup and the official England team was started partly to negate Harry Batt's unofficial England XI trips.

Arthur Hobbs eventually saw the lifting of the ban that he had worked so hard to achieve, but the determination and effort he had put into the women's game had taken its toll on his health. He retired as secretary in 1972 and died of a heart attack three years later on the sea-front at Deal. There were others who shared his dedication and enthusiasm and who were willing to continue with the increasingly difficult administration of the WFA, but Arthur's special empathy for women's football was greatly missed.

WFA recognition

It was UEFA's reaction to the growth of women's football in Italy, and their concern at the success of the unofficial world cups organised by FIEFF, in Italy in 1970 and Mexico in 1971, that led to women's football coming under the respective national governing bodies' umbrellas. UEFA did not wish to organise women's football but as Pat Gregory said, "UEFA woke up and realised if they didn't do something, the whole thing would be out of their control." In 1971, UEFA passed a motion which ended in a vote of 39–1, in favour of member countries taking control of women's football (Scotland was the odd one out) and this became an official UEFA recommendation by November of that year. Most European countries made women's football an integral part of their association. The exceptions were Italy, whose FA did not take control until October 1986, and England, where the FA took over completely only in July 1993. It is interesting to note that those nations that did fully, and positively, integrate the women's game back in the 1970s, such as Sweden, Denmark, Norway and Germany, are among the world leaders today.

With these developments, and the establishment of the WFA, the FA could no longer ignore the fact that women's football had arrived and it was not going to go away. However, although the English FA had voted in favour of taking responsibility for women's football, it was not until May 1983 (and after a directive from the world football governing body, FIFA) that they invited the WFA to affiliate in the same way as men's county FAs. There were 46 county FAs and seven other various groups: the English

Schools FA, three armed services, Oxford and Cambridge
Universities and the Amateur Football Alliance. The WFA would
therefore, in the same way as the others, abide by the FA's rules
and regulations. The FA said they would recognise the WFA 'as
the sole governing body of women's football at the present time'
– a statement that remained in place until 1993. The WFA were
answerable to the FA in exchange for their recognition and were
asked to participate on a joint consultative committee. They
received a small grant and payment of the England team manager's
fees. The FA's official support meant that the WFA was in a
stronger position to approach funding bodies, such as the Football
Trust, for further grants, and it helped to create a more serious
relationship with the media. It showed how women's football
constantly needed the sanction of those men who governed
football in England. However, Pat Gregory feels that it was better
that the FA did not take over completely in the beginning "because
they wouldn't have done anything, whereas we could, at the
WFA, in our limited way, try and develop the game". At least the
UEFA and FIFA instructions had paved the way for better
communications and FA secretary, Denis Follows, was exemplary,
after the initial cold start, in his efforts to 'build bridges' between
the two organisations.

Gradualist versus entrepreneurial development

There are several early examples of leadership problems
encountered by the WFA. Williams and Woodhouse describe the
leadership clash between what they call the 'gradualist approach'
to the development of the game, favoured by the WFA, and
opponents of this 'softly, softly' policy, who advocated a more
high-profile, aggressive and 'professional' launch to the women's
game.[10] The WFA was an amateur association, with volunteer
workers and limited funds. They depended on grants, membership
fees, FA contributions and sponsorship for competitions. By the
start of the 1971–72 season, membership was nearing 100 clubs,
the Mitre Cup competition was in place, they had received a
Sports Council grant and there were plans to start an international
team. They had to ensure that they were only governing amateur
players to comply with FA rules and not jeopardise their funding.
With this fear in mind, the WFA officials had a profound mistrust

of anything commercial or entrepreneurial. I was not alone in thinking that without the advantages of support in terms of resources, both technical and financial – as other countries had – the game in England would not progress. An alternative would have been to follow Italy's example of private business sponsorship, until the governing body was able to resource the game. There was also the wider need to convince the public that women's football was acceptable. Many felt that the involvement of commercial sponsors would provoke the establishment to back the English women's game and accelerate its development. Unfortunately, the WFA continued to set themselves apart.

During the Butlin's Cup in 1969, the *Daily Mirror* had used a rear-view picture of Joan Tench, jumping to head a ball with her shorts falling down, to publicise the final (see p. 214). In the following year, the WFA officials, who were offended by the photograph, insisted on guarantees concerning promotional material and fees for the forthcoming tournament. Apart from the offending picture, all the other newspaper and TV material had provided positive publicity. Despite this, the organisers and the WFA were unable to agree terms and, by way of expressing their disapproval, the WFA threatened to impose a ban on any affiliated club who participated in the competition. Most teams did not enter, but the competition still went ahead. Later at the WFA meeting, in August 1970, no suggestions regarding disciplinary action against those teams that had entered were put forward and the matter was closed. It was ironic that the WFA had started to threaten clubs, players and managers with bans, after fighting so hard with the FA. It was also sad that they had fallen out with the sponsors. Butlin's and the Mirror Group of newspapers withdrew sponsorship altogether from women's football when the competition finished.

The WFA's suspicion of professionalism and commercialism was even more pronounced in their dealings with Harry Batt, as he managed to outmanoeuvre them in their attempt to ban him from entering the 1971 Mexico World Cup. The organisers, FIEFF, had approached Harry Batt, after the WFA had declined the invitation to supply an English XI. Although the WFA were not themselves ready to provide an official England team, they were organised well enough, after the event, to put another ban into place. They objected to Harry Batt's use of the term 'England', and even though he called his unofficial team the 'English Independents', it was sufficient for the WFA to give him a 'life' ban from the association. Several players that went with him received fines and playing bans of up to three months.

A women's World Cup in England?

One of the most disappointing chapters in the history of the WFA was not taking up the opportunity to stage a World Cup in England in 1972 or 1973. I was among those who thought the time was right for the staging of an international event and, when I returned from Italy in 1971, I started to try and get England to catch up with other countries. It was actually a journalist, Ted Hart, who suggested to me the possibility of a World Cup at this time which would also be televised in clubs, pubs and cinemas. To popularise the event Ted Hart said he could guarantee the involvement of West Ham United's three 1966 World Cup stars, Bobby Moore, Geoff Hurst and Martin Peters, who would help as coaches to the England squad, and even England manager, Alf Ramsey, would provide his support. I met Hurst, Ramsey and one of the sponsors, boxing promoter Jarvis Astaire, who confirmed that £150,000 would be available to promote the competition. Geoff Hurst reassured me that it was no gimmick and that they would be deadly serious about coaching the team to ensure England did well. The involvement of such high-profile football personalities as England's World Cup-winning captain Bobby Moore, and hat-trick hero Geoff Hurst, would have helped convince the public, and media, that women's football was a serious participation sport. The backing of such a successful businessman and sports promoter, Jarvis Astaire, would have ensured a financial success and woken people up to the potential of the women's game. The Scandinavian countries and Italy were already well organised in respect of the development of their international teams.

Arthur Hobbs, Norman Holloway and I were excited by the opportunity and everything looked set for a dream launch of women's football in England. However, at a meeting at the Royal Lancaster Hotel in London in March 1972, the WFA representation, including vice-chair David Marlowe and assistant secretary Pat Gregory, had grave reservations about the project. Their major concerns were that they would not have sufficient control of events and that FIEFF would be involved. They suggested that certain nations may not be recognised by FIFA and UEFA, and finally, they said there was insufficient time to prepare the England team. At the next WFA meeting a vote was called and there was a 6–5 majority in favour of staging the event, but the chair, Pat Gwynne, decided to call a second vote because he said the Scottish representative didn't know that she could vote. Therefore, on the second vote the result was 6–6 and Pat Gwynne used his casting vote to carry a 7–6 majority rejecting the proposal. Many people, including Gladys Aikin, Norman Holloway and myself, were bemused by the events. Not only was the vote mishandled, but it appeared a Scottish representative had effectively destroyed England's opportunity to stage a World Cup competition. During this time Ted Hart had assured me, and the WFA, that FIEFF would not have been involved, and that the WFA would have had control over the whole competition so that it would be run in accordance with WFA, FA and UEFA requirements. He had also said that if it was really necessary they could postpone the competition until 1973 to allow more preparation time. He and his sponsors were amazed that such an opportunity had been turned down. In a letter to the WFA officials at this time Hart stated:

> We had hoped that you would look upon a World Cup in this country as an opportunity to put women's football firmly on the map ... to convince the television millions that the women's game, played at its highest level, is both skilful and entertaining. But under the circumstances we now feel it would be financial folly to invest (perhaps gamble would be a better word), £150,000 in support of an organisation that quite clearly doesn't share our enthusiasm for the venture.

So disappointed were Ted Hart and his backers that they actually suggested sponsoring Southampton and other top teams to form a 'breakaway' super women's football league, from which they would select an England team to play in a World Cup in England. Too many people were not prepared to take the risk, which on reflection may have been a pity. Ted Hart and his sponsors were convinced such a league would work and it would at least, they thought, provoke the FA and WFA into developing things more quickly.

Appointment of the first professional WFA administrator

With the World Cup idea rejected, the WFA could settle back down to organising domestic competitions and friendly international matches. Eventually, the administration became too great for volunteers to deal with and Linda Whitehead, who had worked as an administrator at Blackburn Rovers, was appointed as a paid administrator on 24 November 1980. The 1980s will be remembered as the era in which women's football started to become more widely recognised in England. The international team had success in two Italian tournaments: in August 1985 and in the Mundialito (the 'Little World Cup') in July 1988, for which they received the *Sunday Times* award for 'Sports Team of the Year'. Linda Whitehead also received recognition from the *Sunday Times* for her administrative work in dealing with one of the fastest-growing sports in the country. Significantly, the media became more interested in the late 1980s and Channel Four, in particular, provided timely publicity for the game with programmes on the progress of the Women's FA Cup. Live coverage by Channel Four of Leasowe Pacific's (now Everton) 3–2 defeat of the Friends of Fulham in the 1989 final attracted in excess of 2.5 million viewers. It also inspired lots of enquiries to the WFA from girls and women wanting to play and '60 enquiries on how start a women's club'.[11]

The demise of the WFA

In some ways, women's football became a victim of its own success because it did not have the infrastructure to support its rapid growth. The problem was compounded by financial difficulties, and despite all the successes of the 1980s, political infighting within the organisation seemed to increase rather than subside. Tim Stearn had been elected chair in 1984 and some considered that he was chosen on the basis that he was a 'neutral' who could stop some of the political divisions that were undermining the game's development. Four years later, Tim became vice-chair and Richard Faulkner became chair. Richard Faulkner was the first deputy chair of the influential Football Trust, which allocates grants to leagues and non-league clubs for stadium improvements and 'community' activities. It was hoped that he and his Football Trust colleague, Peter Lee, who became treasurer of the WFA, would provide at the helm two high-profile administrators with experience, status and contacts from the world of men's professional football. According to Williams and Woodhouse: 'It was Faulkner's likely influence that the WFA came out with the announcement in 1990, that the Trust had allocated £150,000 to the development of the women's game, some of which would go towards the establishment of a national Women's League for the start of the 1991–92 season.'[12] By 1991, participation rates were increasing with 334 women's clubs registered, accounting for around 9,000 players. But off the field things were getting worse. Richard Faulkner and Peter Lee resigned their posts in a joint letter to Linda Whitehead, on 7 October 1991, which in effect heralded the beginning of the end of the WFA. Tim Stearn took over again as chair from Richard Faulkner, and therefore had the almost impossible task of trying to unite the various groups. He was the last chair of the WFA and the post of treasurer was not immediately filled. Meanwhile, the auditors, Hagley Knight, had been called in to conduct an inquiry into the WFA's accounting problems. David Hunt became treasurer during the final months but his main task soon became working with the FA in winding up WFA Ltd. There were two main problems – one 'political' and the other financial – both, of course, were linked. Women's football was growing but its growth only further highlighted the urgent need for better resources for the development of the game at all levels. At the international level this was illustrated by the fact that other nations, particularly those who had merged with their governing bodies in the 1970s, had become very 'professional' in their organisation and preparation. They expected to receive from England the same high-quality hospitality and organisation as they themselves provided. Before their resignations, Richard Faulkner and Peter Lee had understood, through their Football Trust connections with men's football, that it would make practical and financial sense to respond to the FA's desire for closer links between the two bodies. Richard Faulkner described it as using 'the strengths of the FA in areas where the WFA's administration is weak; in accounting and book-keeping, in the organisation of international matches, in implementing the development programme, and in other activities where the FA can help us whilst we maintain our own independence.'[13] Another problem was the fact that the Sports Council had made a closer relationship with the FA a condition of future grant aid. While the 'old order' of the ex-WFA officers and founder members, most of whom were now honorary life members, such as David Marlowe, Pat Gregory, David Hunt and Flo Bilton, as well as current officer, June Jaycocks, were principally in agreement with this closer association, three of the other current officers were not. Therefore, certain meetings set up with the FA to discuss the links (one for which even FA chair at the time, Bert Millichip, had specially made himself available) were subsequently cancelled.

Personal disappointment

I had been involved from the beginning of the WFA in 1969 as minute secretary, and as assistant secretary for a short while to Arthur Hobbs. I had also had brief spells as vice-chair, and was a member of the development committee in the mid-1980s that soon became defunct. All of these posts had been undertaken when I was playing, and when I retired in 1986, I had hoped I could devote more time to the development of the game. It had not always been easy to penetrate the 'inner sanctum' of national women's football administration and I even recall an official suggesting that I 'get involved with local development'. In 1991 I finally became a WFA officer but it was to prove to be a time during which the organisation was going through its 'death throes'. I was also advising the FA on the transition of power and thus had the privilege of helping start the WFA and the less pleasant task of sealing its fate. Perhaps I should have realised in the autumn of 1991, when it was suggested that I stand as the international officer, that I was being asked to go where others now feared to tread. Certainly it would be no easy matter to follow June Jaycocks, who had been a popular international officer, with players and officials alike, when I had been in the international team. As Pat Gregory said, "June worked tirelessly for the game right from the start in 1969. One of the enduring memories of her, though, is the way she could get through to some of the stuffy gentlemen officials where others had failed – just by smiling. They'd melt at her smile every time." June's cheerful and willing manner had certainly been tested over the years and she finally became sufficiently frustrated with events to resign. It was indicative of the mood in the international team when England manager, Barrie Williams, who had been in post for one year, also resigned. He, too, was apparently frustrated at the lack of resources and the response to his development ideas, including an improved selection procedure for senior, U21 and even U16 players. When I took up the post of international officer in January 1992, the England women's team goalkeeping coach, John Bilton, an ex-goalkeeper for Rotherham Utd, had been appointed by the officers as the new team manager.

The WFA's situation worsened. In May 1992, Tim Stearn issued a report to the council and members recommending: 'The officers take full responsibility for all matters concerning their individual programmes, with all enquiries on these matter being dealt with by them.' Certainly, organising internationals would become incredibly difficult to manage, and like the rest, I had my paid work to fit in as well. By the end of 1992 the FA started to become more involved and the WFA's problems were not only becoming public knowledge but the subject of much conjecture. For example, in December, an article in the *Sunday Times* records how the game was continuing to grow, with 86 new football clubs being formed since July, and with 30 per cent of these clubs catering for the under-16 age level, the age where development was at last happening. Ominously, the *Sunday Times* report added: 'The WFA is in debt. The chairman (male) has resigned, the treasurer (male) withdrawn, the England team manager (male) quit and only the secretary (female) is hanging on.'[14] It goes on to relate how ex-chair, Richard Faulkner was referring all telephone enquiries to the WFA vice-chair who, subsequently, referred all callers to the FA, who described themselves as 'concerned'. The article concludes: 'Linda Whitehead, WFA secretary, said wearily: "It's always the men that cause the problems."'

International team disappointments

I tried to concentrate on my responsibility to the England team, ensuring that some of the bad preparation for international games that I had experienced as a player was not repeated. One of the highlights for me was representing the FA at the first FIFA Women's Football Seminar in Zurich in October 1992. At this seminar I was able to catch up with many of the international developments which had passed England by, such as the 1991 FIFA World Championship – the official title of the World Cup. It was obvious that in terms of development and international results England had been left behind. A clear indication of the higher status afforded women's football in other countries arose at the discussion on coaching, which I attended with England men's team manager, Graham Taylor. He made some supportive comments about women's football being a more open and exciting game compared to most men's football. However, we were unable to respond with the same unison as others there who had actually worked together on women's football development in their countries. For example, Germany and the US were represented by their team coach and top players, Gero Bisanz and Martina Voss and Anson Dorrance and Michelle Akers respectively. Norway were represented by coach Even Pellerud, captain Heidi Store, and an official from their FA, Karen Espelund. Sweden had ex-player and subsequently FA official Susanne Erlandsson, and a much-capped ex-player also working for their FA, Pia Sundhage. Furthermore, earlier in the main auditorium, these players, along with other top ex-international players, were properly introduced to the delegates. It was staggering to see women players accorded such high status by their own associations and by FIFA.

Meanwhile, in England, the U21 team, which the WFA had started in February 1987 under the guidance of ex-England player and Preliminary Licence coach, Liz Deighan, became defunct. The WFA had asked Liz to give up her role as north-west region team coach to take on the U21 team but, four years later, they gave the post to John Bilton and soon afterwards the team folded because of lack of funds. Liz said, "It was vital they kept that squad going" and proudly relates that under her more than 80 players experienced U21 football and that they had won all four international games. More importantly, eight of her team featured in England's World Cup squad in 1995. Liz spoke of her disappointment, especially as she'd given up the regional coaching post to take on the U21 team. She was a star midfield player in the England team that were runners-up in the 1984 European Championship and her passion and enthusiasm are still not dimmed:

> I retired completely from the game in 1993. Managing my club [Knowsley, now called Liverpool] was taking over my life, and starting to jeopardise my full-time job as I was getting so many phone calls at work. I recently asked how I could become involved at a higher level again and was told to get involved locally. I've started helping out a bit at Preston Rangers. The former U21 players who now play for the senior squad, such as Karen Burke, Pauline Cope and Lou Waller, ring me up and tell me how they're doing and that's nice.

Lou Waller was full of praise for Liz and said how she'd helped her and other youngsters take a step towards full international honours: "I was only 18 at the time, and it was so good to step up a level and be coached by a woman who had been a great international player and done it all before – we couldn't help but be inspired." Liz spoke highly of ex-England manager, Martin Reagan, for his support and encouragement of her involvement at the U21 level, and she said he was sorry when she wasn't re-appointed to the post. UEFA have sanctioned an U18 competition but so far only the Republic of Ireland has U16 and U18 squads and Scotland and Wales U16 squads.

The FA take over

Tim Stearn wrote to all the WFA members and officers and tried to allay fears about the WFA's problems, offering reassurance about the WFA's relationship with the FA. In some respects the confusion and breakdown in communication became worse, not only causing public embarrassment, but also, on a practical level, affecting the players of the national team.

By the end of 1992, news of the impending FA and WFA merger was made public. *The Times*'s report on the FA's 'Development of Girls' and Women's Football' conference held in November 1992, stated: 'If the women's game is to succeed, it needs official blessing and Charles Hughes, [the FA's director of coaching and education, who made the opening address to delegates] is expected to announce shortly the WFA will merge with the FA.'[15] The article went on to say that: 'To fulfil the potential, the FA will need expert coaching from individuals like Sue Lopez and Sue Law.' Sue Law is an ex-Millwall and Bromley and England player and National Coaching Foundation (NCF) development officer – the NCF is the 'coaching arm' of the Sports Council. She is quoted as saying: 'I never thought I'd sit and talk about women's football in the same room as Charles Hughes! The way change has accelerated is incredible. But the FA are not silly and they realise that by ignoring women they were overlooking half the population.' The problem was, of course, that we didn't have enough women coaches.

The last WFA international

At the second leg of the European Championship quarter-final against Italy at Rotherham Utd's ground on 7 November 1992, England needed to recover from the first leg 3–2 defeat. The away match, in Avellino, Italy on 17 October 1992, had seen

England bravely recover from being 3–0 down after losing Doncaster's centre-back, Jackie Sherard, early on with damaged cruciate ligaments. At Rotherham, England managed a performance that summed up the sorry off-the-field state of affairs. Carolina Morace, the Italian captain, superbly led her team to a 3–0 victory, completely outplaying the home side.[16] The team's usually reliable defenders managed to concede three goals in the most bizarre manner, including an own goal from Law. Further, Millwall's Lou Waller was sent off for trying to stop a goal with her hand. It was England's final game under the WFA and sadly for Sue Law it was an ignominious end to her England career. She had played bravely, despite agonising back pain, probably not helped by a vigorous pre-match fitness test with shoulder charges from the solid six-footer John Bilton. Sue has done much development work for women's football, including help start Bromley (now Croydon) and she has also provided TV commentary for women's matches. She is now concentrating her talents on her NCF work.

The new set-up

In February 1993, a meeting of the women's football steering committee, which became an FA standing committee, started to address all the issues involved in taking over the WFA. The FA took over the WFA's financial deficit and took responsibility for the administrative staff in the WFA office. The final transition meeting took place at Stoke City's ground in July 1993.

The Women's Football Alliance was established to provide a forum for clubs, along with the post of a women's football coordinator, whose task is to oversee the development of girls' and women's football. The FA's Women's Committee had three representatives from the Women's Football Alliance. There is no special intention to have women representatives on the committee, nor representation from particular regions. Julie Hemsley, a Preliminary Licence coach, Brighton WFC player/coach, and Brighton & Hove Albion assistant community development officer, became the Women's Football Alliance's representative on the FA council and therefore the first woman ever to serve on it. The FA took over the responsibility for the national team and Julie Hemsley was also appointed assistant England manager, and Ted Copeland, the FA's assistant regional director of coaching for the north-east of England, became the England manager. After the

World Cup competition in Sweden, Julie was replaced by Graham Keeley, from the Cheshire FA, as Ted Copeland's assistant. The England team does have a female doctor and physiotherapist. The rest of the FA's Women's Committee is made up of FA executive members and representatives from the FA council's county organisations. During the 1993–94 season, the WFA National Cup, although run by former WFA officers, was brought under the control of the FA and renamed the FA Challenge Cup. In 1996 it became the UK Living FA Women's Cup. In the 1994–95 season the FA assumed responsibility for the organisation of the Women's National League, which was renamed the Football Association Women's Premier League (FAWPL). The League was divided into three divisions: National (the top ten teams) and Northern and Southern (regional divisions of ten teams each). Ten regional leagues feed into the top divisions via a system of promotion and relegation.

Women's football under the direct auspices of the FA is still in its infancy and will inevitably have teething problems. However, during my short involvement with the FA it was obvious that their greater resources and expertise could help the game considerably. It is to be regretted that it has taken so long. Certainly the England team has benefited from being properly resourced and some steps have been taken to address the problems of the Premier League, such as the setting up of a 'briefing day' for clubs that provides workshops on development, coaching and medical education, funding and media coverage. Interestingly, the development workshop information stated: 'Examples of good practice from clubs abroad have shown that their success lies in sound club structures.' There are proposals to rationalise the League structure in the 1997–98 season to provide girls' and women's football with a pyramid development structure similar to boys' and men's football and, further, to involve the county FAs more. This has dismayed some of the regional League volunteers because the county FAs would take over much of the administration. This would seem to have value but vindicates Clive White's observations in the *Independent* that: 'There may remain a degree of suspicion about the FA's motives [for taking over] among some regional administrators who jealously guard the empires they have built up from, or indeed in spite of, the FA.'[17]

In the beginning women's football was encouraged because of its use to raise funds for charities and the war effort, and then it was banned because it was 'not a suitable game for women' and was a perceived threat to men's football. Despite all this it survived the lean years and re-emerged in the 1960s. When it was ultimately controlled by the FA through the WFA, in the 1970s and 1980s, it was not encouraged, developed, or given real financial support. This probably helped to precipitate the WFA's downfall. On reflection, Pat Gregory said of the WFA's demise: "It's sad that perhaps we hadn't succeeded. We put in a lot of work. At least it's now being run efficiently and there's a glimmer of hope in that it's much more available to schoolgirls." We can only speculate at present about how the game will be defined under FA control.

6 The WFA Cup and Southampton's golden years

Early years of the WFA Cup

The national WFA Cup competition, first known as the WFA Mitre Cup, began in the 1970–71 season, replacing Arthur Hobbs's Deal Tournament as the major competition in England. At this time the Scottish and Welsh FAs would not sanction women's football and the WFA permitted them to enter this competition as well. In its first year the competition attracted 71 entrants, including the Scottish side Stewarton and Thistle, the north London club White Ribbon, and EMGALS from Leicester. The teams were put into eight geographical groups to play off for quarter-final places. It was also around this time that a number of individual women became involved in women's football who went on to play significant roles in the development of the sport.

White Ribbon

White Ribbon had been formed in June 1967 by Pat Gregory. A year later Pat helped form the South-East England League with another London team, Spurs, and teams from the Luton area. Pat formed her team in response to demands from other local female football fanatics:

> My father was a Spurs supporter, and my brother occasionally took me to Highbury to watch Arsenal, but I supported Chelsea. I was eventually allowed by my father to go with him to some of the Spurs' matches ... and it occurred to me on one of these occasions, as I stood in the crowd, women don't play football! I wrote to the local paper and asked why can't women play football? The response was lots of girls and women writing in and asking

if they could join my team! Then I started to realise some
of the reasons women didn't play. We couldn't find a
pitch anywhere to train or play on, nor referees to run the
games – all because women's football wasn't affiliated. My
father got cross about this because he said if he pays his
rates, why can't we find a local pitch to play on? Eventually,
Arthur Hobbs came to the rescue by inviting us to the
Deal International Tournament, played at the Betteshanger
Colliery ground, and there we met other teams with whom
we could arrange 'friendlies'. The publicity in the local
press led to one of the local amateur men's clubs offering
us the use of their pitch for training and matches. Their
name was White Star, but in the 1930s there had been a
men's team called White Ribbon and they used to train with
the Tottenham Hotspurs' professional club so we thought
it would be an appropriate name for us.

Pat had never played football before she started the White
Ribbon team at the age of 19 and her initial interest came from
family influence:

I have always liked sport but I'm no good at it. I used to play
everything at school except football. I suppose I liked
football because my house was full of it with my father and
brother being supporters of Spurs and Arsenal. When I
started playing football with White Ribbon I wanted to be
a ballet dancer too. I went to ballet lessons and kept the two
going for about two years, even though I wasn't good at
either. My sister played for us – probably because I made
her. My parents weren't deliriously happy about me playing;
my mother wasn't really happy at all – partly, I suppose,
because I brought a set of dirty kit home every week and
this was pre-washing machine days. The White Star men
used to give us some training but we never improved much
because we had a succession of appalling managers who
knew less than we did.

In 1969 Pat became involved with the newly-formed WFA and
although she kept White Ribbon going for about eight years
in the end, without support, it became too much of a struggle. After
the end of White Ribbon Pat continued to be involved in women's
football. She succeeded Arthur Hobbs as WFA secretary and held
the post of chair for the 1982–83 season. She was for many years

the WFA's UEFA representative and currently serves on the FA's Women's Football Committee. She also works for the BBC's Sports Department, organising the televising of special events, such as Euro '96 and the World Cup in America in 1994.

Flo Bilton and Hull

As pre-Cup preparation for Southampton, the Hull women's football team was invited to play a match at the Southampton Civil Service grounds on 2 May 1971. Flo Bilton was one of two key people who helped women's football start in Hull – the other was Bill Doodie, the chair of the Hull League. Flo Bilton is one of the unsung heroines and one of the greatest supporters of women's football. Flo worked tirelessly as secretary of the Hull League and has continued in that role ever since. She also found time to do a lot of the less glamorous, behind-the-scenes work for the England team, and was very supportive of the players. In the early days of the WFA she also acted as membership secretary. She is respected by everyone in the game and the players were always certain that she had their interest, and that of the game, at heart. However, women's football came too late for her to make much impact as a player, and her only playing involvement was in the early days, with Reckitts, as a goalkeeper:

> I was asked to form a girls' football team to play a 'curtain raiser' to an All Stars Charity match in Hull. The firm I worked for, Reckitts, was very keen on all sport and as I was an active member of the cricket, netball and hockey teams, they asked me to form a women's football team. The match was played on 19 April 1963 against another firm, Smith & Nephew, and we won 2–1. I was well into my fortieth year so I played in goal. The club continued from then on. The girls were all from the firm, and we received a lot of help with getting the pitches, a coach, and kit ... I remember when we got the chance to go down to Southampton. They had become the top team by this time, having lost only four out their 40 matches. They were a credit to the game and, along with Fodens, were two of the best teams I ever saw – they both played good, attractive, clean football – a pleasure to watch. We were no match for Southampton that day. Our most famous player was still a youngster then – Carol McCune, who later became an England full-back and captain.

Stewarton and Thistle

Stewarton and Thistle from Kilmarnock formed in 1961 at the Provost's request to help raise funds for the Freedom from Hunger Campaign. They continued with matches against other Scottish teams and later had success in the Scottish Cup and the Scottish Ladies' Charity Shield. Their captain, and stalwart player, was Elsie Cook, who played at centre-back despite her petite build of five foot four inches. Elsie went on to become secretary of the Scottish Women's FA. Their star player was Rose Reilly who started playing football at the age of seven. When she was 14, and playing in a friendly boys' match, a Scottish League club scout mistook her for a promising male player and tried to sign her for his club.[1]

The inaugural WFA Cup Final 1971

Southampton had scored 34 goals on the way to the final, beating White Ribbon, the London and south-east group winners, 23–0, in the quarter-final and EMGALS 8–0, in the semi-final. Top scorer was Pat Davies with nine goals, and Dot Cassell and I scored seven each. The team had gained much confidence in winning the Deal Tournament the previous July and from their two exhibition matches against Manchester Corinthians at the Empire Pool, Wembley. Southampton met the Scottish side Stewarton and Thistle, in the final. They had beaten Thanet (Kent) and Wanderers (Nuneaton) in the quarter-final and semi-final respectively. The match was played at Crystal Palace National Sports Centre in London, almost the same spot where the men's Cup Finals were played prior to moving to Wembley in 1923. Southampton overwhelmed their Scottish adversaries 4–1, with Pat Davies scoring a hat-trick and Dot Cassell the other goal. It was the biggest occasion so far for the team, with many dignitaries in attendance, including FA secretary Denis Follows. However, the abiding memory for the team was the long grass, which no one had thought to cut. The result of the game was announced on the BBC evening news but there was no other coverage, not even in the national press. The exception in the media was *Goal* magazine, which covered it well with some excellent photographs. The team for Southampton that day was: goalkeeper Sue Buckett;

full-backs Pat Judd and schoolgirl Karen Buchanan (who shackled Rose Reilly for us); centre-backs Jill Long and Barbara Birkett; midfield Maureen Case, Lesley Lloyd (captain) and Dot Cassell; forwards Lynda Hale, Pat Davies, Sue Lopez. Substitutes were Jean Seymour and Louise Cross. At right-back was a prodigy in 14-year-old Karen Buchanan, who is the second youngest player (Southampton's 13-year-old Sharon Roberts is the youngest, in the 1978 final) to have appeared in a Cup Final. She left the game after just one season to go to live in South Africa.

League changes

At the June 1970 WFA AGM there had been seven leagues affiliated and more developed as the number of teams grew. A year later, amid optimistic signs of growth in the game, there were portents of the problems to come. The WFA had fined Southampton for misrepresentation as a league club, which resulted in Southampton joining the Home Counties League for the 1971–72 season. At this time, besides the WFA Cup, there were only regional league and league cup competitions organised – a national league competition was not introduced until 1991. In 1992 there were 18 leagues in England and Wales.

Southampton were disappointed to find they had to win promotion to the First Division from the Second Division of the Home Counties League. As a result the players endured a costly first season that involved much travelling. Nevertheless, they won promotion with embarrassing ease with a 100 per cent record. Although Division One was more competitive, with one or two exceptions, even this league soon became insufficiently challenging. The fact we were meeting a Scottish team for the second time in the WFA 1972 Cup Final illustrated the increasing gulf between Southampton and other English teams. In my secretary's report to the Wessex League (as the Southampton League had become), I asked the WFA to address development problems as a priority. We needed youth leagues to accommodate the growing interest from girls, and a national league of the top ten teams.[2] If I had known then what complications would arise in trying to establish a development structure for English women's football I would probably have packed my bags and gone back to Roma the very next day.

1972 and 1973 Cup Finals

Although the Home Counties League provided few strong opponents, an exception in 1972 was Thame. The ex-Hooverettes star, Paddy McGroarty, was now orchestrating Thame's successes and the two sides illustrated their close rivalry by sharing the Home Counties League Cup after a 4–4 draw in the final. However, it was the WFA Cup that gave the club its greatest challenge. Southampton scored 38 goals in the matches leading to the 1972 final, conceding only five. In the semi-final Southampton defeated Thame, 4–3, and in the final Southampton met Stewarton and Thistle again, who had changed their name to Lees Ladies after their newly-acquired sponsors. The encounter was much closer than the previous year and a crowd of 1,500 at Burton Albion's ground watched a thrilling match which Southampton won 3–2, with two goals from Pat Judd and the other from me.

In their six matches on the way to the 1973 WFA Cup Final, Southampton scored 34 goals including two 7–0 wins, one over Johnsons of Port Talbot and the other in the semi-final against Birmingham. They then completed a hat-trick of WFA Cup Final victories by beating the Scottish team Westthorn United, by 2–0 at Bedford Town's ground, in front of nearly 3,000 spectators. Elsie Cook, who had been sidelined due to pregnancy the previous year, was back as Westthorn's centre-half, in her twelfth year as a player, and Rose Reilly had also transferred from Lees Ladies. This was Rose Reilly's last appearance before her move to Italy. The Southampton team had to rely on some dogged defensive play and the goals were scored only in the last ten minutes, one from midfielder Sylvia Kenway and the other a fine strike by Lynda Hale.

The Southampton players

During 1973 Southampton experienced some changes in players and management. Norman Holloway retired and was replaced as manager by Mike Harvey, a local PE teacher and FA Preliminary Licence coach. Five players had been lost and one of the replacements was Pat Chapman who, with Pat Davies, formed one of the most deadly strike-forces in women's football. Pat Davies was 17 and worked as a valuation clerk in local government. Pat Chapman, a natural left-footer, travelled from Portsmouth to play a season for Tottonians in the Southampton League, as the teams in her home town were not of a sufficiently good standard. She took over my left-sided striker's role and, like Pat Davies, was a talented all-round sportswoman, representing the county at netball and athletics. Pat Davies had started playing at the age of five and Pat Chapman had been encouraged by her father, a keen Portsmouth FC fan. Both, too, were only about five feet tall. Pat Chapman's other great asset was her quick wit and ability to keep the dressing-room full of humour. She became the team's 'wag' and no one escaped her quips. Pat wanted to win and let anyone know if she wasn't happy with the service she was getting on the pitch. I sometimes think I was put behind her at left-midfield because, with a deaf ear, I was often oblivious to her comments. This deafness was especially useful if I beat Pat's close-marking defender with a pass for her to run on to – instead of placing the ball exactly to her favoured left foot. But we had much respect for each other and I felt privileged to play in between two of the finest left-footed players, Pat and Maggie Pearce (née Kirkland). Flattering comments were often made about Maggie and none sums up her talent more than when people genuinely and complimentarily said 'she plays like a lad'. The three of us later combined to make a very successful left side of the England team. The phenomenal scoring feat of our players in the League and Cup competitions prior to the 1973 Cup Final was: Pat Chapman 82 goals in 21 matches, Pat Davies 44 in 16, right-winger Lynda Hale 22 in 18, and, from midfield, I chipped in with 33 in 20. By then the club had won 58 out of 65 matches, with an incredible goal record of 491 with just 44 conceded. The fact we conceded so few goals was due, in part, to having Sue Buckett in the team, perhaps the best and most consistent goalkeeper in English women's football. Her football career began with local Southampton League team, Flame:

> When I started playing for Flame, people thought it was a gimmick. I had played a lot of netball and almost represented Britain at canoeing, but gave it all up for football, although I kept playing badminton – it helped my reflexes. But netball was so restrictive, and I enjoyed playing in a team as opposed to being on my own canoeing. The excitement and atmosphere and great rushes of adrenalin are unique to football. I basically taught myself goalkeeping. I learnt my angles and started to go up to the Dell and watched the goalkeepers. I admired Gordon Banks a lot.

Sue also recalls how the 'gimmick' aspect did little to help the game: "At the time there were silly charity matches with, for example, models calling themselves 'The George Best Girls' and playing against George just for a giggle and for charity." This attitude was reflected in the media coverage. Although media attention was growing it was not wholeheartedly encouraging. Prior to the 1973 WFA Cup Final, for example, the media descended on the Southampton team. Although the local *Echo's* Sue Twell wrote a full-page spread in the paper that concentrated fully on the football, the more difficult media presence came from *Sun* columnist, Peter Batt, who met the team at the Southampton Polygon Hotel. Peter admitted to being biased against women's football:

> The first thing a prejudiced male learns about lady footballers is that he had better take them seriously. Ask them to pose for glamour pictures, as colleague Roger Bamber did, and you are odds on to wind up with a punch up the throat. The dedication to the sport is nothing short of fanatical. Only one of the team is married, the rest quite simply haven't got time for it.

His piece is typical of many journalists' inability to resist the cliché. Most of all, Batt is intrigued by manager Mike Harvey:

> I didn't know whether to feel jealous or sorry for Mr Harvey. He told me 'the biggest problem in ladies' football is managers. They [the clubs] run through them like paper hankies. I've been in the job a year now and the pressures are almost unbearable at times. I need a skin like rhinoceros. You can imagine what I have to put up with from the crowd when I run on the field to give them treatment for injury. [3]

Mike Harvey, therefore, raised in this flippant way a serious problem concerning the image of women's football and that of the men involved. They too experienced – and still do – prejudice towards their support of a women's sport which they carried out on a purely voluntary basis.

The WFA Cup 1973–75

Southampton started the 1973–74 season by gaining the use of Hampshire League side Totton Utd's ground, and by this time had five team members who were England players: Sue Buckett, Maggie Pearce, Pat Davies, Lynda Hale and myself. One of Southampton's main rivals in the Home Counties League would be Crystal Palace, captained by Sue Head, daughter of Crystal Palace FC's manager, Bert Head. Crystal Palace did in fact beat us 3–0 in the Home Counties League competition, which was perhaps a portent of things to come. In the WFA Cup Final, Southampton were to meet their first English opponents – and old adversaries – Fodens. Since losing to them in the final of the 1969 Butlin's Cup we had heard little about their activities. They had briefly left affiliation to the WFA, after the Butlin's/Joan Tench photo affair, but returned to the Three Counties League (with such teams as Manchester Corinthians, Macclesfield and Preston North End), under the guidance of another stalwart of women's football, Mrs Lucy Latham. Fodens were still an experienced team and now had three current England internationals in their side: Sheila Parker, Alison Leatherbarrow and veteran Sylvia Gore. They were keen, anxious to prove they were a team to be reckoned with, and we rather meekly surrendered our three-year grip on the WFA Cup and lost 2–1. It was a great disappointment.

Victory against Warminster

The 1974–75 season was much better for Southampton. We obtained 18-year-old Linda Coffin, a section supervisor at Fareham's Plessey factory, and a hockey player. Her father, Noel, took on the vacant management role. Within two seasons Linda had become England's centre-half. Hilary Carter, along with Pat Chapman and Maggie Kirkland, made up a trio of talented left-footed players. We won the Home Counties League Cup and narrowly lost out to QPR in the League competition, but, more importantly, we won back the WFA Cup. We met Eileen Foreman's Warminster Town in the final at Dunstable Town's ground and won 4–2.

Duel with QPR 1976–78

Southampton beat QPR 2–1 in the 1976 WFA Cup Final with an extra-time goal from Pat Davies in front of 1,500 spectators at Bedford Town's ground. The team enjoyed a double civic celebration with Southampton's men's team which, under Lawrie

McMenemy's management, had also won their FA Cup. I had left the club for a short while, due to internal politics, and missed these events, though I was still playing for the England team. It was Maggie Kirkland's boyfriend, Gordie Pearce, a respected supporter and confidant of Southampton players and management alike, who helped the club overcome the political infighting and smoothed the way for my return. Gordie helped Maggie progress into being one of the finest full-backs ever to play for England and his genuine support for women footballers was a welcome contrast to some of the less altruistic 'supporters' the game had started to attract. I will always be grateful for the way he resurrected my Southampton career.

At the beginning of the 1976–77 season we again had problems in finding a pitch because the pitch at Totton had been let to another club and we couldn't find a replacement. This was resolved when Romsey Town FC's secretary came to our rescue and offered us the use of their excellent facilities. The little market town was to prove ideal, with its enclosed pitch, small stand, and a captive local audience who could be attracted through the town's weekly newspaper, the *Romsey Advertiser*. Publicity was also aided by the chair Mike Squires, who produced a regular home programme.

Additionally, we received much support from the Southampton men's team and I was one of four players who had the chance of some pre-season shooting practice at the most coveted ground in our vicinity – the Dell. Maggie Kirkland, Pat Davies and Lynda Hale, joined me in a penalty shoot-out against Saints' reserve keeper Steve Middleton. This exemplified the Saints' readiness to support our team, and by extension women's football, which they did on many occasions.

Southampton attempt to win the Treble

The 1977 WFA Cup was now called the Pony Cup, after a drink made by new sponsors, Showering. They provided £100 prize money, which was the first time a prize had been offered, and 107 clubs entered the Cup competition. There were now over 275 clubs in England with at least 8,000 players. However, competitive matches were still difficult to find and we easily beat teams such as Thame, who had lost their form, 16–0, and Bracknell, 7–1, and Bristol Bluebirds, 9–0, in the opening round. Our closest opponents this season were the ever-improving QPR team, who boasted four England internationals in goalkeeper Pat Cavanagh, midfielders Josie Lee and the charismatic Paddy McGroarty, and forward Sandra Choat. Before the hectic end-of-season run-in, Southampton took an Easter break in a European Cup Winners' Cup tournament in Menton, France. We beat French champions Reims in the final, having beaten Landhaus (Austria) 3–1, and local side Menton 1–0. This tournament turned out to be one of the few international events organised during the 1970s. They were ad hoc competitions instigated by local teams rather than by UEFA or FIFA.

On our return we faced the challenge of 'doing the Treble' by winning the League, League Cup and WFA Cup. Ready to deny us all of these was the team we had beaten in the previous year's Cup Final – QPR. In the League Cup Final we were 2–0 down to QPR, after an own goal and one from centre-forward Carrie Staley, who always seemed to save her best performances for when she played against us. In the remaining 20 minutes of the game, however, we came back with goals from Chapman and Squires, and after a superb solo effort from Lynda Hale we won the game. The WFA Cup Final was played at Dulwich Hamlet's ground in front of 3,000 spectators. Also in attendance was FA secretary Ted Croker, who was renowned for his cynicism towards women's football. No doubt QPR wanted to avenge the previous year's WFA Cup defeat and they played the best game they had ever played against us. Inevitably Staley scored the winner. Paddy McGroarty and Josie Lee were outstanding in midfield, forwards Ross, Choat and Staley turned our defence inside out, and goalkeeper Pat Napier made up for her lapse from the previous year with such a good performance that Ted Croker gave her the 'player of the match' award. The media were there in greater numbers than ever before. The *Mirror*'s back sports page showed a photo of 21-year-old Carrie Staley holding the Cup under the heading 'What a Carrie-on!' The *Guardian*'s Frank Keating wrote a large report under the headline 'Bridge of thighs', which indicates something of the article's patronising flavour. He admitted that there was some 'jolly good play ... enough certainly to suggest that a lovely, simple game could well gather much more support among the PE staff at girls' schools' but went on to comment that football could be a 'lovely game for women. What they need to do now is to redefine it in feminine terms, not ape the men so much ... so that it complements their nature rather than compromises it.' In particular, he criticised the 'gum-chewing players, holding their groins in the defensive wall [against free-kicks] for instance, and appealing for every throw-in as a matter of course – aping their Saturday heroes on television'.[4] More significant in media terms was the presence of Bob Wilson of the BBC, who filmed some of the match to show prior to the forthcoming London Marathon. At last women's football was getting some TV exposure.

Stung by our Cup defeat, just a week later we took on QPR for a third time, in pursuit of the Home Counties League title at Romsey Town's ground, and managed to recapture our true form. With two headers from Linda Coffin and Pat Davies and a final goal from Pat Chapman, we finally beat QPR 3–2.

Dave Case had returned as manager for the 1976–77 season but stayed only for a year. We also had the disappointment of Linda Coffin 'defecting' to QPR during the summer and it looked, at this point, as though 1977–78 was going to be a difficult season, but it turned out to be the most successful in the club's history. We were fortunate to obtain the services of Charlie Clarke as manager. Charlie was the first Advanced Licence coach to take charge of us and he was a well-respected local manager in men's football. He was not only a great coach and motivator, but he also had the perfect cheerful yet firm manner the team thrived on. Southampton also gained another young player, 13-year-old Weston Park schoolgirl Sharon Roberts, who quickly proved more than capable of looking after herself. Sharon soon became one of the fiercest tacklers in women's football and, some would say, fiercer than her tough-tackling brother Graham, who played for Tottenham Hotspurs. Sharon undoubtedly had the potential to gain international honours. That year we finally won the Treble of the League, League Cup and the WFA Cup that we had striven for since starting to play in the Home Counties League in 1973.

The 1978 WFA Cup Final made our eighth consecutive Cup Final appearance. It was played against QPR at Slough's ground and, unusually for this time, two women officiated, assisting referee Mr Clive White. In the first few minutes, Hazel Ross, QPR's dangerous winger, started one of her incisive runs down the left wing that had previously been the source of many of their goals. However, on this occasion she met one of Sharon Roberts's tough tackles and little more was seen of her. After only eight minutes, Pat Chapman sent over one of her accurate inswinging corners, and found our smallest player, Pat Davies, in the penalty area, who headed the ball into the top corner of the goal. Not long after, Pat

Chapman and Maggie Pearce worked one of their familiar dazzling left-wing build-ups, to lay on a pass for me to score with a low drive. Just before half-time Pat Chapman scored with a stunning 20-yard shot to put us 3–0 up. In the second half we took QPR apart and finished with an 8–2 victory which, up to 1996, was the highest Cup Final score. Pat Chapman scored five goals and received a special trophy. Full-back Maggie Pearce's husband Gordie said, "Ten more trophies should have been made, for in fact, this was a complete team performance." The Saints men's team had regained First Division status and the mayor, Mrs Joyce Pitter, invited both teams to a celebratory reception. The *Echo* printed a photo of Saints' goalkeeper, Peter Wells, with Sue Buckett, both raising their champagne-filled glasses to the city's two successful teams.

The match was televised by ITV as part of Southern Television's *Southern Report* series in which reporter Isabel Maxwell followed the team's build-up to the final. It showed how we held down our jobs as well as devoted so much time to football. It was entitled 'Nice one ... Sue, Sharon, Maggie, Ann, Heather, Grace, Lynda, Pat, "Diddy", Sue and Hilary', mimicking a current popular song about Spurs, 'Nice one Cyril!'. Southampton's sixth WFA Cup victory saw the club reach the zenith of its ambition to be the best and most consistent women's football team of the 1970s. I was the sole survivor of the original Southampton team that had formed for the first match against Portsmouth in 1966.

Managers, money and motivation

Despite Southampton's prolonged success in the 1970s, the club faced many of the problems endemic to women's football. The first of these was the difficulty in sustaining stable management. Southampton had seven managers over the 20 years of the club's existence and it often proved impossible to find men – or women – sufficiently qualified and able to manage the team. With so many players in the team with international experience and, therefore, access to some of the best football coaching from the FA-appointed managers and staff coaches, it was perhaps inevitable that we challenged the ideas of male managers who had not had as much exposure to quality coaching.

Another persistent problem was the expense of playing. Our League programme involved so much costly travel and overnight accommodation that our treasurer, Sue Buckett, estimated that in one year it cost the club £4,000. The infrequent visits by the few top clubs to Romsey meant that only rarely did we attract more than a 100 or so supporters. As we didn't have an entrance charge, and relied on programme sales, our income was low. In all the years of our success we gained only one sponsor, Masters, a vegetable wholesaler, who provided the team with T-shirts advertising their business, plus some cash towards travel, training and pitch hire expenses.

A further problem was the accessibility of FA League grounds for our games. Although the ban had been rescinded, there were still problems when it came to playing on League grounds. In 1979 we found the Football League would not give Southampton FC permission for us to play a short pre-match entertainment game before one of their First Division League games at the Dell. One of our most ardent fans, John Shaw, was so annoyed about the refusal that he wrote a letter to the *Echo*. His opening line read: 'The very successful Southampton lady footballers have shown wonderful form, bless them, but I ask you – a gate of 1,200 for the Cup Final at Waterlooville. It's a disgrace.' He went on to say that he had seen Dick, Kerr Ladies playing on League grounds with big crowds after the First World War and he couldn't see why there was a problem today.[5] The *Echo* printed my response as club secretary in which I explained we'd hoped to build on the successful staging of the England v. Belgium game we had organised at the Dell the previous October (see p. 98) which had attracted nearly 6,000 spectators. Saints' secretary, Brain Truscott, explained the League's reasoning as follows: 'It is not the policy of the Football League to permit organisations to use League grounds on Sunday, except for charity matches and even then, it is not automatic that permission will be granted.' We were in fact requesting use of the pitch on a Saturday. The Saints, who were very supportive, were blocked in this instance by the Football League.

The issue of finding suitable grounds, qualified leaders and being unable to accommodate the increasing enquiries from girls wishing to join our non-existent youth team, were all symptomatic of the problems the game encountered. When an American U18 team, the Texas Sting, requested matches in England on their way to the famous girls' and boys' Gotha Cup tournament in Sweden, I arranged for a girls' team from the secondary school, where I taught PE, to play them. The school team were completely outclassed and lost 11–0. Several young players had joined the Southampton team and undoubtedly learned a good deal from training with a team containing seven internationals, but they all, apart from Sharon Roberts, really needed to develop in a reserve team rather than going straight in at the top against experienced adults. The all-round lack of development for girls' and women's football in the country as a whole meant that a few teams dominated each regional league. Southampton were finding it difficult to motivate themselves to beat the few top teams they encountered each season in the WFA Cup, let alone the weaker teams in the Home Counties League. Additionally, there were few international competitions. Pat Davies became so disenchanted with the lack of development that she retired and took up other sports. She found it more difficult each year to make the necessary sacrifices of long expensive journeys to WFA Cup games, besides the regular commitment to training sessions to keep fit. In an *Echo* report, Sue Buckett highlighted the problem:

> We have won everything there is to win in women's football in this country. Other teams raise their game against us because it would be a feather in their cap to topple Southampton. We mainly do it because of our pride in being a Southampton player and staying at the top but the other problem is the wide age gap – Sharon Roberts was only 13 when she appeared in the 1978 Cup Final – three years younger than the age limit for boys playing senior football.[6]

Little had changed in women's football since the early 1970s. There was still no sign of a national league or sustained development of girls' football. Apart from the FA Preliminary Licence coaching award course, instigated in 1975, there had been no initiatives to encourage women into coaching, refereeing or medical courses. Over the decade, in which Southampton appeared in every WFA Cup Final, they were challenged by a handful of clubs – Fodens, QPR, Warminster, Lowestoft, St Helens and Preston North End. These clubs found it hard to sustain consistent teams. This instability was partly caused by a few of the best players moving to another club or, as in the case of Fodens, an ageing team. The lack of a youth development structure in English women's football meant we had no young women to replace the older players. Girls desperately needed opportunities to play football at school, and clubs needed assistance from other agencies. The adult women's teams, equally, needed a structure

which encouraged development by way of regional and national
league competitions. Equally necessary was a drive to encourage
older players to stay in the game as leaders.

The WFA tried to address some of these problems and obtained
enough grant aid to afford a full-time secretary but, as Williams
and Woodhouse point out, by the early 1980s women's football
in England had enjoyed little success in its attempts to establish
a strong country-wide base for the sport:

> A small number of top players enjoyed some international
> success but found little competition in the struggling
> regional leagues. In 1983, Norwich and England striker,
> Linda Curl, scored a record 22 times in her club's 40–0 WFA
> Cup competition destruction of Milton Keynes. Soon after,
> the emerging Doncaster Belles beat Leek Leaders 34–0.
> Probably wisely, the Belles' next opponents withdrew from
> the tie. The women's game's lack of any strength in depth
> and effective grass roots development was proving to be
> damaging and embarrassing. Who could take the sport
> seriously?[7]

In August 1979, when Southampton took third place in an
international club tournament in Frankfurt, we lost in the early
rounds to the runners-up, West German champions, Bergisch
Gladbach. Winners were Oxabacks from Sweden, a country where
girls could play in schools and where it was normal for towns and
villages to have sports clubs which included girls' and women's
football teams. Women's teams were sponsored much in the
same way English men's teams were, and clearly a more egalitarian
attitude towards women's sport prevailed.

Southampton's decline

By 1980, Southampton's decline had set in. The key players were
ageing and others left to channel their energies elsewhere. Despite
finding ourselves with one of ablest trainer/managers of all, in
Tony Old, we failed to reach the 1980 final, losing to Cleveland
Spartans in the quarter-final. Although we recovered our form
sufficiently the next season to beat St Helens 4–2 in the 1981 final,
it was to be our tenth and last WFA Cup Final appearance. We had
acquired two fine players in Eileen Foreman and Louise Worth
from Warminster, but even with their input we could not recapture
the style and determination of our halcyon days. I retired in

1985 aged 39 after 20 years of playing for Southampton and six years as an England player, with 22 caps. Southampton folded in 1986.

Maggie Pearce concentrated on being a netball coach. Sue Buckett, Linda Coffin, Pat Chapman and Hilary Carter signed on for Red Star Southampton (now Southampton Saints, since their official association with the Saints men's team). Pat Chapman became player/manager and took them to the 1992 Cup Final at Tranmere Rovers' Prenton Park, where they lost 4–2 to Doncaster Belles (who achieved that day their fifth WFA Cup victory). Pat retired in 1993 following a collision with a goalkeeper that needed a cruciate ligament reconstruction and she is no longer involved with football. Sue Buckett retired in 1994, at the age of 51, the oldest player to play in the League. She became qualified in first aid and in 1995 became the Southampton Saints' physiotherapist. She is still prepared to play in goal in emergencies! In 1996, Linda Coffin, Hilary Carter and Jill England were still playing for the Southampton Saints and Lynda Hale was playing for the team she started up called Solent, renamed Southampton when the original Southampton team finished in 1986. Nessie Raynbird became the manager of Southampton Saints in 1995.

The next decade of WFA Cup Finals was dominated by the Doncaster Belles. The team was led by England's most capped player (93 as of October 1996), Gill Coultard, and the team also boasted five other key England players of the late 1980s and early 1990s, such as star striker Karen Walker, centre-back Jackie Sherrard, goalkeeper Tracey Davidson and wingers Gail Borman and Jan Murray, as well as founder member Sheila Edmunds.[8] However, although they contested 11 out of the next 13 finals, they won only six times, compared with Southampton's unique record of eight victories in ten finals. Apart from Arsenal winning in 1993 and 1995, against Doncaster and Liverpool respectively, no other club has won the Cup on more than one occasion. In the 1996 Cup Final, recently-formed Croydon added a thirteenth different name to the Cup with their penalty shoot-out victory, after extra time, against Liverpool. Played in front of 2,122 spectators at Millwall, the event was screened live on Sky TV with viewing figures of one million. The competition attracted just over 200 entries and out of the prize fund, the finalists received £500 (the club, not individual players), the semi-finalists £400 (as do all those involved in the sixth round), the fifth-round teams received £250, fourth £200, and third £100.

Any prize money clubs receive today is obviously welcome but £500 does not stretch far in terms of covering the cost of playing. National League clubs receive a subsidy from the FA towards the cost of accommodation and mileage for away League matches but it still costs players at least £10 each for an away game, while home ground matches incur ground hire and referee's fees. Success in the Cup can still be as expensive for today's players as it was for those playing in the final 25 years ago when no money was available. Perhaps more disappointing is the fact that the competition did not grow as fast as it did in the 1970s. The first final in 1971 attracted 71 entries and by 1979 it had almost doubled, when 134 clubs took part. This early indication of the game's popularity should have provided the base from which women's football could have gone from strength to strength.

7 The England team

In the summer of 1972, the WFA set up an international team committee whose task was to organise trials to select players for the first official England team. Their responsibilities included finding opponents to play, and the provision of training facilities, kit and equipment. As UEFA had no immediate plans to organise competitions, to replace those held unofficially in Italy and Mexico, the WFA looked to neighbouring nations for friendly matches.

The FA appointed FA staff coach, Eric Worthington, an ex-professional player for QPR, as manager of the women's team. The responsibility for appointing managers, and payment of their fees, was always a matter for the FA. They allowed the WFA autonomy in all other aspects of the women's game but maintained their right to step in whenever they thought it was appropriate. As the FA was ultimately the governing body in England, the women's team was representing *them* abroad and it was up to the manager to ensure there was a certain amount of conformity to FA standards with regard to the actual football.

Funds to run an international team came from a Sports Council grant. A small grant came from the FA but there was no specific money from them for preparation, nor help with the provision of kit. The WFA were responsible for meals, accommodation and travel in England and abroad. The contribution towards expenses for travel around England did not always fully compensate for amounts spent and those players who lost wages while on international duty were not recompensed (a situation still true in 1997). There was no formal education about fitness or diet and it was entirely down to each player to show 100 per cent commitment and ensure she was fit and well prepared. The volunteer amateurs who organised internationals had inadequate finances and little experience of match organisation or the needs of international athletes. Training days were few and there was usually no more than a day before a match for the manager to finalise his team. Often, away trips did not allow sufficient time to recover from travel fatigue. Getting adequate training and match kit was nearly always impossible and sometimes farcical. Players trained in their own tracksuits and the WFA had to find suppliers of white shirts for matches, upon which their official motif was sewn. None of the major football suppliers expressed an interest in providing kit for the women's team. International committee member Flo Bilton not only laundered the kit, but actually made the caps by hand. When this became too arduous and impractical, one cap per season was provided, and QPR's Josie Lee didn't even receive one, despite playing in three internationals in 1977. When players retired they eventually received a wooden shield upon which was fixed an engraved metal plate with details of each of their international matches.

When I took over as international officer in 1991, things had not improved. I found that players were unable to wear the new training drill suits because they had not been finished off properly, and were in sizes either much too big or too small. In addition, players did not get to keep any of their international shirts, as is the custom in men's football. When the England team became the FA's responsibility in 1993, things began to improve. The England men's team kit suppliers, Umbro, agreed to supply the women's team and have, reputedly, been generous. For the World Cup in Sweden in 1995, the England players received so much kit from Umbro, including 15 shirts each with their own name on, that they had enough to give away to fans and friends. In 1996 Adidas supplied the team with their new specially designed women's boot 'Equipment Real'. Players also now receive a daily allowance, currently £15 per day for away matches, whereas under the WFA they received nothing.

The first official matches

Eric Worthington selected 16 players for the first England team, for the 1972–73 season, from a trial tournament, sponsored by Lillywhite Sportswear. The tournament was set up as an inter-league team competition containing around 300 players and was won by the Home Counties League team containing over half of the Southampton squad. This system of selection overlooked loss of form and injuries, and anyone in this category, like me, had to wait a whole season for the next selection opportunity. I was fully fit by the time of the first official England match, on 19 November against Scotland, but it was too late. The match was played on an icy pitch, and in the second half during a snow storm, at the Ravenscraig Stadium at Greenock. England won 3–2 with the first goal being scored by Fodens' 28-year-old Sylvia Gore and the other two by Southampton's Pat Davies (17). Three other Southampton players were in the side: Maggie Kirkland (15), Lynda Hale (18) and Sue Buckett (28), and two other Fodens players: Sheila Parker (captain, 24) and Jeannie Allot (16). The other players were Janet Bagguley (17), Paddy McGroarty (25), Sandra Graham (28) and Jean Wilson (23). Five of the Scottish players were from Westthorn Utd Margaret McAulay (captain, 21), Edna Neillis (18), Mary Anderson (18), Marian Mount (18) and Rose Reilly (17). Three others came from Lees Ladies, runners-up in the 1972 WFA Cup Final: Linda Kidd (21), Jean Hunter (17) and Sandra Walker (22). The rest of the team were Jane Houghton (17), June Hunter (19) and Mary Carr (20).

Sylvia says she'll never forget scoring the first ever goal for the first official England team, which was especially rewarding after all the times she had represented an unofficial 'England XI' abroad when she was with Manchester Corinthians:

> Scoring that goal, and beating Southampton in the 1974 Cup Final, are the greatest memories of my football career. I ran the whole length of the Scottish half of the pitch and was so relieved I didn't lose the ball in all the mud, and it was even more pleasing when the Scottish goalkeeper dived and the ball went past her into the net!

Sheila Parker recalls when Eric Worthington told her in training that she would be captain:

> It was a surprise, but I suppose he saw some leadership qualities I had, and I was one of the older, more experienced players among quite a few youngsters. I led them out and played my normal game, and was real proud when we won.

Before long Eric Worthington left England in order to coach in Australia and was replaced by the FA with John Adams. The first match he oversaw was against France in April 1973, at the Stade de Brion. In front of 3,000 spectators, who had paid approximately £1.50p each for tickets, the England team comfortably won 3–0.

Pat Davies scored two goals and Eileen Foreman, in her debut match for England, scored one. The players and officials, Pat Gregory, Flo Bilton and press officer Roger Ebben, were all surprised at how well-organised French women's football was – France had around 400 clubs and 7,000 players. Also the media exposure and attendance was better than anyone from England had expected. Presumably they had not heard about the French opponents to Dick, Kerr Ladies in the 1920s.

John Adams selected the new season's England team by the same tournament trial system in June 1973. The new squad, including me (although I didn't actually play), gathered for the first official match on English soil. This was at Nuneaton, in Warwickshire, on 23 June, a baking hot summer's day, and we beat Scotland 8–0 in front of a crowd of 1,310. There were now many younger players challenging for the strikers' positions and one of this new breed was 16-year-old Pat Firth, who scored a hat-trick in her debut match. Pat Davies and Paddy McGroarty scored two each. John Adams brought Eileen Foreman on, in the last 20 minutes of the game, to exploit her speed against the weary Scottish defenders and she also managed to score a goal. One of the Scottish defenders was the 16-year-old Edinburgh Dynamo centre-half, Sheila Begbie, who 20 years later became the coordinator for Scottish women's football development and assistant international coach. She recalls the match as "my biggest playing nightmare!"

This was to be John Adams's last match managing the team but he had taught the squad well in his short time with them and was highly respected by all the players. In addition to being an excellent coach, he had a sense of humour and the rare quality of being able to get the best out of all his players. With his big, handsome smile, and in a broad Yorkshire accent, he used to say to our centre-back, Wendy Owen, whenever she lost the ball trying to dribble out of defence: "Wendy, I didn't pick you to play football, you just have to stop the opposition playing, and give it to a white shirt." We didn't fully appreciate at the time what a great coach he was and only later, when we read comments he made in the press, did we realise the respect was mutual: 'When it comes to soccer skills, these girls could show the men a thing or two. There are certain aspects of the game they do so well.'[1]

The FA's next appointment was Tommy Tranter, manager of Slough Town of the semi-professional Isthmian League. Like John Adams, Tommy did his best to champion the cause of women's football. In his first match on 7 September 1973, Tommy led the team to victory over Northern Ireland at Twerton Park, in Bath, in a game played as part of the city's 'Monarchy 1000' celebrations. This was the first international women's match to be staged under floodlights. It was also my debut game and the mixture of experience and youth in the team worked well as we overwhelmed the Irish 5–1. The next match, against the Netherlands on 9 November 1973, gave England a 1–0 victory. This was the first women's match since the 1921 ban to be played on a professional League ground, at Elm Park, Reading, in Berkshire. In just one year, the WFA, and its England team, had not only achieved five fine victories but had also made some headway with the FA and Football League (who had responsibility for all the male League teams then) and had, for the first time, the benefit of coaching from top FA coaches.

After a flurry of matches within the first year, there was gap before the team had a chance to continue their success: they did not play again until March 1974, against Wales at Slough's ground, winning 5–0. This was followed by a 3–0 away victory over the Netherlands in May. The Wales match was memorable for the fact that it was sponsored by an egg firm; each player received a complimentary carton of half a dozen eggs.

Flo Bilton oversaw the England team for the WFA and she had the wisdom to see the value of encouraging women to become coaches while they were still playing. Staffed by Tommy Tranter, and in conjunction with the FA, the first women-only FA Preliminary Licence coaching course was organised in August 1974. The expectation was that many England players would attend. However, only captain Carol McCune and I turned up from the England team, along with team physiotherapist, Jane Talbot, and Southampton player Pauline Dickie. We all passed and received our certificates from FA secretary Denis Follows, and were the first women Preliminary Licence coaches in the country.

On 11 November 1974, England beat France 2–0 at non-league Wimbledon FC's ground, and this match was remarkable for both the quantity and improved quality of the national press coverage. The *Guardian*'s Richard Yallop reported on some of the financial aspects of the women's game, which provided an interesting read.[2] We were also particularly flattered by ex-professional player and TV pundit Jimmy Hill comparing us favourably, in the *News of the World*, with the England men's team by saying: 'Take a tip Revie [England's men's manager] – it's time to follow the girls.'[3] He expressed pleasure in watching our shorter-passing game, a hallmark of women's football at the time, and particularly admired our organised 4–3–3 defence system, and the fact that we played with a left-footed left-back and left-winger.

Sweden and Italy challenge England's superiority

Five months later, in April 1975, England went to Basle and beat the Swiss 2–0. Switzerland had lost only to the Netherlands (3–0) in their last seven matches, which included games against Austria (one), France (four) and one other against the Netherlands which they had drawn. England's winning run was to end, however, when they met the new generation of women footballers from countries that had made enormous strides in development. It was no great surprise that the Swedish international team was of a significantly higher calibre. They gave us a football lesson with two conclusive victories, 2–0 away in June and 3–0 at home in September. I did not play in either of the matches but remember the Southampton players returning from these games amazed at the Swedish players' level of skill, as well as their fitness and athleticism. Sue Buckett recalls having witnessed Denmark's progress in Turin in 1969 and she was even more astounded at the advances the Swedish players had made. She also noted how professional they looked, with their team of medical people and trainers, and she predicted that England would be left behind if we didn't start to learn from the Scandinavians.

In May 1976, England defeated the Netherlands again by 2–1 at Borough Park Rugby League ground at Blackpool, and the Swedish lesson was forgotten. This was the first England match to be played in the north of England and there is no explanation in the programme as to why a Rugby League ground was used. Six years after the FA ban had been lifted, and with affiliated pitches available, it was odd that one couldn't be found for an official international match. The WFA comments in the programme further illustrated the dichotomy between the rhetoric and the actual practice regarding the game's development. This programme stated that progress had been made with the FA since the end of the ban but went on to say 'the ties are quite tenuous'. It explained that in spite of FIFA and UEFA directives recommending that member nations control the women's game, the FA had decided to leave the control of the English game to the WFA, giving them 'full recognition and support'. The programme also recorded that there were nearly 300 clubs and 25 leagues at this time.

England used semi-professional football grounds when they beat Scotland (5–1 at Enfield FC) and Wales (4–0 at Bedford Town FC) to win the first Home International Tournament in May 1976.[4] In June 1976, the England team made their first official visit to Italy and played two games over one week, one in Rome and the other in Cesena, near Rimini on the Adriatic coast. WFA officials saw for themselves the progress the Italians had made and the excellent training facilities they had. The first match kicked off at 6 pm, to avoid the heat, in the Flaminio Olympic Stadium in Rome, in front of nearly 10,000 spectators. Italy had played twice as many internationals as England's 14 and, whereas England had already lost four, they had lost only three. England's goalkeeper, Sue Buckett, was gaining her fifteenth cap while 26-year-old Assunta Gualdi (who played for Gorgonzola) was winning her twenty-fourth. The Italian team had a number of veteran international players and Italy's star player that evening was 22-year-old Elisabetta Vignotto, playing her twelfth international game – she went on to gain 110 caps. Italy deservedly beat England 2–0, although some of the England side had struggled with the humid weather and hard ground. In between this match and the next at Cesena, the squad had two novel experiences: the first was an audience with the Pope at the Vatican; and the second a chance to see a television recording of their first match and observe how much more skilful some of the Italian players were. In the second game in Cesena, with ten minutes to full time, the score was 1–1, but Italy's higher stamina and fitness levels earned them their eventual 2–1 victory. The audience with the Pope had not provided a miracle! The Italian players were clearly benefiting from having a national league that gave them regular competitive football and for this reason they were envied by many of us. Jeannie Allot pursued this desire to play in a competitve league and went to play for Dutch team ZW Rotterdam in 1976.

England had one game, a 0–0 draw against France in Paris in February 1977, before their return match against Italy. This was on 15 November 1977, again at Wimbledon FC, and it marked Italy's first visit to England. The match attracted the biggest sponsorship so far, with £1,000 from Sir Fred Pontin, chairman of the holiday firm. It also attracted more press attention than the first Wimbledon fixture against France, stimulated by the fact that the England men's team were also playing Italy, at Wembley, the following evening. The London *Evening Standard, Evening News,* as well as the national newspapers, the *Daily Express, Daily Mail, Daily Mirror* and the *Guardian,* all had several column inches both before and after the match. With no blonde-haired replacement for Jeannie Allot (who was always picked out by the press for this reason), they turned instead to the dark-haired Italians for their photos.

It was to England's credit that they gave an outstanding performance, despite a freezing cold evening, in front of a relatively small crowd of 1,493. The only regrets were the low attendance and that the margin of the victory, England winning 1–0 with a goal scored by Sheila Parker, was not larger. The media's post-match reports were a joy to read. Most enjoyable of all was the report from the *Daily Express* journalist, John Morgan, which opened with:

> Ladies, I apologise unreservedly and wholeheartedly. I went to Wimbledon to watch England play Italy expecting to snigger. I went with all the usual male prejudices about soccer being 'unfeminine'; that the girls would break down and cry if someone kicked them or if the referee was a bit nasty and did not allow a goal. I saw instead the best game of football I have seen since those famous Wolves managed by Stan Cullis terrorised Europe in the 1950s … There was no 'aggro', no obscene chanting, no 'acting' or cheating by the players, and soccer of a standard that those of us over 40 years of age remember watching as school-kids.[5]

The first women's match on a First Division ground since 1921

England played Belgium at the Dell in Southampton, on 31 October 1978, and won 3–0. This may have seemed an unspectacular achievement but it was, for several reasons, a significant event in the history of women's football. The match, organised by Sue Buckett and myself, was the first to have been held on a Football League First Division ground since before the FA ban. Southampton FC were happy to give us the venue and the game attracted the largest sponsorship ever received by the WFA for a match, of £2,000 from Martini & Rossi, who had a local factory. The attendance of 5,471 remains a record for any women's game (not part of another event) under the control of either the

WFA or FA.[6] Additionally, we received personal backing and promotion from the indomitable Southampton manager, Lawrie McMenemy. While his predecessor, Ted Bates had always been supportive of the Southampton women's team on a practical level, Lawrie McMenemy was willing to make the important public gestures which helped to convey the message that women's football was acceptable. He was happy to pose for promotional photographs with Southampton's five England players: Sue Buckett, Pat Chapman, Linda Coffin, Maggie Pearce and myself. Before the kick-off the players had been introduced to Ron Greenwood, England's men's team manager, and we were all conscious that it was a special occasion. The players responded by producing excellent football and St Helen's Liz Deighan even received praise for her display from Ron Greenwood, who described her as 'the female Kevin Keegan'. Many said then, and years later, that it was one of the best women's internationals ever staged in this country. Personally, I was thrilled to have had the opportunity to play at the Dell after so many years as a supporter. The Saints' men and women proved to be pioneers in showing the mutual advantages in professional men's teams and local women's teams working together – as many now do today.

Changes in management and team

Several of the original England players retired at the end of the 1978 season. They included the first international players such as Janet Bagguley, Sylvia Gore, Wendy Owen and the Southampton duo Pat Davies and Lynda Hale. The latter two had played non-stop football for the past twelve years, including eight WFA Cup Final appearances. This exodus allowed in a fresh generation, among them Debbie Bampton, Gill Coultard and Marieanne Spacey, all of whom have had distinguished international careers – and who are still playing.

The eleventh Italian European Tournament, held in Naples in July 1979, was to be my last international appearance. Like many players, I had become frustrated at the game's lack of leadership and decided to concentrate on getting my coaching qualifications. The tournament was held over two weeks and the competing nations were: Italy, Denmark, Sweden, Finland, France, Switzerland, the Netherlands, England, Northern Ireland, Scotland

and Wales. Tommy Tranter had resigned and the manager of Cleveland Spartans, John Sims, had been a late replacement. The tournament was well organised, played at top professional grounds, and while we easily beat Finland 3–1 and Switzerland 2–0, Italy outplayed us with their 3–1 victory at the Stadio San Paolo. In the play-off for third and fourth place, we drew 0–0 with Sweden at Scafati, but lost 4–3 on penalties. Denmark, who had gone from strength to strength since their win at the unofficial World Cup in Mexico, beat Italy 2–0 in the final.

John Sims did not remain as manager for long and England played one match under temporary manager Mike Rawdin: a 2–2 draw with Denmark at Hull City's Boothferry Park, on 13 September 1979. Then Martin Reagan took charge. He was an ex-professional who had played at a number of clubs and obtained his FA Advanced Coaching Licence in 1955. He remained in the post for ten years and, as well as being the most successful team manager, he did his best to address some of the far-reaching and fundamental problems associated with the women's game. Things had not progressed as well as the WFA had hoped and Reagan says of the first months: "I met with Pat Gregory, and David Hunt, and I gathered that there had been some confusion since Tommy Tranter resigned a few months earlier, and it seemed that we'd have to start again from scratch." His first year was not successful, with a defeat by Belgium, 2–1, easy wins over Wales, 6–1, and the Republic of Ireland, 5–0, but yet again difficulties with the Scandinavians, a 1–1 draw at home to Sweden.

Martin Reagan recognised the huge problems in managing the national women's team – greater than most of those encountered in men's football. These included: identifying the talented players; affording sufficient pre-match preparation time; overcoming injuries and other reasons for non-availability, such as employment demands; and raising players' fitness levels for international games. To this end, England became the first Home Countries nation to put their national women's team on a fitness programme. A grant of £6,000 was obtained from the Sports Council and, for the first time, players were able to take six fitness tests and receive individual fitness programmes over a period of two years. This took place at the FA's Human Performance Centre at Lilleshall National Sports Centre in Shropshire.

While Martin Reagan could influence things to some extent, like past managers he was frustrated and told me later:

There were models to be seen abroad, but from outside the WFA there seemed to be little interest. Those with the power and the authority, for whatever reason, were not aware of the needs, or committed to improvement. There was a desperate need at this time for greater awareness and support from other footballing bodies, who were in a position to render much more help in developing the women's game more actively.

Martin cared deeply about football, and women's football in particular, and he had some positive ideas, which he suggested early on, about the development of girls' and women's football through the counties. Some 15 years later, his development ideas have become policy. The FA strategy document, 'Women and Football', published in 1995, recommends that the counties appoint referees, register clubs and lead the launching of a ten-county FA pilot scheme to introduce girls' small-sided leagues, through liaison with local borough sports development officers. Martin also lamented the demise of the regional system which had been used to identify talent, and the failure – over 20 years or more – to involve experienced former players in the game, especially as coaches and administrators.

UEFA Championships and Italian tournaments 1982–1993

For the first ten years England played between three and six matches a year and a total of only 43 matches. Most of these were 'friendlies'. Their only competitive matches were the Three Nation Home Championship with Wales and Scotland in 1976, the European Tournament in Naples in 1979, and the Three Nation Tournament in 1981 against Japan and Denmark (organised to help stimulate interest in women's football in Japan). In 1971, UEFA had set up a committee for women's football, composed exclusively of male representatives, and by the time this committee folded in 1978 they had failed to organise any international competitions. A new committee was set up in 1981; this time it included two women members – Pat Gregory and Hannelore Ratzeburg from Germany – and the first UEFA-organised women's championship took place in 1982–84.

Martin Reagan's greatest achievement was undoubtedly getting England to the final of this inaugural UEFA Championship. When the team went to Gothenburg for the first leg of the final in May 1984, they were overwhelmed by the presence of the national press and television. The game was televised live; Sweden won 1–0. For the second leg, two weeks later at Luton Town's ground, the Swedish team arrived with a TV crew and 36 press personnel. By contrast, the game was barely mentioned in the English press. England led 1–0 at full time but, with no extra time allowed, lost 4–3 in the penalty shoot-out.

Sweden were not the only team beginning consistently to challenge the England side. The West German team had been newly formed in 1982 and in their first encounter beat England, 2–0, in the Italian Tournament, on 22 August 1984. England's other results in the tournament were a 1–1 draw with both Italy and Belgium and then a 2–1 and 3–1 defeat of Belgium and Italy respectively, but they didn't reach the final rounds.

For the second UEFA competition (1985–87), England once again took on less demanding UK opponents in the early stages and defeated Scotland 4–0 and 3–1, Northern Ireland 10–0 and 8–1, and the Republic of Ireland 6–0 and 4–0. England then turned to the 1985 Italian Tournament and won it, having drawn 1–1 in the qualifying rounds with Italy, and beaten international newcomers, USA, 3–1. They then went on to defeat the hosts in the final.

However, in the UEFA competition, Scandinavian opposition proved harder to beat and England lost 3–2 in extra time to Sweden in the semi-final. In the play-off for third and fourth place, England lost 2–1 to Italy, and in the final, Norway beat Sweden 2–1. This was to be England's last appearance at this stage of the competition. In the third UEFA Championship (1987–89) they encountered Finland, winning 2–1 and drawing 1–1; Denmark, winning 2–1 and losing 2–0; and holders Norway, losing 2–0 and 3–1. Germany became UEFA champions for the first time, beating Norway 4–1 in Osnabruck, Germany, in front of 22,000 spectators – with many locked outside the stadium unable to get in. England did win the Italian 'Little World Cup' a second time in July 1988, by beating the USA 2–0 and Italy 'B' 3–0, drawing 1–1 with France, and defeating Italy 2–1 in the final.

Sweden were to inflict another defeat on England, on 23 May 1989, when they beat them 2–0 at Wembley, the first goal coming in the sixth minute, scored by Pia Sundhage (winning her eighty-third cap) and the second from Lena Videkull. It was the first time an English women's team had played at Wembley, but the game became infamous for another reason. The match was very poorly staged, which did not please the WFA's Swedish guests. Women's football in Sweden was, of course, under the control of the Swedish men's FA and therefore communications probably would have gone direct to the FA in England, and then, subsequently, to the WFA. The Swedish FA had one of Europe's top officials in Lennart Johansson (the UEFA president in 1996), and this may have made things worse for the WFA. Certainly, the failure to stage the game at the professional level expected by foreign teams, such as Sweden, did nothing to help the WFA's cause in keeping control of women's football and merely added to the ongoing problems that eventually brought about their demise.

In 1990, a friendly was successfully staged at Wembley against Scotland on 12 May, in which England won 4–0 and the mercurial Marieanne Spacey scored an outstanding goal. In the fourth UEFA 1989–91 Championship preliminary matches England beat Finland 4–0 and drew 0–0, and beat Belgium 3–0 and 1–0. Although they lost against Norway 2–0 and drew 0–0 at home, they qualified for the UEFA quarter-final. In the 1990 Italian Tournament, England struggled among the elite of women's football and managed only one victory, 1–0 against the USA's 'B' team. They lost to UEFA champions West Germany by 3–1, and USA's 'A' team by 3–0.

Following the Italian Tournament, England met West Germany again in the UEFA quarter-final and their opponents confirmed their status as the best European nation by demolishing England 4–1 at High Wycombe, in November 1990, and 2–0 in Bochum in December. In the final, Germany beat Norway 3–1, with Denmark placed third and Italy fourth. The failure to reach the UEFA semi-finals meant that England did not qualify for the FIFA inaugural World Cup in China in 1991, and it also led to Martin Reagan losing his job as manager. Martin was informally invited to meet Richard Faulkner, the WFA's chair, and told that the committee thought it was an 'opportune' time to make a change in the position of manager. Martin feels his dismissal was poorly handled:

> The sudden and complete cessation of involvement in something which had taken up so much time and effort, caused great regret. The manner of my leaving was very disappointing and the way in which it was handled left a

lot to be desired. On behalf of the WFA I had always demanded very high standards from players, in activities, or behaviour; these standards were not reflected in my leaving

Reagan's only major regret was not qualifying the English team for the first FIFA World Cup, but his overall thoughts on women's football remain positive:

> My abiding memory is one of the happiness of women players taking their full and rightful part in this wonderful game – their attitudes and their determination to succeed in spite of the odds being against them. With this attitude, and given the right opportunities, the future of the women's game is assured and I hope England's women will eventually reach their rightful place in world terms.

Martin's England team record speaks for itself: played 70, won 37, lost 19, drawn 14; scored 152 (average 2.17 per game), goals conceded 68 (average 0.97 per game). UEFA Championships: 1984, finalists, losing on penalties, and 1987 fourth place.

Barrie Williams took over from Martin Reagan in 1991. The new manager was reminded of the gulf between British teams and the best. England beat Scotland 5–0 but lost 3–1 to the USA. The team then enjoyed two draws with Denmark, 3–3 and 0–0, and 2–1 and 2–0 defeats of the USSR – both in friendly matches. The two games against the USSR had been played at Brighton & Hove Albion's ground and at the Dell, Southampton. I watched the match at the Dell and was soon aware that all was not well with the organisational side of things when Pat Gregory personally handed out programmes to the meagre crowd just before the kick-off. International officer June Jaycocks resigned, to be followed shortly by Barrie Williams. I then took over from June Jaycocks as international officer, working with new manager John Bilton. Further communication problems between the WFA and the FA's Human Performance Centre had led to an interruption in the players' fitness monitoring programme and, due to lack of finances, the England team could not get sufficient training days together.

As in the past, the preliminary rounds of the 1991–93 UEFA Championship did not prove too difficult for England with 1–0 and 2–0 victories over Scotland, and over relative newcomers Iceland by 4–0 and 2–1. However, England's last game organised by the WFA, the 3–0 defeat by Italy at Rotherham, showed yet again that whenever a top nation was encountered England spluttered. I watched the match, alongside the FA's officials, as they were poised to take over. It was a sad and poignant finale for the last WFA England team. Italy eventually became runners-up in the competition, losing 1–0 to Norway in the final.

In the 1993–95 UEFA Championship England came top in their qualifying matches, winning easily against Belgium and Slovenia, and drawing 0–0 twice against Spain, with a 29 goals for, 0 against goal record. For once, England avoided meeting one of the better European teams in the quarter-finals. They met Iceland (whom they had beaten 6–1 on aggregate in the qualifying rounds in 1992), and this time won 4–3 on aggregate. In the semi-final, however, they could not avoid Germany and in December 1994, they lost 4–1 at Vicarage Road, Watford FC's ground, and lost again 2–1 in the second leg. The *Telegraph*'s Kate Battersby lamented the lack of coverage from the rest of the media in view of the game's importance. Perhaps this was why only 937 supporters turned up. She thought women's football would gain more credibility, and a greater atmosphere to games, if internationals were staged as an extra attraction before a men's FA Premier League game. In the game itself, she noted that some of the Germans were outstanding, such as Heidi Mohr and Martina Voss, and that England ran out of steam in the second half.[7] Germany went on to beat Sweden 3–2 in the final.

In the 1995–97 UEFA Championship, Italy qualified, having won the qualifying group by 14 points to England's 13, following a 1–1 draw against England at Sunderland in November 1995, and a 2–1 victory in Italy in March 1996. England beat the other two nations in the group; they had a 5–0 defeat of Croatia at Charlton's ground in November 1995 and a 3–0 defeat of Portugal at Brentford's stadium in May 1996. Unlike in 1993, England had an opportunity to qualify for the quarter-finals but lost 3–2 on aggregate to Spain, who qualified from the 'B' group of seeded teams. When they played Spain over two legs, in September 1996, England lost 2–1 in Mantilla, and could only draw 1–1 at Tranmere Rovers' ground in front 3,500 spectators.[8] New manager Ted Copeland had told me several weeks prior to these two matches that he was optimistic about the future and felt that England were catching up with the best. He said when he took over from John Bilton, in 1993, players had had no concept of playing as a unit, there was too much individuality and fitness was poor. He felt that players needed to understand the commitment required at international level and he had been impressed with the fact that the Norwegians and the Germans are athletes and take their game seriously. He saw opportunities for improvement in women's football, especially as there was more money available now, and because of the FA's development schemes, such as mini-soccer (FA centres, organised and run locally by FA Preliminary Licence coaches, for boys and girls to play small-sided football with the aim of developing their skills) and the 'new generation' of coaching courses, which became available from August 1996.[9] When asked about junior international teams, he said that the FA's Women's Committee would make the decision after UEFA had organised a tournament and if sponsorship deals could be found. With regard to opportunities for women coaches in the future, he said he didn't discriminate between male and female – they just needed to be good coaches.

Missing the opportunities and ignoring the talent

The England team succeeded in the early years, despite meagre resources, thanks mainly to the great commitment of players, managers and volunteer officials. Unfortunately, by the time FIFA and UEFA competitions were in put in place, England could no longer compete with nations which had already adopted a more professional approach to an amateur game. England had done well to achieve runners-up place in the inaugural UEFA Championship in 1984, and to have been losing semi-finalists in 1987, as well as winning the 'Little World Cup' in 1985 and 1988. However, these successes were not capitalised on and they heralded yet another false dawn. The players of this later period, the second generation of English players in the modern era, have felt much the same frustrations as the first.

The captain in 1997 is Debbie Bampton, who won her first cap against the Republic of Ireland in May 1978 (she had 89 caps by October 1996), and led England in the World Cup in Sweden in 1995. She took over the captaincy from Carol McCune when Carol retired in 1985. Gill Coultard took over the captaincy in 1991 when Debbie was injured. Debbie regained the post from Gill in 1995.

Debbie's potential to be an international footballer was not recognised by her PE teacher, who told her that there was no future in women's football and that she should pursue her other sporting talents of judo (for which she was an England trialist), and athletics, at which she represented her county. After playing in her first 11-a-side team, Barnfield, in Kent, she went on to play for Maidstone, Lowestoft, Howbury Grange, Millwall, Trani (Italy), Millwall again, Wimbledon, Arsenal and now Croydon. As player-manager, Debbie led Croydon to the League and Cup Double in the 1995–96 season. She told me that she went to Italy before there was a national league in England and found the standard was far ahead that of English club football. In the 1990s, she felt England were catching up with Italy, but commenting on the teams in the Sweden World Cup she said, "Norway were in a different class to the rest ... and Germany are just like their men's team – very professional, strong, athletic, a bit robotic but very effective technically ... all the top nations' players are wonderful athletes." As to why England have been left behind she said, "Lack of sponsorship; the fact we didn't progress for at least ten years; not enough coaching at club level; lack of youth development; and lack of facilities and floodlit pitches for training." What she would like to see, immediately, is the setting up of U18 and U21 England teams and for clubs to be sponsored to have qualified coaches and better training facilities. Ideally, she would like to see women's football become semi-professional.

Gill Coultard came into the England squad at the age of 16, in the 1978–79 season, and received her first cap, also against the Republic of Ireland, in May 1981. As of October 1996, she had 93 caps and had captained Doncaster Belles through many of their successful years in the 1980s and 1990s. The other mainstay of the England team, over the past 15 years, has been Marieanne Spacey. She was prevented from playing in the boys' school team but joined British Oxygen's women's team in the London area when she was 13 in 1979. When she joined Friends of Fulham, Marieanne found the manager, Fred Brockwell, was able to develop her skills. She became one of the first to benefit from professional clubs that had closer links with women's teams, such as Wimbledon, and her current club Arsenal (one of the most envied clubs regarding facilities, with an indoor 'Astroturf' training pitch). Arsenal's Vic Akers is the only paid manager, and physiotherapist, of a women's team and has the full-time role of overseeing the development of girls' and women's football at the club. Marieanne told me, "We're fortunate that the directors are supportive and we have the best set-up of all for a women's football team. We have training facilities and can train two nights a week, plus we have kit and boots, and subsidised transport and hotels; although we pay around a £1 a week, match subscriptions etc., it all goes for the team's benefit." Marieanne has always been an honest spokeswoman for the game and talked to me about her development, or lack of it, in the early days: "I regret not being able to learn skills when I was at school and I was lucky to have so much support from my father, and other male members of my family. My Dad has followed my career and came out to Sweden for the World Cup." She says of her Friends of Fulham days that she remembers the great camaraderie within the team and with the opposition: "We'd give a 100 per cent on the pitch but be friends afterwards. At England level, we weren't happy with things like the inadequate expenses, which made us out of pocket, and we knew things could be better organised because other nations were getting it right. But we just had to get on with playing." According to Marieanne her career highlights are winning the Italian Tournaments in 1985 and 1988, her goal at Wembley in an exhibition game against Scotland in 1990, and 'doing the Double', the National Premier League Championship and the FA Women's Cup, with Arsenal in 1992–93 and 1994–95. She adds: "The World Cup in Sweden should have been a highlight but I was disappointed because we could have done better against Norway. We all need to be a 100 per cent dedicated."

The longevity of these three players' careers – like those of many before them – speaks volumes for their skill, fitness and dedication, but it is also a reflection on the lack of development from the late 1970s onwards. Furthermore, it's an even greater loss to the game that of more than 150 ex-England players, only a handful stayed in the game in a coaching capacity or in any other way. They enjoyed access to some of the best coaches, and top international experience, and could have been encouraged to gain FA coaching, physiotherapy or refereeing qualifications, and been well placed to coach and teach the next generation. It wasn't until the FA appointed three female football development officers, in the late 1980s, that the idea of 'women-only' Preliminary Licence courses got tried again.

The UEFA Championship runners-up place in 1984 remains the pinnacle of England's achievements, as they have never reached another UEFA final, failed to qualify for the inaugural FIFA World Cup in China 1991, and reached only the last eight of the second World Cup in Sweden in 1995 but could not qualify, like the other quarter-finalists, to play in the Olympics in 1996.[10] They have failed to reach the last eight of the UEFA Championship to be held in June 1997.

After 25 years, since it officially started, the England team finally has the financial input, technical resources and promotional back-up that the top European women's teams have enjoyed for many years. The problem is that the skilled and dedicated players, such as Coultard, Bampton and Spacey, are unlikely to be able carry England into the next World Cup in the USA in 1999. After Spain put England out of the UEFA Championship finals, Ted Copeland organised an England training weekend, in November 1996, and brought a number of younger players into the squad. Yet the absence of a stepping stone, a junior international squad, is a big handicap for young players, who will find the transformation to international play difficult. They move from being one of the best players in their clubs, with small crowds, to being just one of 22, often playing in front of thousands of spectators at huge stadia. Apart from learning new team tactics, they need to grasp what is entailed in being an international athlete in terms of diet, fitness and mental preparation. Several top nations have had junior international teams for some time, and Sweden, for example, have both U16 and U20 levels. Undoubtedly, a stronger, elite player development structure is necessary if England are to find a way of breaking the cycle of defeats every time they encounter the strong, well-trained, and appropriately resourced teams from Europe and other parts of the world. There are more opportunities for girls to play football but without an effective player development structure, and an army of well-trained coaches to work within it, then the players' performances will still generally remain at a low level. It is not easy for clubs to find quality coaches and what's needed is a nationwide network of effective and comprehensive elite performance development centres. Many male coaches already work with women players, but the best tend to concentrate their work in men's football, where there is higher status and greater financial rewards. Funding must be targeted on training and supporting aspiring women coaches, and helping those wanting to improve. Talent development and deployment of quality female, as well as male coaches, is a strong feature in other nations' development models, such as those of the USA, Scandinavia and Germany. Why can't we forsake our insularity – a factor recognised over the years by a number of individuals involved in the women's game – and adopt some of the model development ideas from abroad?

Why, in this country particularly, has women's football been perceived as a threat to the men's game, while in other nations it's seen as beneficial? If we are to reach their standards, we must quickly take up the ideas adopted by them way back in the 1970s.

Jean Seymour heading a goal in her first trial game for Dick, Kerr Ladies (Preston) in April 1946.

Doris Ashley, captain of Corinthian Ladies (with her father, Percy Ashley, behind her) receiving the Festival of Britain Trophy from Bert Trautman of Manchester City at the Capital Cinema Manchester, 1952.

Dick, Kerr Ladies v. Wythenshawe, Belle Vue, Manchester, May 1950.

BACK (left to right): Margaret Thornborough, Betty Sharples, Lily Parr, Joan Burke, Sheila Pinder, Nancy Thomson, Stella Briggs, Alfred Frankland (Manager)

FRONT (left to right): Doreen Richards, Jean Lane, Joan Whalley, Alice Hargreaves, Barbara Gilbert. (Photograph courtesy of Gail Newsham, *In a League of their own!*)

Sylvia Gore training at Wembley stadium before
the first official England team departed for
Greenock for the inaugural match against
Scotland, November, 1972. *Photograph Douglas
Arent.*

Eileen Foreman, who played for Warminster
(1972–1981) and Southampton (1982–1984) and
for England (1972–1981).

Practice session for Sue Lopez with England's
1966 World Cup hat-trick hero, and West Ham
United player, Geoff Hurst, in 1972.
Photograph Sunday Mirror.

Gordon West, Everton and England goalkeeper, congratulates Sylvia Gore from Fodens on her selection to play in a 1972 England veterans side against the 1983 team, for an exhibition game at Wembley Pool Arena, November 1983.

Pat Chapman of Southampton receiving the runners-up shield in the EUFA England v. Sweden final at Luton FC in May, 1984.

Sue Lopez, in 1990, training future players in a
Hampshire school, assisted by Southampton FC
apprentice professional players.

England captain Debbie Bampton playing
against Germany in European Championship
semi-final at Watford's ground, Vicarage Road,
December 1994.

Sonia Denoncourt from Canada refereeing US v.
China in the Women's World Cup in Sweden,
1995.

Carolina Morace of Agliana Imbalpaper playing
against Milan in September, 1995.
Photograph Rainer Hennies.

Gro Espeseth, captain of
Norway, receiving the winner's
cup in Women's World Cup,
Sweden 1995. *Photograph
Bildbryan.*

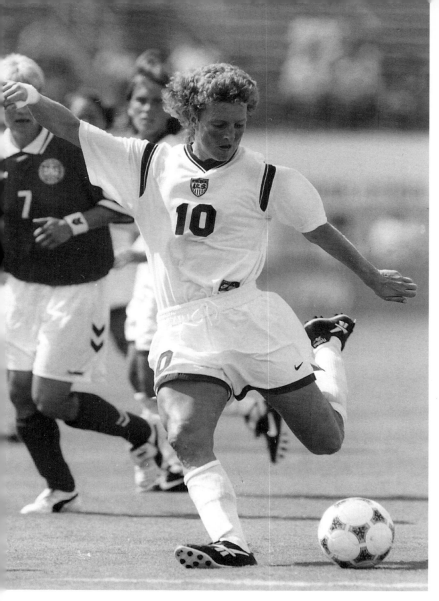

Michelle Akers, playing for the US in a Olympic
championship match against Denmark, July,
1996. *Photograph J. Brett Whitesell.*

Inaugural WFA Mitre Cup winning Southampton team, at Crystal Palace National Sports Centre in London, 1971.
BACK (left to right): Pat Judd, Louise Cross, Karen Buchanan, Sue Buckett, Maureen Case, Lynda Hale, Dott Cassell.
FRONT (left to right): Lesley Lloyd, Jill Long, Sue Lopez, Barbara Birkett, Pat Davies, Jean Seymour.

The Roma team touring the US in 1971.
BACK (left to right): Monika Karner, Elena Dell'Uomo, Rosalba Lonero, Sue Lopez, Patrizia de Grandis, Carla Alliegro.
FRONT (left to right): Olga Amerini, Maria D'Auria, Stefania Medri, Mirella Angeletti, Lucia Gridelli (Captain), Anna Accaputo, Antonella Carpita.

First official England team pictured at Wembley stadium prior to journey to Greenock where they beat Scotland 3–2 on 18 November, 1972.
BACK (left to right): Lynda Hale, Maggie Pearce (née Kirkland), Julia Manning, Paddy McGroarty, Wendy Owen, Sheila Parker (Captain), Jean Wilson, Sue Whyatt, Eric Worthington (Manager).
FRONT (left to right): Jeannie Allott, Janet Bagguley, Sue Buckett, Pat Davies, Eileen Foreman, Sylvia Gore, Sandra Graham. *Photograph Douglas Arent.*

Women's Football Association Pony Cup in 1977 and the winning team from QPR who beat Southampton 1–0 in the final.
BACK (left to right): Josie Clifford (née Lee), Annie Richardson, Jean Cantrill, Jacqueline Green, Pat Napier, Carrie Staley, Cora Francis.
FRONT (left to right): Maggie Flanagan, Sandra Choat, Paddy McGroarty (Captain), Hazel Ross, Pauline Gardiner, Pauline Dickie.

Support from the Saints players for the women's team in the WFA Pony Cup final in 1977.
(Left to right): Ted MacDougall, Ann Squires, Steve Williams, Sue Lopez, Alan Ball, Sue Buckett, Maggie Pearce (née Kirkland), David Peach and Lynda Hale. *Photograph Southern Daily Echo.*

The five Southampton players in the England squad, with Laurie McMememy, playing Belgium at the the Dell in 1978.
(Left to right): Linda Coffin, Maggie Pearce (née Kirkland), Pat Chapman, Sue Lopez, Sue Buckett. *Photograph D.W. Hampton.*

Southampton's last WFA Cup Final in 1981 at St. Helen's Rugby Club.
Southampton beat St. Helens 4–2.
BACK (left to right): Tony Old (Manager), Jackie Richards, Nessie Raynbird,
Jill Long (Physiotherapist), Jill England, Sharon Roberts, Hilary Carter, Ann
Squires, Sharon Hubbard, Stephanie Harris.
FRONT (left to right): Sue Lopez, Linda Coffin, Sue Buckett, Heather Kirkland,
Pat Chapman, Mel Baker.

The England squad prior to their departure from Heathrow to Japan for a
tournament between Japan, Denmark, Italy and England, November 1981.
Left to right: Sports Council Representative, Flo Bilton, Vicky Johnson, Tony
Brightwell (Physiotherapist), Leslie Taylor (travel agent), Sheila Parker, Janet
Turner, Angie Gallimore, Gill Coultard, Liz Deighan, Linda Curl, Linda
Coffin, Eileen Foreman, Chris Hutchinson, Terry Irvine, Carol Thomas (née
McCune), Terri Wiseman, Tracey Doe, Maureen Reynolds, Debbie Bampton,
Annabelle Hennessy (Doctor), Martin Reagan (Manager), Pat Gregory (WFA
Official).

The England team. England v. Sweden, Wembley, 1989
BACK (left to right): Martin Reagan (Manager), Hope Powell, Brenda
Sempare, Jackie Sherrard, Terri Wiseman, Tracy Davidson, Debbie Bampton
(Captain), Karen Walker, Jan Murray, Marieanne Spacey
FRONT (left to right): Marie Harper (née Stanton), Linda Curl, Gill Coultard,
Joanne Broadhurst, Kerry Davis, Jane Stanley.

England team, 1996.
BACK (left to right): Justine Lorton, Tina Mapes, Kelly Smith, Vicky Exley,
Tara Proctor.
MIDDLE (left to right): Charlotte Cowie (Doctor), Maureen Marley, Pauline
Cope, Claire Lacey, Carol Harwood, Mandy Johnson (Physiotherapist).
FRONT (left to right): Ted Copeland (Manager), Karen Burke, Gill Coultard,
Debbie Bampton, Becky Easton, Sian Williams, Graham Keeley (Coach).
Photograph Action Images.

8 Lessons from foreign fields

This chapter looks at the leading women's football nations and highlights some of their development successes.[1] Also included are Northern Ireland, the Republic of Ireland, Scotland and Wales, who have been involved in international women's football since the 1970s. Although France were annual challengers to the Dick, Kerr Ladies during the 1920s, played in tournaments in the early 1970s, and have reached the finals of the 1997 UEFA Championship, information on the national team's activities is scarce.

Italy, Denmark and Sweden were the pioneers of the game in the modern era of women's football, followed by Norway. The 1980s saw the rapid development of the game in Germany and the USA, and now other nations are emerging as talented opponents in the international arena: China, Brazil, Japan and New Zealand. New teams from these countries competed in the first official World Cup in 1991 and the second World Cup in Sweden in 1995, except New Zealand – who were ousted by Australia. Participation in Australian women's soccer is growing by 30 per cent each year, and since Australia is hosting the 2000 Olympics the Australian Women's Soccer Association is aiming for gold by preparing its international squad with intensive training at national team camps.[2] The fact that China came fourth in the Sweden World Cup, and, remarkably, were runners-up in the inaugural 1996 Olympic competition, indicates that they are becoming one of the world's elite. Norway, World Cup winners in 1995, had to be content with third place in the Olympics after defeating Brazil. The Brazilian team's participation also indicates a future challenge to the world's best. Japan is another country determined to join the top nations. It is the only country since 1992 to have a women's fully professional League. The Japanese League has attracted foreign players, mostly from the USA, and other countries such as Norway's international Linda Medalen.

Many other nations are at earlier stages of development, such as Mexico, Jamaica, Trinidad and Tobago, South Africa and Greece. Xanthi Konstaninidou has been instrumental in getting the women's game in Greece established through the organisation of leagues, and teams – of which there are now 30. Women's football was recognised by the Greek FA in 1988 and when there was a possibility of Athens hosting the 1996 Olympics a national team was formed. She is also the first woman to obtain a Greek coaching licence.

In the 1970s, Italy and Sweden competed with Denmark and England to become the leading football nation. Since the start of UEFA Championships in 1982, with finals in 1984, Italy's only major achievement has been second place in 1993, and they failed to qualify for the World Cup in Sweden. Still led by the phenomenally successful captain and star centre-forward, Carolina Morace, they have finally shown signs of a revival by qualifying for the quarter-finals of the UEFA Championship, 1997, winning their group ahead of England, Portugal and Croatia. Sweden have also faltered. They won the first European championship in 1984, were runners-up in 1987 and third in 1989, but their contribution to the game's advances goes beyond results on the field of play. They have led the way, with Norway, in expanding opportunities for women – as referees, coaches and administrators. Denmark is another country that has struggled to maintain its early dominance in the 1970s.

The various ways the game has developed in different countries obviously reflect a nation's football culture and its broader social and cultural differences. These influences can be seen in the gender relations, the education process and the way in which the media present the game. Obviously funding plays a crucial role, but there also appears to be some correlation between the success of a nation and the extent to which it involves women as leaders, and the degree of autonomy provided. Norway and Germany not only had the most successful players in the 1995 World Cup but also two of the top administrators. Karen Espelund is a member of UEFA's Women's Football Committee and in 1996 became the Norwegian FA's vice-president with responsibility for the development for women's and men's football. She is also a member of Norway's FA's executive committee, along with five men and two other women, Inger Marie Vingdal and Bente Skogvang. Hannelore Ratzeburg leads the German FA's women's committee and also serves on the women's committees of FIFA and UEFA. After the Olympic Women's Football Tournament, two women took over as coaches for the Swedish and German national women's teams. Germany's Tina Theune-Meyer became national coach, and captain Sylvia Neid replaced her as assistant coach. The world's most capped woman player with 146 caps, Pia Sundhage, retired after the Olympics to become Sweden's U20 national coach and Anna Signeul took over from Pia Sundhage as U16 national coach. In the USA, April Heinrichs and Lauren Gregg were assistant national coaches to the 1996 Olympic champions team. USA players Michelle Akers and Mia Hamm are two of the world's best role models among a team of role models, in terms of attitude, skill and fitness. Akers, scorer of a record ten goals in the 1991 World Cup, and Hamm lead the way as modern-day stars of women's football.

The examples given by women in Scandinavia, Germany and the USA show that women's football is becoming less isolated and offer models of development that are not mere replicas of men's football, but born out of an understanding of the needs of the girls' and women's game. Fortunately, too, FIFA and UEFA continue to do much to encourage women's football and women leaders in the sport. In December 1996 UEFA announced that an inaugural European U18 women's competition will commence in August 1997. This should provide the encouragement for more of the 33 national associations who participate in the European championship. FIFA demonstrated their support for women leaders by inviting Carolina Morace and Canadian referee, Sonia Denoncourt, to the 'Task Force 2000' assembly of top experts at a meeting in Zurich in November 1996.

The cross-cultural project 'Sport in the Lives of Women', undertaken by a group of European and Scandinavian academics, looks at the part sport plays in the lives of sportswomen, including female footballers, and will provide useful in-depth information on women's football developments in those countries.[3]

BRAZIL

Population: 156 million (1995)
Governing body: Confederacao Brasileira de Futebol, Rue
Alfandega, 70, PO Box 1078, 20.070–001 Rio de Janeiro.[4]

Landmarks

1981 – First women's tournament organised, on Copacabana
Beach, Rio de Janeiro.
1982 – First international match, v. Spain.
1983 – First official championship, played in Rio de Janeiro.
1988 – First official Brazilian team participated in FIFA's unofficial
World Cup.
1991 – Won the Confederación Sud Americana de Fútbol
(CONMEBOL), South American Championship.
– Placed ninth in the first FIFA World Cup.
– Radar Club won the sixth National Championship.
1995 – Placed ninth in the second FIFA World Cup.
1996 – Placed fourth in the inaugural Olympic Tournament.

Participation and development

Only two states in Brazil organise women's football competitions.
In 1991, there were 20 clubs and 300 players and by 1995 there
were 420 clubs with 1,800 players. Like many of the outstanding
men players, women have access to beach soccer. Special pitches
are reserved for them, which provide an unorthodox but effective
way of gaining football practice and Copacabana beach in Rio de
Janeiro has many such pitches. The Saad team from Sao Paulo,
sponsored by a Lebanese businessman, has a well-organised girls'
section which competed in the Dallas Cup, USA, a youth
tournament for boys' and girls' teams which attracts many top
teams from all over the world.

National team

The national team first played in the FIFA unofficial World Cup
in 1988. They beat Norway, the Netherlands and China and
gained third place. To qualify for the 1991 World Cup, Brazil
played Chile and Venezuela, beating them 6–1 and 6–0
respectively. Brazil went on to achieve ninth place in the
championship, which proved to be a turning point in the Brazilian

women's game. Most of the national team came from the Radar Club in Rio, who were national champions from 1983 until 1987. The Brazilian Federation allocated £266,000 for the next World Cup preparations, and there was a greater representation from other clubs: Vasco da Gama (Rio de Janeiro), Euroexporte (Sao Paulo) Euroexporte (Bahia), UNASA EC (Maranhao). They achieved ninth place again, but qualified for the 1996 Olympics (instead of England).

Having spent several months in special training camps prior to the Olympics, the Brazilian team more than justified their inclusion with outstanding results in the preliminary rounds. They drew with world champions Norway 2–2, World Cup runners-up Germany 1–1, and beat Japan 2–0. They narrowly lost to China in the semi-final 3–2, conceding two goals in the last seven minutes, and lost to Norway in the play-off for third and fourth place.

The recent growth of women's football in Brazil was explained by the ex-professional player and national women's team coach, Ademar Fonseca, and reported by Andrew Longmore in *The Times*: 'There are a lot of talented girls playing football, all with exactly the same feel and ability for the game as the boys, but there is still something against the idea of women playing football.'[5] Fonseca said that forward Roseli, who starred in the Swedish World Cup, learnt her football in the streets with her brothers, until they wouldn't play with her any more because they couldn't get the ball away from her. In his report, Longmore predicted that with their skill and speed, Brazil would learn from their international experiences and would soon threaten other nations. Their presence in the Olympic competition proved him right and the Brazilian Federation's commitment of backing and resources brought deserved rewards. Following the performance of the women's team in the Olympics, Jose Fahad, president of the Sao Paulo State Soccer Federation, announced in an interview on television that the Federation was creating a plan to encourage more opportunities for girls to participate in soccer. He said that plans will be made for a women's soccer championship and all the top men's professional clubs will be required to open a space for women's training sessions and must form women's professional teams. It is hoped that the other state federations will follow this example.[6]

CHINA

Population: 1.2 billion (1996)
Governing body: The Football Association of The People's Republic of China, 9 Tiyuguan Road, Beijing.[7]

Landmarks[8]

AD 25–220 – Frescoes from Donghan Dynasty illustrate women playing football in Congshan, Henan Province.

AD 610–917 and 969–1297 – Under the Tang and Song Dynasties, women's football developed from an individual sport to a team sport.

1644–1911 – Qing Dynasty stopped women's football.

1920s – Women's football advocated in schools in south-eastern coastal area.

1981 – Eleven teams participated in an invitation tournament in Chuxiang, Yunnan Province.

1982 – All China Women's Football Invitational Tournament introduced.

1983 – All China Invitation Tournament attracted 27 teams.

1983 – First International Women's Football Invitational Tournament in Guangzhou.

1984 – First Xi'an International Women's Football Tournament.

1986 – All China Women's (U16) Football Tournament organised.

– National Team tours Europe.

– Won the sixth Asian Cup Championship.

1988 – First All China Undergraduate Women's Football Championship (school football) was held at Penglai County, Shandong Province, with eight teams.

– Chinese team won the World High School Women's Football Championship in Brussels, Belgium.

– FIFA Women's Championship in Guangzhou.

1989 – Won the seventh Asian Cup Championship.

1990 – Won the Women's Football Tournament of the Asian Games.

1991 – Won the eighth Asian Cup Championship.

– Quarter-finalists in inaugural World Cup.

1993 – Won the ninth Asian Cup Championship.

1994 – Won the Women's Football Tournament of the Asian Games.

1995 – Placed fourth in Sweden World Cup.

1996 – Runners-up in inaugural Olympic Women's Football Tournament.

Participation and development

Women's football has come under the Chinese FA since the mid-1980s, when there were approximately 300 women players. By 1996 it was estimated by Becky Wang Bin, of the Chinese FA, that there were around 800 women players, mostly students. It is extraordinary, given China's international success, that they achieve this with such a small number of players. According to Becky Wang Bin, some people in Chinese society still do not approve of girls and women playing football.[9] They play in a national league, which has been in operation since 1986, with the following divisions: the First Division with 12 teams is national and the Second, Third and Fourth Divisions are regional. They have leagues for U15 and for U12 national teams. There are no separately organised clubs but city and provincial teams exist. For example, Guangdong Province, where the 1991 World Cup was held, has a team.

National team

China is the strongest Asian women's team but the distance from other top nations has meant that they either had to bring a World Cup to their doorstep, or travel. In 1986 they toured Europe and in 1988 they hosted the first FIFA competition as a trial for the inaugural World Cup in China in 1991. The 1991 competition was watched by a total of 510,000 spectators and the final attracted an audience of 63,000. China lost narrowly to Sweden in the quarter-finals in front of 55,000 spectators in Guangzhou. In the 1995 World Cup they came fourth, losing 2–0 to the USA, having lost to Germany 1–0 in the quarter-final.[10]

China undertook a rigorous preparation schedule for the Olympic tournament in 1996. The Football Association of China gave its full support to the team, arranging 18 international competitions in preparation for the Olympic Games, and technical adviser and vice-president of the China FA, Chen Chengdu, was brought to help national coach Ma Yuanan. He devised a series of strategies and tactics for the team; physical strength played a key role. They participated in the Algarve Cup in Portugal in March and spent four months in training camps in the USA.

They participated in the US Cup in May 1996 (an annual invitation tournament organised by the USSF) and proved themselves to be second only to the USA. They beat Japan 3–0 and Canada 5–0, but lost 1–0 to the USA in the final, in front of 6,081 spectators in Washington, DC. Haiying Wei and Lirong Wen, both from Beijing, were voted 'All-Tournament Stars'.[11]

In the Olympic tournament China confirmed their dedication to their game by coming runners-up to the USA. In preliminary rounds they defeated Sweden 2–0, Denmark 5–1, and drew with the USA 0–0. In the semi-finals they came back from being 2–1 down, with only seven minutes left, to defeat Brazil 3–2. They conceded only three goals in the tournament before the final with the USA, which they lost 3–1. The quality of play from both teams was outstanding, with China illustrating how far they have come since the first unofficial FIFA World Cup in 1988.

DENMARK

Population: 5.5 million (1995)
Governing body: Danish FA, Idraettens Hus, Brondby Stadion 20, 2605 Brondby.[12]

Landmarks

1969 – Runners-up in an unofficial European Tournament, Italy.
1970 – Winners in unofficial 'World Cup' in Italy.
1971 – Winners in unofficial 'World Cup', Mexico.
1972 – Danish FA set up a Women's Committee to organise women's football.
1973 – First organised leagues.
1974 – First official international, against Sweden.
1979 – Won unofficial European Championship, Italy.
1991 – Placed third in European Championship.
  – Placed third in World Cup.
1993 – Placed third in European Championship.
1995 – Placed sixth in World Cup.
1996 – Placed eighth in Olympic Tournament.
1997 – Qualifiers from Group Four for European Championship.

Clubs: 1,602

Players: U18 – 23,360; U25 – 8,450; Over 25 – 4,883; Total: 36,693

Danish champions
1973 – Ribe Boldklub
1974 – Ribe Boldklub
1975 – Femina
1976 – Ribe Boldklub
1977 – Femina
1978 – Ribe Boldklub
1979 – Ribe Boldklub
1980 – Femina
1981 – B1909
1982 – Hjortshoj-Ega IF
1983 – B1909
1984 – Hjortshoj-Ega IF
1985 – B1909
1986 – Hjortshoj-Ega IF

1987 – Hjortshoj-Ega IF
1988 – Hjortshoj-Ega IF
1989 – Hjortshoj-Ega IF
1990 – Hjortshoj-Ega IF
1991 – Hjortshoj-Ega IF
1992 – B1909
1993 – B1909
1994 – Fortuna Hjorring
1995 – Fortuna Hjorring
1996 – Fortuna Hjorring

Early development

Danish women's football became organised in the mid-1960s by the Danish Women's Football Union, and from 1969 was formed into two leagues, east and west, with the winners of each group facing each other in a play-off to establish a champion club. Femina became the champions in 1969 and represented Denmark in the four-nation European Tournament in Italy, where they were the runners-up to the hosts. In 1970 Denmark won an unofficial 'World Cup' beating Italy in the final 2–0 in Turin. In 1971 they retained their 'World Cup' title and won 2–0 in the final against Mexico in an unofficial world tournament in Mexico. In 1972 the Women's Football Union applied to be accepted by the Sports Confederation of Denmark, which already included the men's Football Association. However, it was considered more appropriate for women's football to come under the Danish FA rather than have two different football associations within the Sports Confederation. Under the auspices of the Danish FA, the national team won the unofficial European Championship in 1979. Although they have figured strongly in all the official European Championships and both World Cups, they have never equalled the success of the unofficial competition days.

Participation

The first organised competition under the Danish FA was in 1973 and today there is a national Super League of ten teams, as well as a First Division with ten teams, and a Second Division with ten teams each in east and west geographical zones. For several years the Super League championship has been dominated by Fortuna Hjorring, an independent club. At the end of the 1995 season,

Fortuna Hjorring retained their league title on goal difference by beating rivals Hjortshoj-Ega 4–2 in the final, watched by a crowd of 3,200. Internationals Christina Bonde and Lene Madsen scored Fortuna's goals, three and one respectively. Madsen and Hjortshoj-Ega's Gitte Krogh were the league's top scorers with 45 goals each. In the 1995 World Cup more than half the national squad was from these two teams, including Helle Jensen from Fortuna, who captained her country in the competition.

The league is structured as follows: veterans (over 33 years); seniors 17–33, juniors 14–17; girls 12–14; lilleput 10–12; miniput 8–10, micropput 6–8; and poder 6. At U12 boys and girls can play in mixed teams. The youth structure consists of six local regions with their own league system. The U16 league champions play in a national competition to establish a Danish champion. U12 and young players are permitted to play only seven-a-side football.

League matches attract around 100 spectators but Super League team Fortuna regularly attracts approximately 400 and when there is a decisive match, there can be around 5,000 present. The national team's record attendance in Denmark is 5,800 but it is usually approximately 1,000.

National teams

Every year the U20 and U16 teams play in the Nordic Cup which is considered to be the strongest tournament for U20 national teams. Participating countries in the 1996 competition included Sweden, the Netherlands, Norway, Finland, Iceland, Germany and the USA. After qualifying for the 1991 World Cup, Keld Gantzhorn took charge of the senior team. Gantzhorn was also head coach for the 1995 World Cup team with another male, Poul Hojmose, as his assistant. After the Olympic Tournament, Gorgen Heidemose took over as head coach from Keld Gantzhorn. Currently the top Danish players are: forward Helle Jensen, midfielder Lisbet Kolding (Hjortshog-Ega), and goalkeeper Dorthe Larsen (Fortuna). All Danish women players are amateurs, although the Danish FA compensates them for lost earnings while on international duty, including when they are away at training camps.

Denmark had a female referee's assistant Gitte Holm officiating at the World Cup in Sweden in 1995 and at the 1996 Olympics. The team was unfortunate to be in the same preliminary group as the Olympic finalists and lost 3–0 to the USA, 5–1 to China, as well as losing to Sweden 3–1, which left them in last position in the tournament.

The Danish insurance company, Topdanmark, has been the official sponsor for all national female teams since March 1988 and in 1996 this sponsorship cost £80,000 for the year. All of Denmark's World Cup matches in Sweden 1995 were shown on Danish television as well as the final between Norway and Germany. Every Monday three or four of the main newspapers print information about the women's leagues, especially the Super League's results.

Like Norway, Denmark have established a good youth structure but, unlike them, have not produced the female leaders and role models on and off the pitch, and have trailed behind other nations. Keld Gantzhorn told me that he realised that Danish women's football has started to fall behind its neighbours in gaining equal access to the best coaches and resources. He felt that winning an international title was necessary to gaining this support.

GERMANY

Population: 80 million (1995)
Governing body: Deutscher Fussball-Bund (DFB), PO Box 71 0265, D-60492, Frankfurt am Main.[13]

Landmarks

1955 – Deutscher Fussball-Bund (DFB) ban women's teams from playing on DFB-affiliated pitches.
1970 – October, DFB rescind ban, and give official permission for women's football to be played.
1974 – First Women's Championship.
1977 – Hannelore Ratzeburg represents women's football on DFB committee.
1981 – First Women's Cup Final.
1982 – First official international, v. Switzerland (5–1).
1989 – Germany beat Norway 4–1 in the European Championship Final at Osnabruck in front of a record crowd for a European women's football competition of 22,000.
1991 – Win European Championship by beating Norway 3–1.
     – Placed fourth in 1991 World Cup.
1995 – Win European Championship by beating Sweden 3–2.
1996 – Placed fifth in Olympic Tournament.
1997 – Qualifiers as Group 1 runners-up for European Championship.

Organisation of national championships
1990 – Introduced a First Division of 22 teams split into a northern and southern group.
1992 – First Division enlarged to two leagues of 11 teams (two additions from the former German Democratic Republic (GDR).
1993–96 – First Division reduced to two leagues of ten teams. Regional championships for U12 and U16 players.

German champions
1974 – TuS Worrstadt
1975 – Bonner SC
1976 – Bayern Munchen
1977 – SSG Bergisch Gladbach
1978 – SC Bad Neuenahr
1979 – SSG Bergisch Gladbach

1980 – SSG Bergisch Gladbach
1981 – SSG Bergisch Gladbach
1982 – SSG Bergisch Gladbach
1983 – SSG Bergisch Gladbach
1984 – SSG Bergisch Gladbach
1985 – KBC Duisburg
1986 – FSV Frankfurt
1987 – TSV Siegen
1988–89 – SSG Bergisch Gladbach
1990 – TSV Siegen
1991 – TSV Siegen
1992 – TSV Siegen
1993 – TuS Niederkirchen
1994 – TSV Siegen
1995 – FSV Frankfurt
1996 – TSV Siegen

German Cup winners
1981 – SSG Bergisch Gladbach
1982 – SSG Bergisch Gladbach
1983 – KBC Duisburg
1984 – SSG Bergisch Gladbach
1985 – FSV Frankfurt
1986 – TSV Siegen
1987 – TSV Siegen
1988 – TSV Siegen
1989 – TSV Siegen
1990 – FSV Frankfurt
1991 – Grun-Weis Brauweiler
1992 – FSV Frankfurt
1993 – TSV Siegen
1994 – Grun-Weis Brauweiler
1995 – FSV Frankfurt
1996 – SC Klinge Seckach

National team's record
From 1982 to February 1996: Played 116, won 79, drawn 13, lost
24. Goals scored 317, against 105.

Participation in girls' and women's football
Teams
1971 – 1,110 teams.

1980 – 2,457 teams.
1985 – 3,493 teams (2,543 women's teams and 950 U14 girls' teams).
1990 – 2,902 teams (1,902 women's teams and 100 U14 girls' teams).
1990 – U19 national team introduced.
1991 – 3,109 (including the GDR).
1992 – U19 national team becomes U20.
1993 – U16 national team introduced.
1995 – 4,415 teams (1,847 women's teams and 2,568 girls' teams).

Players
1991 – 475,658 women, 45,371 U16 girls, total 521,029.
1995 – 490,923 women, 121,921 U16 girls, total 612,844.

History

The first attempt to render women's football socially acceptable in Germany was at the turn of the century. A group of women started playing women's football seriously in Frankfurt in the 1920s but such was the ridicule of the public that they turned instead to the sport of rowing – which led to the city becoming the centre for women's rowing in Germany. The next attempts to play in an organised fashion were made by two women from Hamburg, Ingrid Heike and Ildiko Vaszil. They founded a club but the DFB was strongly opposed to women's football and in 1955 banned women from using pitches of affiliated DFB teams – in much the same way as the FA had banned women's teams in England in 1921. As the DFB are reluctant to acknowledge that women were playing football at all at this time, information about how many teams were in existence is scarce. The first female clubs were formed in the provinces and, in July 1955, a women's football interest group was established in Duisburg. This resulted in the formation of the West German Women's Football Association, in Essen, in August 1955. West German businessmen sought to become involved in promoting West German women's football in the same way as businessmen had become involved in Italy. They drove, and some would say, exploited, women's football in the late 1960s and early 1970s.

The first international match took place in September 1956 in Essen when Germany beat the Netherlands 2–1, watched by 18,000 spectators, over a 1,000 of whom were Dutch fans. On seeing how well-attended the women's matches were, the West German managers were quick to realise that money could be made by staging more international events. Erich Brodbeck, in *Niedersachsen Fussball*, recalls: 'This was the signal for managers who sensed big business in women's football. After organising matches around West Germany, they decided to have a European Championship in Berlin in 1957.'[14] However, they experienced a similar difficulty in obtaining suitable pitches and Eberhard Wittig, writing in the newspaper *Tagesspiegel*, records that there was great controversy over the planned use of certain venues.[15] Wittig was one of the few journalists of that era to promote women's football and not only did he support the players' commitment to their sport but strongly castigated the DFB for their high, petty and anachronistic attitude towards the women's game.

Despite the DFB's ban, and consequent attempts to veto the use of large grounds in Berlin, the 40,000-capacity Poststadium was made available for the 'European Championship' in 1957. It was organised by the International Ladies' FA, which had been set up in Nuremberg on 28 August, and which had its headquarters in Luxembourg. A lawyer, Dr Bernaritz, was appointed general secretary with an annual salary of 10,000 Swiss francs. The participating teams in the competition were: the Netherlands, Germany, Austria, Luxembourg and England (represented by Manchester Corinthians and lead by 33-year-old Doris Ashley). Standards of health and fitness were not so rigorous at this time, illustrated by the fact that after England had beaten the Netherlands 2–1 in the opening game, they had a short break when, according to the report in *Tagesspiegel*, 'some of them smoked cigarettes furiously'. Further, matches were also more relaxed and, with the help of three Dutch team members, they agreed to a 15-minute-each-way exhibition game against the West Germans in order to entertain the crowd of 3,000.[16] The Austrians were delayed by fog and arrived too late for the championship, so they played the Dutch for third place. England beat West Germany 4–1 in the final.

Developments since the 1970s

Women's football in West Germany did not really take off until the late 1960s and the upsurge of interest led the DFB to lift their ban in 1970. Official permission was given for women's matches to be played prior to men's professional matches. For example, *Neidersachsen Fussball* reported that on 16 May 1970, in rainy conditions in Kaiserslautern, before a Kaiserslautern FC and FC Cologne match, the Landau and Augsburg women's teams attracted 18,000 spectators. It was a meaningless men's match as far as the league was concerned and the reporter estimated that around 10,000 spectators were there to just to see the women play.[17] Matches were often played as part of a town's 'Volkfest' (annual people's fair) and in 1970 a match in Delmenhorst attracted 7,000 spectators, filling the town's stadium.

In 1974, a West German championship was established and by 1981 a knock-out competition was in place. In 1985, a regional league was started in the west of the country, consisting of teams from three states, and in 1986 a regional league began in the north with teams from four states. This was followed, in 1990, by the formation of a regional north-east league, consisting of teams from the GDR and Berlin. The rest of the country still has state leagues as secondary leagues under the National League, north and south. Most clubs are sections of local sports clubs, with girls' and women's football being just one of several sports played.

A number of the current national league clubs started in the late 1960s and early 1970s. TuS Worrstadt, formed in 1969, won the first national championship in 1974, and Bergisch Gladbach, formed in 1973, won the national championship in 1977, and the inaugural national Cup competition in 1981 and 1982. Even in conservative Bavaria, women's football is popular and Bayern Munich, who won the national championship in 1976, went on to become runners-up in 1979, and runners-up in their two Cup Final appearances in 1988 and 1990. The most consistently successful teams have been Bergisch Gladbach in the 1980s and TSV Siegen in the late 1980s and 1990s. Cup Finals have been played in the Berlin stadium prior to the men's Cup Final matches since 1985. The success of German women's football, with well-run clubs, has attracted players from countries such as Hungary, Poland, Russia, Switzerland, the USA and Canada.

Funds for women's football come from subscriptions and sponsorship. The amount women's teams in the national league receive ranges between £13,000 to £21,000 a year, including around £8,000 a year 'TV money'. Television companies give money to the FA and they decide what kind of sum clubs will receive. Some of the top players receive money and are helped with accommodation and a job. There is not, however, a national standard and each club sets its own terms and conditions. Players at FSV Frankfurt, for example, have so-called 'amateur contracts'. Sylvia Neid, who captained the 1995 German World Cup squad, and other experienced national players, Voss, Mohr, Meinert and Fitschen, had an opportunity to play in the Japanese professional women's league, reportedly with offers of US$40,000 each per season. The German FA, however, ruled that any player wishing to be selected for Germany in the Olympics should play in Germany. Playing for the national team was too attractive an opportunity for any of them to move to Japan.

The DFB's Women's Football Committee of seven women, under chair Hannelore Ratzeburg, is responsible for women's football. Hannelore Ratzeburg, a former player in the 1970s, and a teacher by profession, is not only Germany's top women's football administrator – she is a member of the German FA's executive committee – but also serves on both FIFA's and UEFA's women's football committee. Her astute leadership has played a large part in the successful development of German women's football. She has recently co-written a history of the last 25 years of the German women's game.[18]

National team

Since 1982, the national women's team has enjoyed sustained progress. In the 1991 World Cup they came fourth and in 1995 were runners-up, losing 2–0 to an outstanding Norwegian team. They won the European Championship in 1989, 1991 and in 1995 beat Sweden 3–2 in the final at Kaiserslauten in front of 8,000 spectators.

The national team's steady rise – in only 14 years – to become the second best European women's football nation, behind Norway, is a testimony to the DFB's serious aspirations to be world beaters. They provided the necessary funds to resource the team's preparations and in 1982 appointed Gero Bisanz, one of their most highly qualified and respected coaches, to take charge of the squad's development. Bisanz is a professional sports instructor who played and coached for FC Cologne. Since 1970 he has been the DFB's head of instructor training and in 1981 became the men's national 'B' team coach. In 1996, Bisanz admitted in *FIFA Magazine* that at first he was not very keen on taking over the women's team but had a change of attitude:

> It became clear to me that there was no reason why women should not play football ... women are eager to find things out. They want to learn. In the men's game I have sometimes noticed that this desire was lacking. Women are also prepared to make personal sacrifices and to train just as hard without any financial rewards.[19]

Bisanz also emphasised the critical importance playing for the national team had in improving players' standards throughout the women's game:

> At the beginning, the women's game was characterised by the desire to copy the men's game as far as possible and that's what happened, whether it was training methods or going down to the pub for a beer and a cigarette afterwards. Women's football was just a pastime. But the creation of a national team started people thinking about improving performance, and things began to change. Club teams used to train one or twice a week, but now it's at least three times and the national team have an extra session or two on top of that.[20]

He acknowledges that while he used the same training methods for women as for men, he allowed for the obvious physical differences. *FIFA Magazine* asserts that Bisanz 'is arguably the expert in women's football'.[21] Certainly, the continuity of Bisanz's association with the team, along with Tina Theune-Meyer as assistant coach for the past ten years, has served the national team very well. He was rewarded in 1995 with the Silver Needle of Honour from the DFB, and in 1996 with Germany's Cross for 'Services in the Promotion of Women's Sport'. When the German team achieved only fifth place in the Olympic tournament, some observers claimed that the team did not prepare well enough to cope with the heat and humidity of Georgia. They won only one game, against Japan 3–2, lost 3–2 to Norway and could only draw with Brazil 1–1. Whatever the reasons for their disappointing performance, it should not be allowed to overshadow the record of one of the most consistently successful national coaches. Bisanz retired from the post after the 1996 Olympic tournament, but he will be remembered as much for his enlightened attitude to women's football as his overall achievements with the women's national team.

The national team comes under the direction of the DFB's head coach and ex-international player, Berti Vogts, who has overall responsibility for all national teams. Tina Theune-Meyer took over as head coach of the women's team on Bisanz's retirement, and is directly in charge of senior and U16 teams. Tina Theune-Meyer played for GW Brauweiler and she has gained the DFB's highest coaching degree, Fussball Lehrer. She was assistant national team coach from 1986 and since 1990, she has been in charge of the U20 team. Ex-national team captain Sylvia Neid retired from the game to become Theune-Meyer's coaching assistant, in charge of the U20 team. She hopes to progress from her B licence coaching award up to Fussball Lehrer. Their appointments represent the positive attitude of the DFB towards women and Bisanz confirms the commendable choice:

> The DFB wanted to set an example with this decision. Frau Meyer has been in the business for ten years and she knows all about it. She will certainly grow into the job. By choosing Sylvia Neid as her assistant, the DFB is also sending out another signal. It is certainly unique for there to be a [woman] full-time trainer and [a woman] full-time assistant. This should help women's football, and it's a step in the right direction, for the ultimate aim should be for the women's game to look after itself.[22]

Regarding the game's development he said:

> The women's game will continue to develop positively if junior teams get the right attention and coaching. As far as the professional game goes, the standard will have to be right, and then the TV companies, sponsors etc., will come along of their own accord. I would like to see clubs trying to get more support so that players have more time and better conditions for training. And I will propose again that women trainers should have at least an A Licence. Only with better trainers and much more training will the standard of play improve.[23]

Coaches

Germany has developed girls' and women's football in a 'step by step' approach with football education for the youth players and coaches. Since the ending of the ban in 1970 and the first international in 1982, Germany's national team's progress has shown an enviable, sustained, upward trend. In the all-time ranking for the World Cup, Germany are placed third, having reached fourth place in 1991 and runners-up in 1995.

In the past, initiatives to teach females how to coach football were motivated by the idea that they would then be able to coach boys. In recent years it has been made apparent that female students are willing to learn because of their interest in the sport alone. Horst Muller, who has been a football coach at the Sports Institute at the University of Hannover for many years, confirms that, since the beginning of the 1970s, there has been a trend towards more female students training to teach football. He says: 'Today, on my training courses, every third to fourth participant is a woman, and most are interested in football teaching. I think this is a good trend and a big change from the early days when it was such a novelty to train women students in football.'[24]

The DFB pursues a policy, in both men's and women's football, of encouraging ex-internationals to train as coaches. Anne Trabaut, a player/coach of Haarbach, was a pioneer international player and DFB A licence coach. She played in the first official West German international in 1982 against Switzerland and also assisted Gero Bisanz as trainer. She now teaches in a gymnasium in Ratingen rather than pursuing a career with the DFB. Some other older players have gone into coaching, such as Mirella Cina, who is manager of TVS Worrstadt, and Rose Breuer, who is coach at the same club. As well as Tina Theune-Meyer, three other women have gained the highest German coaching award of Fussball Lehrer: Margret Kratz, who plays for VFR Saarbrucken and works for the regional FA of Saarbrucken district; Ulrike Ballweg, player/coach of the Klinge Seckach national league team, who has a full-time job as a coach in the Baden FA; and Monika Staab, who played for two seasons with English club Southampton in the late 1980s, and who is now coach of the national league team SG Praunheim-Frankfurt. Five of the 20 national women's league teams have female coaches.

Media

Germany is one of the few nations that has its own women's football magazine, *dieda, Das Frauenfussball-Magazin*, which started during the 1993–94 season. It's a glossy magazine that gives comprehensive coverage of all aspects of the German women's game. Its editor, Monika Koch-Emsermann, has been a B licence coach since 1976, and was a player and coach with FSV Frankfurt for 20 years. Contributor Rainer Hennies is Germany's most prominent women's football journalist. Despite Hennies's efforts, and the existence of *dieda*, like Gero Bisanz he thinks media coverage could be better, especially in view of the national team's success.

In general the regional media do promote women's football, by giving short reports on national league games on regional television stations, especially when local teams provide them with information. Local businesses like to sponsor women's teams for publicity purposes and local television companies are happy to show matches in order to gain the advertising revenue.

German national sports papers cover only women's national league results and report on special events such as the European, World and Olympic Championships. The 1995 World Cup group matches were shown on television between 10 pm and 11 pm, with between 30 to 45 minutes' coverage. From the quarter-finals onwards all matches were shown live. The final between Germany and Norway attracted over 5 million viewers, 14 per cent of every household, which was 27.5 per cent of the television market. Prior to this, the best viewing figures had been when Germany beat Sweden in the European Championship in March 1995, with 2.33 million viewers, 23.1 per cent of the market.[25]

Also in 1995, FSV Frankfurt women's team achieved the League and Cup Double with a side containing several of the national team who, a week earlier, had been runners-up to Norway in the World Cup. However, German TV did not cover Frankfurt's match live and instead broadcast a summary of the game later. In July 1995, *Der Sportjournalist*, the official publication of the Association of German sports journalists, gave Gero Bisanz the opportunity to put forward his ideas on why his national team struggled to receive the media coverage it deserved. Bisanz said that the media have a duty to help out but at the same time would like to see, along with many of the women's club trainers, a professional women's national league that would enable players to achieve attractive, quality football more easily. He felt that the overall daily newspaper reports, which take information from the press agencies, were good, and that the World Cup coverage was superb. Nevertheless, he said, 'Television, and the special press, in particular, *Der Kicker*, still failed to find the right approach to the achievement of the women's national team.'[26] Bisanz accuses the press of 'sloppy research' and gives an example of the erroneous reporting of the World Cup matches when a well-known television reporter told the nation that 'Our girls have come third' although they had, in fact, reached the final. As a result many did not switch on to watch the match. In the same article, one of the editors of *Der Kicker* responded to this criticism by saying that women's football does not attract a readership. Bisanz refuted this; he felt that from his observations of people and of play in men's football, the opposite was true:

> I have the feeling that many good specialist journalists, who write about the men's game, are frightened to have anything to do with women's football. They are scared they may no longer fully be respected by their colleagues or trainers in the professional game. Although professional players and trainers have publicly acknowledged the performances of the women's national team, myths are still cultivated within journalism regarding gender issues. Today's sports journalism should rise above such stereotyped thinking ... men's professional football should not be compared with women's football, as this is not the case in any sport. The media should not be permitted to portray the reality as they wish to see it, but should report the facts as they stand. Women's football is well represented and often better than the degree of attention awarded by the media.[27]

ITALY

Population: 57.8 million (1995)
Governing body: Federazione Italiana Giuoco Calcio, Via Gregorio
Allegri 14, CP 2450, 1–00198 Roma.[28]

Landmarks:

1968 – Federazione Italiana Calcio Femminile (FICF) founded in
     Viareggio.
     – First FICF Championship – won by Genoa.
     – First international match v. Czechoslovakia.
1969 – Second FICF Championship – won by Roma. Ten clubs in
     national league.
     – Unofficial European tournament in Turin. Italy beat Denmark
     3–1 in the final.
1970 – FICF splits and the Federazione Femminile Italiana Giuoco
     Calcio (FFIGC) founded in Rome.
     – International victories over France (represented by Reims) by
     2–0 each game.
     – Gommagomma (Milano) win first FFIGC championship.
     There are 14 clubs in national league. Real Torino wins the
     smaller Torino-based championship.
     – First unofficial 'World Cup' staged in Italy. Denmark beat Italy
     2–0 in the final.
1971 – FICF and FFIGC unite and form national league of 14 clubs.
     – Competed in unofficial 'World Cup' in Mexico.
1972 – February, the unification is ratified and the association
     becomes Federazione Femminile Italiana Unificate Autonoma
     Giuoco Calcio (FFIUAGC).
     – Forty-six clubs complete in four regions with a play-off of
     regional winners.
1973 – Championship consists of two leagues.
1974 – Roma Club disbanded due to financial difficulties.
1976 – FFIUAGC becomes Federazione Italiana Giuoco Calcio
     Femminile (FIGCF).
1980 – October, Italian FA (FIGC) accepts FIGCF as an 'associate
     member', retaining its autonomy within the FIGC.
1984 – Placed third in European Championship.
1986 – FIGC incorporates FIGCF completely within the amateur
     section.
1987 – Placed third in European Championship.

1989 – Placed fourth in European Championship.

1990 – Marina Sbardella appointed president of the Italian Women's Football Committee with responsibility for running women's football under FIGC.

1991 – Placed fourth in European Championship.

– Placed sixth in World Cup.

1993 – European Championship hosts, in Cesena, and runners-up, losing 1–0 to Norway in the final.

1997 – European Championship qualifiers as winners of Group 3.

Italian champions

1968 – Genoa (FICF)

1969 – Roma (FICF)

1970 – Gommagomma Milano (FFIGC – Roma)

– Real Torino (Torino Championship)

1971 – B. Gabbiani Piacenza (FFIGC – Roma)

– Real Juventus (Torino Championship)

1972 – Gamma Tre Padova (FFIUAGC, shortened in 1976 to FIGCF)

1973 – Gamma Tre Padova

1974 – Falchi Astro Montecatini

1975 – Milan

1976 – ACF Valdobbiadene

1977 – ACF Valdobbiadene

1978 – Jolly Catania

1979 – Lubiam Lazio

1980 – Lubiam Lazio

1981 – Alaska Lecce

1982 – Alaska Lecce

1983 – Alaska Lecce

1984 – Alaska Trani

1987 – Lazio

1988 – Lazio

1989 – GB Campania

1990 – Zambelli Reggiana

1991 – Zambelli Reggiana

1992 – Milan Salvarani

1993 – Zambelli Reggiana

1994 – Torres FOS

1995 – Agliana Imbalpaper

1996 – Verona Gunther

There has been an Italian Cup since 1971, and in the early days the winners were: Roma (1971), Falchi Torino (1972), Falchi Astrol Torino (1973). Records are incomplete and the next confirmed winners are Zambelli Reggiana, who won the Cup and League in 1993.

Participation
1991 – 10,000 players
1993 – 9,760 with 376 clubs
1995–96 – 11,000 players with 350 clubs

Development

Italy was the first country to have a competitive national championship and the early development of women's football in Italy owes much to the entrepreneurs who helped push the game forward when conventional ways of sports development were closed. After disputes between the two federations, the league of 16 teams in Serie (Division) A and the two leagues of 16 teams in Serie B came under the control of the Italian Football Federation (FIGC) in 1986 and under a women's committee in 1990. For the 1996–97 season Serie B was divided into three leagues.

The top clubs are sponsored and players receive expenses, and some even receive salaries. Verona Gunther, who won the Italian Women's Championship in 1996, are sponsored by a group of pharmaceutical companies. For publicity purposes they appointed a dog, a German shepherd called Gunther IV, as 'president' of the club and he attends all matches as the 'club's benefactor'. Despite Gunther IV's presence, Verona's success in 1996 was due to Carolina Morace, Italy's most famous female footballer, who was top scorer in the league with 39 goals. She reputedly earned £40,000 in 1995 from the club, excluding sponsorship endorsements and her television work. In previous years she helped a number of teams achieve championship wins, including: Agliana Imbalpaper 1995, Torres FOS 1994 and Zembelli Reggiana 1993 and 1991. As of November 1996, Carolina Morace had scored 100 international goals and had 138 caps.[29] She also contributes to the widespread print and television media coverage of Italian women's football, as a television presenter of a TV football programme. Along with her, another key personality in the Italian women's game is Marina Sbardella, who was appointed

– in August 1990 – as the president of the Italian Women's Football Committee. She is a sports reporter for Tele Montecarlo (TMC) – Italian Network, and produces and presents most of the important sports programmes. Women's football is transmitted live by TMC and covers the whole country. Sbardella also serves on FIFA's Women's Football Committee. In a country less famous for equal opportunities than those of Scandinavia, Morace and Sbardella illustrate how it is still possible to attain leadership roles. Pina Debbi is also a reporter for TMC and the Italian FA's women's football press liaison officer. She has the task of facilitating the women's committee's objective of improving the promotion of the women's game.

In the early days, the national league competition, and the higher status of the Italian game, proved a great attraction to foreign players from Scandinavia, Germany, France and England. The style of Italian women's football was similar to the men's, with greater emphasis on technique and short passes and less on the physical strength required for strong tackling and sending the ball long distances, a hallmark of the English game. Those women players who transferred in the 1980s were able to enjoy earning salaries in full-time competitive football and no longer had to be concerned with losing their amateur status. England players Kerry Davis, Debbie Bampton and Sian Williams have all played in more recent years for Italian league clubs.

National team

The Italian team led the development of international competition from 1968. The country's early development of a national league was of clear benefit to the national team and produced some of the greatest women footballers of all time. Among these in the 1970s were Roma's Stefania Medri, Genoa's Maria Grazia Gerwein, Piacenza's Luciana Meles and ACF Valdobbiadene's Elizabetta Vignotto. The national team flourished, competing in the numerous competitive and well-resourced tournaments supported by Italian businesses.

Italy dominated most international competition in the early years and their successful international team played a key part in stimulating the formation of others. After the first international match at Viareggio on 22 February 1968, in which Italy beat Czechoslovakia 2–0, they next met and drew 2–2 with Denmark, the only international team they found difficult to conquer (by 1993 Italy had played Denmark 17 times winning, only three and drawing four, with 15 goals for and 32 against). Italy met Denmark again in the final of the first four-nation European Tournament, in Turin in November 1969, and in front of 10,000 spectators at the Stadio Communale won 3–1. In 1970, the team played two friendly internationals, both against a French team, mostly made up of the Reims club side, with Italy winning both games 2–0. In July 1970 Italy hosted the first unofficial 'World Cup' and competed with several other nations, including England (mostly made up of Harry Batt's Chiltern Valley team), Denmark, West Germany, France and Mexico. Denmark beat Italy in the final, 2–0, in front of 35,000 spectators. In 1971 Italy embarked on a unique trip to Tehran to play two matches against an Iranian women's team, winning both games, 2–0 and 5–0. Their playing record during this early period illustrates how much international experience they gained; in 1971 they played Denmark twice again, losing 2–0 and 1–0, and in 1972 played Yugoslavia three times, winning two, 3–0 and 1–0, and losing one 3–2. They were defeated by Spain at home twice, 5–0 and 3–0, and won away in Spain 5–1 and 4–1, and in 1973 they beat Czechoslovakia 1–0, 2–0, and 3–0.

In the 1970s many nations started to come under the umbrella of their national governing football bodies and therefore began to gain significant support and appropriate resources. This was not the case in Italy, or England, but the Italians continued to receive offers of sponsorship and backing from businessmen which enabled them to continue to be a leading force. In England, under the auspices of the WFA, the women's game struggled. Overall, Italy have played 15 matches against England, winning nine times, drawing three, with 34 goals for and 15 against.[30] England's performance improved in the mid-1980s and they beat Italy at two major events: in the Italian Tournament finals 3–2 in 1985, and 2–1 in 1988, in the 'Little World Cup'.

Ironically, after the national team came under the Italian FA, in 1986, they enjoyed little international success. Their best European Championships result was runners-up to Norway in 1993. They only just managed to qualify for the inaugural 1991 World Championships and in China beat Chinese Taipei 5–0, and Nigeria 1–0, but lost to Germany 2–0. They did not qualify for the

European Championship semi-final places in 1995 and therefore did not qualify for the World Cup in Sweden.

Italy's failure to qualify signalled a reappraisal of their situation, and, in particular, the need for stronger, grassroots development with younger players. Italy have qualified for the finals of the 1997 European Championship and it would be encouraging to see a renaissance of the Italians' international team.

JAPAN

Population: 124 million (1995)
Governing body: The FA of Japan, Second Floor, Gotoh Ikueikai
Building, 1-10-7 Dogenzaka, Shibuya-Ku, Tokyo 150.[31]

Landmarks

1980 – National Championship with 16 teams.
1981 – First appearance in the fourth Asian Cup.
1989 – National League with six teams.
1991 – National League with 10 teams.
   – Placed twelfth in the FIFA World Championships.
1992 – Professional League introduced.
1995 – Placed eighth in the FIFA World Championships.
1996 – Lost in the preliminary rounds of the inaugural Olympic
   Tournament.

Participation and development

Teams from elementary schools, high schools and university
level, play national championships, and Japan has a full-time
professional women's league, introduced in 1992. The participation
figures for 1996 were approximately 1,000 teams and 20,000
players. Yomiui Seiyu Beleza have been League Champions four
times, and Matsushita Panasonic Bambina once. Japanese women's
football clubs are sponsored by businesses and the league has
attracted many foreign players. Star Norwegian forward Linda
Medalen plays for Nikko Securities team in Tokyo. The amounts
players receive in salaries are reported in the press as being
anywhere between £20,000 and £50,000 a year.[32]

National team

In Japan's first international match in 1981 in the Asian Cup, they
lost 1–0 to Chinese Taipei, and 2–0 to Thailand. In September
1981, they held a three-nation tournament in Tokyo and lost to
Denmark and 4–0 to England. In the 1991 World Cup they came
twelfth, having lost 1–0 to Brazil, 8–0 to Sweden and 3–0 to the
USA in the preliminary rounds. They qualified for the 1995
World Cup in Sweden, with China from the Asian group, and came
eighth, losing to Germany 1–0, Sweden 2–0 and beating Brazil 2–1
in the early rounds. In the preliminary rounds of the 1996
Olympic tournament they lost to Brazil 2–0, Germany 3–2 and
4–0 to Norway.

THE NETHERLANDS

Population: 14.5 million (1994)
Governing body: Koninklijke Nederlandsche Voetbalbond (KNVB), Woudenbergseweg 56–58, Postbus 515, NL 3700, Amzeist.[33]

Landmarks

1896 – Sparta (Rotterdam) tried to organise a team to play against an English XI but was banned by the KNVB.
1924 – Another attempt to organise the match with England, but the ban continued.
1955 – Dutch Ladies' Soccer Association founded.
  – A national league of 14 clubs organised.
  – September, first international match against Germany.
  – KNVB ban women from using pitches of clubs affiliated to KNVB.
1971 – After UEFA request of all nations, KNVB take control of women's football.
1973 – November, first official international match against England at Reading. England win 1–0.
1974 – First international match at home at Groningen, losing to England 3–0.
1995 – DVC Den Dungen national champions for fifth consecutive season.
1996 – SV Saestum national champions.

Domestic competition

Despite the KNVB's ban on the use of their pitches, women's clubs were playing in regional leagues up until the KNVB took over on 9 September 1971. The Dutch Ladies' Soccer Association disbanded and a National Committee of Ladies' Soccer was formed which drew up new guidelines. These included rules on minimum age, measurement of the pitch, size of the ball, and the duration of game (initially two halves of 35 minutes). Also included were such issues as hairstyles – these were not to endanger the safety of other players. There are now approximately 1,000 teams who are part of men's amateur clubs. Although the women's teams have some access to facilities and administration, unfortunately they are given the worst pitches and have to play at inconvenient times. Around 75 per cent of the teams have no reserve or youth section and the talent is too diluted to create competitive matches (one of the independent women's clubs, DVC Den Dungen, won the national championship every year since 1991 but disbanded in 1995). By reducing the number of clubs (there were 1,500 in 1983 and 1,100 in 1994) the KNVB is trying to ensure that there are more talented players in individual teams. They encourage mixed football up to the age of 16 – mixed leagues (girls' teams play boys' teams) and mixed teams (boys and girls playing together in one team). There is a 'pyramidal structure' with a National League Premier Division at the top since 1994–95 with local and regional leagues organised in 20 districts.

Coaching and development

Despite the fact that Dutch women have shown a keen interest in the game and have been playing since the end of the last century, their development has been curtailed. There are no minimum qualifications required to coach a women's team, (unlike in male football), although around 20 per cent do have fully qualified coaches. The lack of media coverage, even in regional newspapers, and the national team's lack of success in either the European or World Championships, compounds the difficulties. One of the most well-known women players, and one of the most qualified female coaches, is Vera Pauw. She is an international player, who used to play for Den Dungen, and she works with KNVB helping to develop women's football.

NEW ZEALAND

Population: 3.5 million (1995)
Governing body: Women's Soccer Association of New Zealand (WSANZ), PO Box 2606, Christchurch.[34]

Landmarks

1975 – Won the Asian Confederation Cup in Hong Kong.
1980 – Founding member of Oceania Women's Football Association (with Papua New Guinea, Australia and Fiji). They decided to organise an Oceania Women's Tournament every three years.
1991 – Oceania Football Confederation put a women's committee in place.
– Placed eleventh in inaugural FIFA World Cup in China.
– Linda Black added to FIFA's list of international referee's assistants.
1994 – Runners-up behind Australia in the FIFA World Cup Oceania group.
1995 – Josephine King of WSANZ elected to FIFA's Women's Football Committee.

Participation
1995 – Senior, approximately 5,000 players; Secondary/Youth approximately 3,300 players; Junior, approximately 300 players.

Teams
Senior – 261 playing in competitions; Secondary/Youth – 235 playing in competitions; Junior – 22 plus playing in the New Zealand Junior Football Association (NZJFA).

Domestic competitions

Women's football is the second most popular team sport for women (after netball) and is the sport with the highest growth rate in the country. WSANZ is affiliated to Soccer New Zealand (SNZ). WSANZ develops and controls all women's soccer in New Zealand under the direction of SNZ.

There are regional leagues, a National Knock-out Cup competition, a Senior National Tournament, U19 regional and inter-regional tournaments, U17 regional tournaments, an U15 National Tournament – organised by the NZJFA, and a Secondary Schools National Tournament.

National teams

There are national teams at Senior, U20, U17, NZ secondary schoolgirl levels and the national team and U20 players take part in coaching courses.

In the preliminary rounds of the China 1991 World Cup, New Zealand lost to Denmark 3–0, Norway 4–0 and China 4–1 and came eleventh overall. Australia narrowly qualified over New Zealand by goal difference in the Oceania qualification matches for the 1995 World Championship in Sweden.

Leading players and officials

Lesley Boomer is the executive officer of the WSANZ and co-ordinates all aspects of the women's game in liaison with SNZ. She also serves on the USA Women's Soccer Foundation Board of Directors. The most capped players are Maureen Jacobson (59), Wendy Sharpe (50), Debbie Pullen (40), Alison Grant (36), Vivienne Robertson (35), Donna Baker (35) and Barbara Cox (33). There are five female Level III coaches Barbara Cox, Kathy Hall, Anne Smith, Roz Wallace and Nora Watkins – 33 Level II, 36 Level I and 51 Level 0.

NORTHERN IRELAND

Population 1.6 million (1995)
Governing body: Irish Football Association Ltd (IFA), 20 Windsor Avenue, Belfast BT9 6EG.[35]

Landmarks

1976 – Northern Ireland Women's Football Association (NIWFA) formed in November.
1977 – May, league of three divisions formed.
  – First international (v. Republic of Ireland).

Participation
There are only three Divisions, Premier, First and Second, with 23 teams and approximately 450 players. There is a knock-out cup competition open to all teams and although there are no girls' teams the affiliated players' ages range from 9 to 57 years!

Development

Northern Ireland's national team is the least developed and funded of all the UK teams and has not been able to participate in the European Championships. In the last few years they have forged a partnership with the IFA, and a coaching and development structure is being put into place. This has resulted in seven new teams being formed for the 1996–97 season. The IFA now funds the provision of coaching equipment and pitches. One of the stalwart volunteers is Chris Unwin, who is vice-president of the NIWFA and president of the Post Office Combined Ladies FC.

NORWAY

Population: 4.3 million (1995)
Governing body: Norges Fotballforbund (Norwegian FA), Postboks
3823, Ullevaal Hageby, N-0805, Oslo.[36]

Landmarks

1975 – A Women's Football Committee set up to organise women's
    football.
1976 – Norwegian FA officially take over organisation of women's
    football.
1978 – First official international (v. Sweden).
1979 – First Regional League organised.
1987 – First National League championship organised (10 teams).
1989 – Even Pellerud takes charge of the National Women's
    Team.
    – Runners-up in European Championship.
1995 – Bente Skogvang officiates at Sweden World Cup.
1996 – Karen Espelund elected vice-president of the Norwegian FA.
    – Bente Skogvang officiates at the inaugural Olympic final,
    USA v. China.

National team record
1987 – European Champions – hosted by Norway.
1988 – Unofficial World Champions (FIFA invitational tournament
    in China).
1989 – Runners-up European Championship.
1991 – Runners-up European Championship.
    – Runners-up World Cup.
1993 – Winners European Championship.
1995 – World Champions.
1996 – Third in inaugural Olympic Tournament.
1997 – European Championship qualifiers, winners of Group 1.

Participation in girls' and women's football
In 1995 there were 1,830 affiliated clubs and 64,000 players
    17+: 22,000
    13–16: 19,000
    U12: 23,000

Domestic competition

There is a National League, plus two divisions sub-divided into six
regions. There is a league system down to Division Five, and a

Veterans League for players aged 28 and over. At the end of 1995 TK Trondheims-Orn led the other nine teams in the National League and were runners-up in the Cup, losing to IL Sandviken (Bergen). The Cup Final in Oslo's Uylleval stadium attracted 6,211 spectators and IL Sandviken's winning goal was scored after extra time by Norway's national team captain Gro Espeseth. The girls' Youth Leagues are based on the same age levels as in boys' and men's football: 'mini' (under 10), 10–12, 12–14, 14–16, junior (16–19), senior from 16 years. The country is divided into 19 regions, the region is divided into smaller districts. There are special rules adapted to children's football.

The top league is non-professional and has ten teams. Players receive compensation for lost wages for international matches and when attending training camps. When teams qualify for the top league they have to follow Norwegian FA guidelines regarding their finances, which includes submitting budgets every half year. The rest of the league is divided into a First Division of six leagues and with ten teams and other Divisions organised by district FAs.

Top club project

This project was started in 1990 with support from the Norwegian FA, and involves the teams in the top league. In 1994 three teams, Asker, Sandviken and Trondheims-Orn, were included and received £10,000 from the NFA, with the proviso that the money be used to employ a consultant for marketing purposes in order to increase their income. The rest of the teams received £2,000.

In 1995 four more teams were included in the deal, and the rest again received the lesser amount. In 1996 eight teams were included (Asker, Hangar, Kolbotn, Klepp, Sandviken, Setskog/Harland, Sprint/Jeloy and Trondheims-Orn). The NFA provided £7,500 plus sponsorship from companies, Norvesen, Norwegian Salmon and O'boy, who agreed to give each team £2,000. In return the clubs fulfil marketing activities for the sponsors: advertisements in newspapers, at the stadia and on the players' kit, and loudspeaker announcements at matches. The Norwegian FA continually makes visits to clubs to ensure the teams are fulfilling the project's aims and further developments are being prepared after 1996. Having marketing consultants has increased each club's revenue and attracted sponsorship. Clubs outside the project have seen the benefits and are now starting to employ consultants themselves.

National team

England, with a comparatively long history of playing women's football, were surprised to lose their first match with Norway 3–0 at home in Cambridge in October 1981. Norway went on to beat them four times, with England's best achievement being a 0–0 draw in Manchester in 1990. In the 1995 World Cup group match England were brushed aside 2–0 by Norway, who went on to become World Champions. How has such a small nation with a population of only 4.3 million managed to make football the most popular sport for women? Their rise to dominance has seen them appear in four European Championship finals, winning in 1987 and 1993, and being runners-up in 1989 and 1991, and all three World Cups, winning the unofficial competition in 1988, being runners-up in 1991, and winners in 1995. In the inaugural Olympic tournament, they achieved third place, losing to the USA 2–1, on the golden goal rule.[37]

Norwegian women's football has flourished in a society where gender stereotyping is discouraged. Norwegian FA official Dag Otto Winnaess was the only male at the Women's Soccer Foundation's 'Links to Leadership' conference held in Seattle in December 1993. He explained that at the Norwegian FA they talk only of football and do not use the prefix 'women's or men's'. He enjoyed telling of the time when a Norwegian FA delegation of men and women went to England. The English FA assumed the Norwegian women in the group were there to provide secretarial support and could not believe they were, in fact, some of the top Norwegian football administrators. At the World Cup in Sweden, Norwegian Coach Even Pellerud was asked why women's football was so successful in Scandinavia. Pellerud replied, 'Because the Nordic countries very early respected women. We are much more even between the sexes.'[38] Women's football has, therefore, been developed along parallel lines with the men's game and has not been stifled by a debilitating struggle constantly to justify women's rights to play, administer, coach and referee their own game. Norwegian football has women in influential, decision-making roles, taking up three of the eight places on the Norwegian FA executive. In 1996 Karen Espelund was elected vice-president of the Norwegian FA, with responsibility for leading the elite football programmes for women and men. She also serves on UEFA's Women's Football Committee. Inger Marie Vingdal represented Norway at a Scottish Women's Football seminar in 1992. There she talked about the importance of the Norwegian FA's inclusion of girls' and women's football in the overall development of the game and hardly ever distinguished between the two genders. Indications of this parity in status, as well as resources, with the men's game are illustrated by their top officials. Women's national team coach Even Pellerud not only shares the same philosophy of modern football as Egil Olsen, the men's national team manager, but they work from the same office at the Norwegian FA headquarters. Olsen watched the women's matches in Sweden, praised the team for their achievement in winning with a 23–1 scoring record, and commented on how advanced Norway was compared to most of the other women's teams. Norway is not content to have 1.4 per cent of its population playing women's football and being European and World Champions; the country is equally concerned about spreading its development philosophy worldwide. At the Women's Soccer Foundation's 'Leadership' meeting held in Gavle during the World Cup in Sweden, Inger Marie Vingdal, Karen Espelund and Bente Skogvang were all there, raising issues about media reporting of the game.

The Norwegian development model

At UEFA's Youth Conference in 1995 Karen Espelund outlined seven key areas to development:

1. There must be total integration into the association, at all levels, including the executive board, committees, administrative and footballing expertise.
2. There should be well-organised club systems and regional organisation so that resources, including footballing knowledge and expertise, can be immediately used. Norway has used the well-proven structure from boys' football.
3. A league system should be organised at age levels the same as in boys' and men's football.
4. Existing rules and regulations should be adjusted, including freedom for girls up to 16 years to play for boys' teams with identical rules and regulations for both.

5. The need for female coaches, leaders and referees should be addressed. In the same way girls and women want to play football they also want to take part in these other activities. Many former players have excellent backgrounds after their careers finish and they must be invited to courses to educate them and give them opportunities. This is an important responsibility for national and regional associations. Clubs must give women opportunities to participate. Role models are important, showing other females the possibilities. In this way they must ensure all promotional material contains girls and women.

6. The Scandinavian countries, Germany and Italy have a history of success in the international competitions and they encourage their best players to be role models who represent elite attitudes and standards through many years.

7. Lastly, there should be continuity of key personnel at national team coach level, board members, administrators and top club leaders.

In respect of girls' football, Espelund said:

> FIFA and UEFA have provided the essential elite international championships to which nations can aspire to achieve, and were looking to establish a UEFA U18 championship to help the youth development [now set for 1997]. Within each country a solid organisational structure is important. This includes using both parents, as not surprisingly, mothers often want to take more part in club activities. Each group of ten to 15 players needs a coach and leader and should play in a separate age system of leagues, with a special emphasis on girls' football in schools. Flexibility in the way we organise football, including the opportunity for girls to play in boys' teams if there is no established girls' football, and they use seven or five players per team, not eleven. Girls' football is anyway taught in Norwegian schools and the Norwegian FA endeavours to influence educational programmes.[39]

National team players

The national team has been in every final round of the UEFA European Championships since their first success in 1987 when, as hosts, they defeated Sweden 2–0 in the final in front of 8,500 spectators. They have a good mixture of youth and experience. Gunn Nyborg played in all Norwegian internationals up to and including the 1991 World Cup final, when she reached her hundredth cap and captain Heidi Store had 145 caps as of October 1996.

In 1988 they won the unofficial World Cup in China, beating Sweden 1–0 with a goal from Linda Medalen, watched by a crowd of 30,000. Their progress was halted by a 4–1 defeat by Germany in the 1989 European Championship final and they appointed a new coach, Even Pellerud. The national team then played as many as 15 international matches in 1990 in preparation for the first FIFA World Cup in China in 1991, which Norway narrowly lost 2–1 to the USA. They regained the European Championship in 1993 by beating hosts Italy 1–0. The match was watched by 8,000 spectators and broadcast live by the national TV companies of Italy and Norway. Although this was followed by defeats in the US Cup in 1994, the Algarve Cup in 1994 and 1995 and in the European Championship semi-final in 1995, Pellerud had his team on course to win the second World Cup in Sweden in 1995.

The team needed to be at the peak of their fitness for the competition and attended training camps from January until the tournament began in July. In the competition they played six matches in 14 days (contrasting with the 1994 men's World Cup where the finalists played seven games in 29 days) based on a rigid system of zonal defence, a hard-working midfield and long balls to pick out their outstanding strikers, Linda Medalen, Hege Riise and Ann Kristin Aarones. Other players, including Gro Espeseth, remained from the team that had played in China, where their game had relied on passing combinations compared to the USA's one-on-one situations. Despite losing team captain Heidi Store who had been suspended (having gained two yellow cards in previous matches) in the final against Germany, Norway looked the stronger team both mentally and physically. Their determined running and long passing game suited the saturated pitch and with goals from Riise and Pettersen they won 2–0. Their overall score was 23 goals with only one against. Riise, Espeseth and Aarones received the Golden, Silver and Bronze Balls respectively, and Aarones also received the Adidas Golden Boot as the best goalscorer (6) and Riise the Silver Boot (5). Sixteen countries broadcast the final live, including Norway, and the Swedish press gave the championship a lot of good coverage.

Inaugural Olympic tournament

In the Olympic preliminary matches Norway beat Germany 3–2 and Japan 4–0, but could only draw with Brazil, 2–2, before losing a semi-final encounter with the USA. In the clash of the former and present World Champions, watched by 64,000 spectators, and by a TV audience of two million in Norway, they succumbed to a rather controversial penalty decision for handball, after Linda Medalen had put them in the lead in the eighteenth minute. Michelle Akers scored the penalty with only 14 minutes left and Shannon MacMillan scored the 'golden goal' winner in extra time. Norway had to be content with third place, after beating Brazil 2–0 in the play-off.

When Gro Espeseth visited the USA in December 1995 to promote the game and run 'soccer clinics' for girls, she emphasised the responsibilities involved by saying: "You don't miss an important training event to attend a wedding ... I train five or six times a week with my team, Sandviken, and up to seven days a week on my own. If I get a chance, I train with men so that I can be challenged to improve my skills and fitness."

With this example of dedication by their players, and the strong leadership from their association, it is not surprising that Norway are the top women's football nation.

REPUBLIC OF IRELAND

Population 3.5 million (1995)
Governing body: Ladies' Football Association of Ireland (LFAI),
80 Merrion Square, Dublin 2.[40]

Landmarks

1973 – First international match (v. Northern Ireland, won 4–1).
1982 – First European Championship match (v. Scotland, lost 3–0).
1991 – The FA of Ireland (FAI) formally assimilated the LFAI in its structure.
1992 – Withdrawal of international team from European Championship.
1994 – Implementation by the LFAI with support by the FAI of a development programme.
  – Introduction of U16 and U20 level national team.
1995 – Re-entry of international team to participate in the European Championships 1995–97.
  – U18 team won Gothia Cup, Sweden.
  – U16 team played in inaugural LFAI-initiated British Triangular Tournament in Ireland.

Participation
There are 13 affiliated leagues, with approximately 250 teams, representing almost 5,000 players. There are also competitions at U14, U16, U18, Intermediate and Senior level, an annual inter-league representative tournament at U18, Intermediate and Senior level, as well as the President's Cup, an inter-club competition for league winners on an annual basis.

Development

At the start of the first European Championship in 1982, there were eight leagues. Since the FAI took over, in 1991, rapid progress has taken place. Following the 10–0 European Championship defeat by Sweden in 1992, the FAI agreed to provide funding for a development plan, and the team withdrew from the competition for three years to concentrate on raising participation levels and standards of elite players. The programme led directly to the formation of U16, U18 and U20 teams and the re-formation of the senior team for the 1995–97 European Championships. The

Republic of Ireland has the most comprehensive national team development structure of all the British Isles teams. Women's football in the Republic benefited from the success of the men's team being the only British Isles team to reach the 1994 World Cup Tournament in the USA. The extra revenue gained from this event helped provide the funding for the women's development programme. The LFAI is governed by a council which is composed of representatives of each of the affiliated leagues, and the council meets four times a year. Day-to-day operations of the association are overseen by a seven-member volunteer executive, elected by council, and members have different functional areas of the organisation, including international affairs, national competitions, coaching and under-age development. The other three positions are: treasurer, secretary and president. All, except two, are female, including the president, Niamh O'Donoghue, who also has a place on the FAI's senior council and is a member of the executive. She has been one of the key leaders of Irish women's football. Others formally represent women's football on the coaching, national finance, international and referees' committees of the FAI. The executive works closely with the FAI and uses their headquarters in Dublin.

National team

Until the implementation of the development plan for women's football in mid-1993, the Republic of Ireland had little or no international success. In the plan all the national squads were placed under the responsibility of Michael Cooke, who was assimilated into the coaching structure of FAI director of coaching. Development panels of elite players were established at senior and under-age levels. One of the most significant developments was in identifying talented players at U16, U18 and senior level, and then addressing their fitness needs. Each player had their own training programmes, plus access to appropriate training facilities, and squad members were tested and monitored every six to eight weeks. The Republic re-entered the new B group of the European Championships in 1995 with a squad of 24 players, ranging in age from 17 to 33 years. In group five they twice beat Faroe Islands, Wales and Scotland, but could not overcome the experienced group-winning Belgian side, who beat them twice. The Republic had scored 20 goals but had ten against in the whole competition.

SCOTLAND

Population 5 million (1995)
Governing body: Scottish Women's Football Association (SWFA),
4 Park Gardens, Glasgow G3 7YE.[41]

Landmarks

1968 – First organised league started in Glasgow.
1971 – Stewarton and Thistle runners-up in English Women's FA
   Cup Final at Crystal Palace.
   – The SWFA formed.
1972 – First international match (v. England) at Greenock.
   – Lees Ladies runners-up in the WFA Cup Final.
1973 – Westthorn Utd runners-up in the WFA Cup Final.
1992 – Sheila Begbie appointed Women's Football Coordinator
   by Scottish Sports Council.
1996 – First U16 international match (v. Republic of Ireland).

Participation
Senior: approximately 600 players
   U18: approximately 80 players
   Senior: 28 clubs in three leagues (two of 10 and one of 8)
   U18: 5 clubs in one league
   U16: 27 clubs in two regional leagues, north and south
   U13: 42 clubs in three regional leagues, north, south and
Aberdeen
   Schools, 74 clubs in four regions, Glasgow, Lothian, Central and
Aberdeen
   Universities, seven clubs in one league

Development

The SWFA was formed on 17 September 1972 and initially worked
in association with the Women's FA of England. The SWFA is the
only women's association not officially affiliated to their men's
FA and development has been slow. In 1992, Team Sport Scotland
(Scottish Sports Council) introduced several Team Sport
Coordinators' posts including one for women's football. Ex-
Scotland captain, Sheila Begbie, was appointed Women's Football
Coordinator to develop girls' and women's' football in conjunction
with the Scottish Football Association (SFA). Approximately

six months after Sheila took up her post the SFA invited her and the SWFA to be housed within their office headquarters rent-free. The SWFA have autonomy regarding all member clubs so long as they play within the 'Laws of the Game and Article' of the SFA. The SWFA's administration is led by executive administrator Maureen McGonigle and a part-time assistant. They run the international team and the senior leagues. The junior regional leagues are responsible for their own administration. Sheila Begbie, Maureen McGonigle and the SWFA Committee (who are all female, although this is not a policy decision) work closely with the SFA, which provides support and financial backing.

At the time of the first international with England in 1972, there were ten teams in Scotland and although participation rates have only slowly improved there has been a significant improvement at youth level. Mixed football is allowed only up until a girl or boy is 12 years of age. Girls can, however, now find competitive football in the new U13 and U16 regional leagues and U16 international team that started in 1996. Some women's teams are attached to men's clubs or to sports and youth clubs and several teams have female coaches. Highland League team Cove Rangers have their own women's team, and pay expenses, but the rest of the teams are all totally amateur. The First Division League and League Cup-winner for the 1994–95 season was Hutchinson Vale. The other leading First Division teams are Clyde and Cove Rangers.

The status of the women's game has been raised through links with the SFA and support of individuals such as the ex-men's national team manager, Andy Roxburgh and current manager Craig Brown. From the men's professional game, both Gary Locke of Heart of Midlothian and Ray Stewart of Stirling Albion have also been supportive. Gary Locke coaches Eskmill Ladies and Ray Stewart helped establish St Johnstone Ladies.

One of the first joint 'Team Sport Scotland', SFA and SWFA initiatives was to hold a conference 'Heading for the Future' to consider the future of women's football in Scotland, which took place in Edinburgh in March 1992. The aim was to learn how the game was being developed in the USA, Norway and England and to receive the views of over 100 Scottish delegates. USA and Norway sent national team manager Anson Dorrance and executive committee member Inger Marie Vingdal respectively. I was invited to represent England and do a coaching demonstration. Other initiatives included the introduction of soccer sevens in schools and communities backed up by promotional videos and booklets and in November 1992 a four-nation five-a-side tournament in conjunction with Glasgow City Council. Scotland A and B reached the final of the tournament that was held at the Kelvin Hall International Sports Arena in Glasgow in front of 900 spectators. In 1994, USA captain Michelle Akers, and ex-husband Robbie Stahl, were invited to do coaching demonstrations with Scottish players, a further initiative arranged by Sheila Begbie.

National team

Their first match was on 18 November 1972, when they lost 3–2 in the inaugural international for both England and Scotland at Greenock. The manager was Robert Stewart, a former professional with Kilmarnock and St Mirren. Scotland played two more friendly matches against England, losing 8–0 and 2–1 before meeting them again in the first European Championship qualifying games in 1982. They lost 4–0 in Dunbarton and 2–0 at Elland Road, Leeds. In the next European Championships they met England again, losing 4–0 at Deepdale, Preston in 1985 and 3–1 at Raith Rovers FC in 1986. Their lack of success continued, losing three more friendly matches against England, 3–0 at Raith Rovers FC in 1989, 4–0 at St Mirren in 1990 and 4–0 in the second women's match at Wembley in May 1990. Scotland's performance seemed to be improving and in the 1992–93 European Championship encounters, Scotland only narrowly lost to England by 1–0 at Walsall and 2–0 in Perth. Scotland went through a disappointing time in the European Championships, especially in 1993–94 when they lost all six games. This included an 8–2 defeat by newcomers Portugal and a 4–0 lesson from Italy in April 1994, at Stirling in front of 1,200 spectators. National coach Peter Clarke was replaced at the beginning of the 1994–95 season by Millar Hay, a former professional with Queen's Park and Clyde, with Sheila Begbie as his assistant. In the 1995–96 championships the Scottish side started well with a victory over the Faroe Islands 7–1, but then lost to the Republic of Ireland, 2–0 and 4–2. In the first half of 1996 they were beaten by Wales 5–1 and Belgium 6–1. They completed their group by beating the Faroe Islands 3–0 and Wales 3–2 but were beaten 3–0 by Belgium, finishing third with nine points, with 17 goals for and 23 against. In January 1997, the national team embarked on a prestigious trip to play friendly matches in Brazil.

The South Americans, having achieved an unexpected fourth place in the inaugural Olympics, confirmed their status by beating Scotland 5–0, 6–1 and 7–1.

Players and coaches

Elsie Cook was one of the pioneers in the game and was the first secretary of the Scottish Women's FA in 1971. She was centre-half and captain of Stewarton and Thistle, leading them to the WFA Cup Final in 1971. Her colleague, Rose Reilly, was an outstanding right-winger in all three WFA Cup Finals, playing for Stewarton and Thistle, Lees Ladies (Stewarton and Thistle under a new sponsorship name) and finally Westthorn United. Disappointed with the lack of progress in her country, she left in 1973 with other players such as Elsie Cook, to find success in Italian women's football. While Cook returned home, Reilly stayed on. She played for Milan and Catania, in Sicily, where league gates were regularly 8,000 and Trani (Bari) with gates sometimes as high as 12,000. Rose became so popular and successful that she took Italian nationality and played for the national team 20 times, scoring 13 goals. She has also played for Napoli, Prato and Agliana. When she opened a sports shop in Trani in 1986, Agliana flew her from Trani to Agliana to play and paid someone to run her shop while she was away. In the Italian national leagues players were earning around £25,000 per season and she doesn't regret leaving Ayrshire, saying: 'When I was a wee girl of seven, this was my dream – to play professional football – and I made it come true!'[42] In Italy she won eight First Division championship ties, five Cup Winners' medals and was top scorer for four seasons.

So far, Scotland has not produced another Rose Reilly, although a promising new group of young players are coming through, such as PE student Nicky Grant and Scottish captain, 21-year-old Pauline MacDonald, both of whom play for Cove Rangers. An indication of how difficult it is for players to improve their fitness and skills at club level is indicated by the fact Pauline trains with a men's Division Three side, Forfar, to ensure she gets adequate training.

Women can obtain the same coaching licences as men up to B grade. There are 10 grade B, 37 grade C, and 60 grade D. Sheila Begbie, with the backing of the Scottish FA, has encouraged women to become coaches by organising several women-only SFA C and B Licence courses.

Media

The Scottish media are fairly supportive of women's football, especially since it established links with the Scottish FA. In 1992, the four-nations five-a-side tournament at the Kelvin Hall received positive media comment. The *Scotsman* quoted Craig Brown as saying, 'The skill factor in women's football is better than many believe and this tournament confirmed that.'[43] BBC Scotland's football specialist is Hazel Irvine, who has commentated on women's football matches for the BBC and Channel 4, and who provided commentary for the tournament. The *Scotsman*'s reporter, Natasha Wood, reported on Scotland's 1–1 draw with Australia (1995) but also highlighted the difficulties a minority female sport has in a predominantly male-dominated area, in trying to promote the game.

SWEDEN

Population: 8.8 million (1995)
Governing body: Svenska Fotbollforbundet, Rasunda Station, Box 1216, S–17123 Solna, Sweden.[44]

Landmarks

1970 – Regional competitions started.
1971 – 17 of Sweden's 24 district associations organise women's competitions.
1972 – First National Championships (won by Oxabacks IF).
1973 – First international match v. Finland (0–0)
1975 – Pia Sundhage's first international match at the age of 15.
1978 – Swedish FA took responsibility for women's football.
1979 – Lost 0–1 in quarter-finals to winners (Denmark) of unofficial European Championship Tournament in Italy.
1980 – Ulf Lyfors becomes first full-time professional national women's team coach.
1981 – Inaugural National Cup competition (won by Jitex, who also won the league).
1982 – First women to officiate in top league.
1983 – Premier League divided into just two regional groups.
1984 – First winners of the inaugural European Championship (defeating England 4–3 in a penalty shoot-out after full time, with the score 1–1 on aggregate).
1985 – Swedish woman official takes charge of an official international match (Hildegun Granlund).
1986 – First U16 international (defeating Norway 2–0).
1987 – Runners-up to Norway in European Championship (lost 2–1 to Norway).
1988 – Two National Leagues divisions merge into one.
  – First woman in the world to become National Coach (Gunilla Paijkull).
  – Runners-up in FIFA unofficial World Tournament in China.
  – Nordic Girls' Tournament started.
1989 – Third place in European Championships beating Germany 4–0 (held in Germany).
  – Swedish Women's Football Year (1989–90).
  – Inaugural Algarve Cup organised by the FA's of Sweden, Denmark and Norway in collaboration with the Portuguese FA.

1990 – Start of U20 national team and Nordic Tournament for U20 matches.

– Sweden plays its hundredth match – Gunn Nyborg plays in all of them.

1991 – Third place in 1991 World Cup (beating Germany in play-off).

– Start of Nordic Club championship.

1992 – Bengt Simonson takes over from Gunilla Paijkull as national team coach.

1994 – Project Group Women's Football set up by the Swedish FA to develop women's football and especially to develop more female leaders at all levels.

1995 – Runners-up to Germany (3–2) in European Championships.

– Ingrid Jonsson becomes first woman to referee a FIFA final.

1996 – Ex-Swedish national coach Gunilla Paijkull is first woman to serve on FIFA's Technical Coaching Instructors' panel.

– Placed sixth in the inaugural Olympic Tournament.

– Marika Domanski-Lyfors appointed national team coach.

– Pia Sundhage appointed national coach for the U20 national team.

– Anna Signeul is appointed coach of the U16 team.

1997 – Sweden, group 4 winners, co-host the European Championships with Norway.

Participation and development

Football is the biggest sport for women in Sweden and there are 3,242 clubs. Sweden's participation rates have grown remarkably since 1970 when 725 women players were registered. In 1990 it soared to 33,000. The figures for 1996 were, women aged 15 years and over, 40,000 and U15 girls, 120,000, making a total of approximately 160,000.

As in the case of Norway's achievements, much of Sweden's success is due to social factors and equal opportunities. Sweden has encouraged women into leadership in politics, business and sport. In football, the Swedish FA started a project called Group Women's Football to develop the game at all levels, but especially to create more female leaders, particularly women coaches. Susanne Erlandsson, a sports teacher by profession and former international player, is the project's chair and is the first and only elected woman of the Swedish executive board. She takes part in all of the board's decisions including those concerning men's football. In recognition of her achievements in football, she was awarded the prestigious Victoria Prize as the Female Sports Leader of the Year, 1995.

In Sweden, grassroots development has been helped by the fact that most village sport revolves around the football club, which usually has club sections for girls and women. Around 1975 mixed-gender football was also permitted in schools. Women coaches are encouraged initially to go on special women-only training schemes, progressing later on to mixed courses. Level 4 is the highest grade and so far three women and 24 men have achieved this level. Five of the Premier League teams have female coaches, one Level 4 and four others, all of whom are at least Level 3.

National Championships

There is a Premier League of 12 teams, and three First Divisions of ten teams each. There are nine Second Divisions of ten teams each and Division Three, Four and Five consisting of local teams. The National Cup Tournament is called the Folksam Cup. It has been in existence since 1981 and 177 teams entered in 1996. Oxaback IF have won it six times. There are also local and district competitions for U8–U10 players, and a national club competition for U15 and U16 teams.

The Swedish Premier and First Division clubs pay some of their players pocket money and organise jobs and apartments for them. Each club is permitted a maximum of three foreign players. The USA's Julie Foudy, Kristine Lilly and Michelle Akers have all played for Tyreso FF and some of Tyreso's matches have attracted around 1,000 spectators. Alvsjo Alk (Stockholm) won the national championships in 1995–96.

National team

As well as having a senior national team since 1973, Sweden has had an U16 team since 1986, and an U20 team since 1990. Selection for the national squads starts at district level, then at regional training camps throughout the country. From these camps a final 20 or 25 women are selected for the national team.

In 1988 Gunilla Paijkull became the first woman to coach a national team and took Sweden to the unofficial FIFA World Cup as well as the official inaugural World Cup in China in 1991.

The team's first international match was in 1973, when they drew against Finland 0–0. In their first matches with England, just two years later, they beat the English side, 2–0 and 3–1. It was England's first defeat in ten games since they had started an official team in 1972 and Sweden subsequently went on to be England's most feared opponents, defeating them in nearly every international encounter. In the 1979 unofficial European Tournament in Italy, Sweden beat England 4–3 on penalties after a 0–0 draw, to take third place in the competition.

The major turning point for the national team was the defeat of Italy both at home and away in the inaugural European Championship semi-finals in 1982–83. A record crowd of 5,162 attended the Linkoping Stadium for the second-leg victory (3–2) and the match was watched by the legendary Swedish male player Nils Liedholm. Liedholm, who played for Sweden in the 1958 men's World Cup in Stockholm, was then coaching the Italian men's team, Roma, but came to offer his support to his compatriots. His presence and subsequent positive comments about the game helped to enhance the reputation of women's football in both Sweden and Italy. (The healthy respect for women's football held by men like Liedholm is echoed by the predominantly male Swedish FA's executive, who suspended some of the men's 1995 Premier League games in order to free the stadia for the Women's World Cup 1995.)

After winning the European Championship in 1984, Sweden have been runners-ups twice and third once. In 1987 they beat England 3–2 in the semi-final but lost 2–1 to Norway in the final. In 1989 they lost 2–1 to Norway in the semi-final and beat Italy 2–1 to take third place. In March 1995, Sweden lost the final 3–2 to hosts Germany. In the 1991 World Cup in China Sweden lost 4–1 to Norway in the semi-final but beat Germany 4–0 to take third place. They qualified as hosts for the 1995 World Cup but surprisingly lost the opening game against Brazil 1–0 and finished only fifth overall. They recovered their form in the next game, beating eventual runners-up Germany 3–2, but inconsistency continued. They secured a 2–0 victory over Japan but in the quarter-final could only manage a 1–1 draw after extra time against China and lost 4–3 on penalties. In the Olympic tournament they were unfortunate in the preliminary rounds to meet both of the ultimate finalists, and lost 2–0 to runners-up China and 2–1 to winners USA. They comfortably defeated Denmark 3–1, but this only gave them fifth place overall.

Their international record stood at: played 165, won 106, drawn 29, lost 30 by 1995.

Players and officials

Pia Sundhage is Sweden's most experienced player. She made her debut in 1975 and is Sweden's most capped player, male or female. She has even had her picture on a Swedish stamp. Pia has played in most positions for her country and when she retired after the China World Cup 1991 she made a comeback in a 'sweeper' role in defence. Since 1990 she has combined her playing career with coaching (U16 national coach) but retired from international competition after the Olympics. She was appointed head coach of the U20 national team in 1996 and continues as player/coach for her club team Hammarby IF of Stockholm. After the Olympics, another well-known ex-player, Marika Domanski-Lyfors, the former assistant national coach, took over from Bengt Simonson (who had been head coach for the past four years) to become Sweden's second female, and eighth in total, to hold this top position. Marika won the Swedish championship twice as a player with Jitex in 1981 and 1984. Ex-national player Anna Signeul became head coach for the U16 national team in 1996, which makes Sweden unique in having women national team coaches for three teams. Anette Borjesson, who also had a distinguished career with the national team, made her debut for Sweden against England in 1975, and won a European Championship medal in 1984. She gives much credit to the Swedish FA for providing the funds to develop the game.

Since Michelle Akers left Tyreso, England's striker Karen Farley is one of the best-known of the few foreign players currently playing in the Premier League. She came to Sweden for the 1990–91 season from Ashford Town LFC and played for south-east Sweden team, Lindsdal, along with another current England international Tina Mapes, who later returned to England. At the time the England team coach did not know of Karen's existence. She later signed for Hammarby IF, who helped her find a job and an apartment in Stockholm. At the end of the 1995 season she had helped them win the Cup and fourth place in the league, by scoring 27 goals. She does not earn much from her work and nothing from playing football, but stays in Sweden to take advantage of a competitive league, as well as top-class training with well-educated coaches. She told women's football journalist, Thorsten Frennstedt, 'In England we don't usually get paid for lost salary and the employers are not happy to give time off for international matches. Now you realise what we have to deal with in England.'[45]

Sweden has become one of the most successful countries in producing world-class female officials. The leading exponent is Ingrid Jonsson, a 36-year-old sports instructor and headmistress, who became the first woman to referee a FIFA final. She has been extremely active and involved in setting up special courses and training programmes for women referees.

Media

When Sweden came to England for the second leg of the inaugural UEFA European Championship final in 1984, they amazed everyone at the Luton Town ground when they arrived with a TV crew and 36 press personnel. For the first leg in Stockholm the game had been televised live.[46] As in Germany, the local newspapers cover their teams' progress well, and at national level, for the 1995 World Cup, there was a lot of media exposure. The top journalist is Thorsten Frennstedt, who works for *Nya Mal* (*New Goals*) magazine, which had its tenth anniversary in 1996.

USA

Population: 258 million (1995)
Governing body: United States Soccer Federation (USSF),
1801–1811 S. Prairie Avenue, Chicago, Illinois 60616.[47]

Landmarks

1979 – University of North Carolina (UNC) starts a women's
soccer programme under head coach Anson Dorrance.
1980 – First national championship.
1981 – First Association of Intercollegiate Athletics for Women
(AIAW) national championships (won by UNC).
1982 – First National Collegiate Athletic Association championship
(won by UNC).
1985 – First national team match (lost 1–0 to Italy in Jesolo,
Italy).
– US Soccer Federation began naming a 'Female Athlete of the
Year' (Sharon Remer).
1986 – First domestic international (2–0 win against Canada in
Blaine, Minnesota).
– Anson Dorrance became head coach of the national team.
1988 – Michelle Akers receives annual endorsement from Umbro
USA.
1991 – Won the inaugural FIFA World Cup in China (2–1 against
Norway).
1993 – Runners-up to China in first appearance at World University
Games.
– International Olympic Committee agree to admit women's
soccer as a full-medal sport at the 1996 Atlantic Olympic
Games.
1994 – Runners-up to Norway in the Algarve Cup.
– Won the Chiquita Cup (tournament organised in USA with
four nations).
– Anson Dorrance retires as head coach and is replaced by
assistant Tony DiCicco.
1995 – Placed third in the second FIFA World Cup in Sweden.
1996 – Won the inaugural Olympic Tournament (2–1 against
China).
– December, UNC beat Notre Dame 1–0 at the National
Collegiate Athletic Association (NCAA) Division 1
Championship Program finals in Santa Clara to become US
champions for the thirteenth time.

History

Men's soccer was developed in the college system towards the end of the nineteenth century in some of the east coast colleges, such as Princeton. Although the USSF was one of the first organisations to be affiliated with FIFA in 1913, the game has never been able to challenge the traditional professional male sports of baseball and American (gridiron) football. The Professional American Soccer League started in 1921. There are now four professional leagues and a new Major League Soccer national league of ten professional teams started in April 1996. The lack of a successful men's national team has left a void which the successful women's national team has been happy to fill. The only downside is that for some it confirms the status of soccer as a game best suited to women while gridiron football is for 'real' men. The USSF's most well-known achievement has been the successful hosting of the 1994 men's World Cup, when the team lost to eventual champions, Brazil. In 1961, the Confederation of North and Central America and Caribbean Federations (CONCACAF) was recognised by FIFA as the governing body of soccer in this region and under which the women's national team plays World Cup qualifying games.

The history of USA women's soccer is not very long. Although Dick, Kerr Ladies played in the USA, after the 1921 ban, there is no evidence of any matches against women's teams. Research by Shawn Ladda of Columbia University indicates that women started to play on the east coast in the 1950s.[48] At this time special 'field days', where students were given time for instruction in physical recreation, were the only opportunity most college women had to be involved in sports. Soccer for women was almost unheard of and where it was played, it was usually used as drill for field hockey or played prior to hockey matches. During the 1950s and 1960s some colleges in Vermont and Canada played intercollegiate matches, and Brown University in Rhode Island started the first official varsity soccer programme in 1977. The first conference tournament, the Ivy League, was held in 1978, and the first regional tournament, the Eastern Association of Intercollegiate Athletics for Women, took place in 1979.

There were many 'firsts' for women's soccer in the 1980s. The first national championship between Cortland State and Colorado College took place in 1980. The first Association of Intercollegiate

Athletics for Women national championship was held in 1981 – won by UNC – and the first National Collegiate Athletic Association (NCAA) championship was held in 1982, with UNC again the winner.

Participation and development

In 1991 the USA's female participation rate in football was 39 per cent of the entire football playing population. Figures for 1994 estimated that six million females were playing the game, which was the largest number of any nation.[49] It is estimated that now nine million girls and women are participating.

There are three youth soccer programmes, which are independent of each other. The smallest is the Soccer Association for Youth (SAY), with seven divisions and 350 leagues. The national headquarters is in Ohio, and the association is affiliated to the USSF. The next largest is the American Youth Soccer Organisation (AYSO) with seven divisions and 40,000 teams. Their national headquarters are in California and they are also affiliated to the USSF. The largest is the United States Youth Soccer Association (USYSA), which in 1995 had 2.3 million boys and girls playing. The USYSA is the USSF's youth division. The Soccer Industry Council of America figures indicate that in 1984 in the U19 combined boys' and girls' SAY, AYSO, USYSA figures were 1,473,943 participants. For the same group in 1995 the figures were 2,983,826.[50]

In the 1994–95 season, the number of girls participating in high-school soccer was 191,350, compared with 272,810 boys. Soccer is the fifth most popular high-school sport for girls but there are 2,000 fewer high schools sponsoring girls' soccer than boys' soccer with 7,445 boys' programmes and 5,463 girls' programmes (48 out of 50 states reported). Some of these girls are, however, playing for boys' teams. Only a third of the high schools that sponsor girls' basketball sponsor girls' soccer with 16,616 basketball programmes compared to only 5,463 soccer programmes. California, with 683 high schools sponsoring girls' soccer and 20,349 participating, is the number-one state for soccer and represents the largest participation rate for girls' high-school soccer in the whole country. The state has approximately 1,785,000 participants, including boys, girls, men and women, playing soccer. According to the National Federation of State High Schools

Association, only 36 per cent of all high-school athletes are girls, despite the fact that enrolments are approximately equal.[51]

Title IX and the college system

The extraordinary participation figures, and the fact the national team had existed only for six years before it won the inaugural World Cup in 1991, highlights the importance of cultural acceptance of the sport, and how much better gender equity has worked in the USA compared with England's impotent Sex Discrimination Act (especially in the Theresa Bennett case (see pp. xii, 226–7). Unlike some European nations, the USA has not had to overcome years of tradition which defined football as unsuitable for women. Furthermore Title IX of the Educational Amendments of 1972, which sets out to ensure that women receive equal funding in colleges and other institutions, has helped the college system become the perfect vehicle for the growth and development of the game. However, enforcement has been truly effective only since a new law was enacted in 1992 to make the original law more efficient. The Supreme Court of the United States unanimously agreed to permit students to receive compensation from schools and school officials for sex discrimination. A total of 75 universities and colleges started new women's teams between 1992 and 1995. This compares well with the next highest increase for a new women's sport, which is 19 new teams in fast-pitch softball. The college system is fed by volunteer-led recreational football which is often mixed-gender.

Collegiate soccer

There are two governing bodies; the larger and more prominent is the NCAA and the smaller, the National Association of Intercollegiate Athletics (NAIA). Formal competition is the NCAA Division I, II and III. Division I and II colleges can provide athletic scholarships to student-players, although not all do. Division I can give eleven scholarships, and Division II can give nine. Division III is not allowed to provide scholarships to any student-athlete. The NAIA offers national championships, but this organisation is small and does not offer scholarships at all. In 1981 the NCAA had 77 teams in Division I, II and III and by 1995 there were more than 600 teams. Despite Title IX, less than 24 per cent of college sport operating budgets are actually allocated to women's sport.

The Women's Soccer Foundation (WSF) research suggests inequality in other areas of college sport:

less than 18 per cent of money spent on recruiting goes towards recruiting female athletes;

less than 1 per cent of coaches of college men's sport are women;

less than 49 per cent of college women's sports programmes are coached by women;

only 34 per cent of all college athletes are women despite the fact that male/female enrolments in college are approximately equal;

less than 33 per cent of collegiate athletic scholarship dollars are awarded to women athletes.[52]

However, the numbers of NCAA-affiliated universities who have added women's soccer have risen dramatically. The top universities, particularly from Division I, receive the most publicity in the press and television coverage. The 1995 Division I semi-finals and final were broadcast on cable television. The interest in college soccer is illustrated by its growing popularity over gridiron football. A total of 445 colleges field women's soccer teams, compared with 862 fielding men's teams, while only 562 field gridiron football teams. The first NCAA Championship tournament was held in 1981 and has been won an incredible thirteen times by North Carolina. The success of UNC has permeated down to local youth soccer and *Soccer* magazine records that in North Carolina state youth soccer had grown from 10,500 in 1986 to 40,000 in 1994.[53]

The problem for the USA is that Division I collegiate soccer is the highest level of competition available, surpassing any club soccer, which tends to be more recreational than competitive. Therefore, when players leave college there is no club league system at a similar level. It was for this reason that players, including Michelle Akers, played in Sweden's competitive national league. Others played in the Japanese professional league, and one signed up for a German team for the 1996–97 season. National team player Julie Foudy complained, in *USA Today* in August 1994, about the one-sided CONCACAF qualifying matches and that the USA would not maintain its number-one status because it had no national domestic league system.[54]

The pyramid development system for the young players, however, is excellent. There are district, regional, state and then national Olympic Development Programs at U14, 15, 16, 17 and

19, from which players are selected for the national squads at U16, U20 and senior level. The senior squad has been in place since 1985, the U20 since 1992, the U16 since 1994. Without these programmes, young players would go straight into the senior squad and while Mia Hamm made, at the age of 15, a successful senior debut at national level, most would benefit from developing through the ranks of the junior squads.

Many colleges and universities have female head coaches. With salaries at Division I level in the region of £18,000 to £30,000, soccer coaching has become a serious career for women in the USA. Many of the victorious 1991 World Cup USA national team players gained top coaching positions and in 1996 there were 32 women USSF A Licence coaches (equivalent to the FA Advanced Licence).

National team

A national team was first selected in 1982 following progression through representative state and regional teams. The USA women's team's first appearance was in July 1985 at the Olympic Festival in Baton Rouge, Louisiana under the direction of coach Mike Ryan. Two months later the team made its international debut at the Italian Tournament that had, up until that year, been attended solely by European teams. The USA lost 1–0 to Italy and to England 3–1, and lost 1–0 and drew 2–2 in games with Denmark. Blaine, Minnesota was to host the first domestic international, when they beat Canada 3–0, 2–0 and lost 2–1, during July 1986.

Under the direction of UNC coach Anson Dorrance from 1986, the USA made steady progress, playing numerous tournaments all over the world. These included an appearance in the 1986 World Tournament in Italy where they beat China (2–1), Japan (3–1), Brazil (2–1), and only lost 1–0, again to Italy. They played the top European nations, Norway and Sweden, in a tournament in Minnesota in July 1987, beating Norway 3–0 in the first game and Canada 4–2, but found they were no match for Norway a second time, losing 1–0 to them and 2–1 to Sweden. In August and December 1987 they went to East Asia to play soccer nationals of China, Japan, New Zealand and Taiwan. Of their seven matches, the US won four, drew one, and lost only to New Zealand 1–0 and Taiwan 2–1. In March 1988, they drew with Sweden 1–1 in another Chinese tournament, and in the Italian Tournament in August they defeated up and coming West Germany, who had been steadily improving since their first official involvement in international football in 1982. They lost to Italy 2–1 and England 2–0. In 1990, the USA team won all of their six matches, including defeats of Norway 4–0 and 4–2, West Germany 3–0 and England 3–0. In 1991 they won the Varna (Bulgaria) Tournament which put them in a good position for the World Cup CONCACAF qualifying rounds. The nations of CONCACAF were no match for the USA and they won easily by beating Mexico, Martinique, Trinidad and Tobago, Haiti and Canada, scoring 49 goals and conceding none, with Michelle Akers top scorer with 11 goals. They proceeded to prepare for the World Cup by playing a series of friendly matches against France, England, Denmark, the Netherlands, Germany and China, and two matches against Norway in the US, both of which they lost 2–1 and 1–0.

Inaugural FIFA World Cup – China 1991

One of the reasons behind the USA's success was having sufficient financial backing from the USSF, and with no club championship commitments, they were able to spend the necessary time in the training camps and play preparatory international games. While there are obvious advantages for the European nations, who have club championships and regular competition, it has sometimes proved difficult to fit in all the domestic matches and find time for national team training. Furthermore, club-level coaching and facilities can be inconsistent with those available at national level and to ensure they are sufficiently fit for the national team, players need to do extra individual training. The USA's championship preparation was second to none. From January 1991, the squad of 24 players came together for two training camps of five days each in January and February, and then three more week-long camps in July, August and November. As well as technical skill and tactical intelligence, Anson Dorrance looked for players with a capacity for self-discipline and an ability to fight and play for each other. This is the similar recruitment idea of the successful Ajax team of Amsterdam, whereby the boys they select for their development programme require the attributes of speed, good personality, intelligence and technique, which is commonly known as SPIT. When the team was not at the training camps, Dorrance organised a personal development and training schedule so that they could maintain all-round fitness, and high technical standards. Dorrance had been used to coaching male college teams, and told *Soccer* magazine in 1995 that he had to teach women the value of competitiveness, aggression and dominance. He also said he liked the way the women listened better than men, and felt that they are much more conscientious and open to learning new ideas, whereas men often had preconceived ideas of how things should be.[55]

In the early-round matches, the USA beat Sweden 3–2 and then easily overcame Brazil 5–0, Japan 3–0, Chinese Taipei 7–0 and surprisingly overwhelmed European champions Germany 5–2 in the semi-final. They played and beat Norway in the final, 2–1, in front of a crowd of 63,000. Michelle Akers scored first and then Linda Medalen equalised in the twenty-ninth minute. Akers scored the winner, and her tenth goal in the competition, two minutes from time. Michelle Akers had also recorded a FIFA championship record with five goals in the match against Chinese Taipei, and received the Gold Boot award. Carin Gabarra (née Jennings) received the best player award, winning the Golden Ball. Their collective total of goals scored was 25, with only five against, and Akers, Jennings and captain April Heinrichs had scored 20 of them. A total of 510,000 spectators had attended the 26 matches and the final was watched by FIFA president, João Havelange, who commented: 'As president of FIFA it was a special pleasure for me to watch these young ladies playing with such flair and such elegance, and according to the reports of the many media representatives present, making the game into a celebration ... women's football is now well and truly established.'[56]

The USA and Norway had set the highest of standards in the competition and women's football had earned the respect and backing of FIFA. Anson Dorrance and his USA team had been superb ambassadors for the game and on their return home, President George Bush invited the team to the White House to congratulate them personally on their achievement. In just six years, the USA had acquired the title of World Champions and were now public role models for all aspiring women football players throughout the world.

Anson Dorrance departs

Anson Dorrance resigned as national coach after the CONCACAF World Cup qualifying rounds in Montreal, Canada, in August 1994. Under his guidance the USA women's team had won 65 matches, lost 22, and drawn 5. To ensure continuity, he was replaced by one of his assistants, ex-professional goalkeeper Tony DiCicco. DiCicco retained Dorrance's assistant, Lauren Gregg, and appointed China World Cup captain, April Heinrichs, as another assistant to help prepare them for the Sweden World Cup in 1995.

The team had no difficulty in winning the CONCACAF qualifying matches, but in Sweden they could achieve only third place. Their opening match was an indication that all was not well: they drew with China 3–3. They recovered to beat Denmark 2–0 and Australia 4–1, and defeated Japan 4–0 in the quarter-final. However, their play was not as deadly as it had been in China. They lacked having Heinrichs in the team, Gabarra had a back injury and Michelle Akers was not 100 per cent fit. With a gruelling schedule of six matches in just 12 days (in the men's World Cup competition they allow greater rest time), players had little time to recover from each match. Akers had experienced a hard season in the Swedish League, and was trying to recover from an illness, later diagnosed as Chronic Fatigue Immune Dysfunction Syndrome. Early on in the championship she also suffered an injury and did not play at her best in the crucial semi-final match, which they lost 1–0 to Norway. Other nations had worked hard to counteract the USA's previously successful attacking style, but at the same time the USA team lacked stamina and confidence. Without the off-field leadership of the charismatic Anson Dorrance and the on-field inspiration of April Heinrichs, the team seemed uncomfortable with the burden of title-holders. Compared to the 16 goals Akers and Gabarra had scored between them in China, they scored none in Sweden and Mia Hamm, who replaced Heinrichs, scored only two. Norway went on to defeat Germany 2–0 in the final. The USA took third place beating China 2–0 in the play-off.

Inaugural Olympic Tournament

Since 1991 the USA had become one of the leading nations in the promotion and development of the women's game and it was the determination of people involved with soccer in the USA that finally persuaded the Olympic Committee to introduce women's football as a medal sport in the 1996 games.

Marty Mankameyer, who became the first woman to serve on the USSF's board of directors, began enlisting support as early as

1984 and Marilyn Childress, president of the Georgia Amateur Soccer Association, was instrumental in her attempts in lobbying the Atlanta Committee for the Olympic Games (ACOG). The cause was enhanced by the success of the 1991 World Championships in terms of high attendances and quality of play, and in 1993, Marilyn Childress organised a match between the USA and Germany in front of 5,532 fans in Atlanta, in order that the ACOG could see for themselves the popularity and quality of international games. The WSF's volunteers circulated petitions encouraging fans to urge their congressmen to support the resolution, which was eventually passed on 18 September 1993. It was further endorsed later by President Bill Clinton, who received the USA's co-captains, Julie Foudy and Carla Overbeck, by special invitation to a reception prior to the start of the event.

It's a tribute to the USA coaches, administrators and players that they did learn from their relative failure in Sweden and returned to form to win the inaugural Olympic gold medal. The USA squad for the Olympics was based at a camp in Florida for six months from January 1996, until the Olympics started in August. During that time they played several friendly matches, including the US Cup, which was a four-nation tournament between China, Japan and Canada, with the USA beating China 1–0 in the final in Washington, DC. The USA matches attracted capacity crowds of around 5,000 with the final attracting 6,081 even though the match was transmitted live on television. Most incredible of all was the fact that when the USA women's and men's teams met the Norwegian women's and men's teams in Jacksonville in February 1996, the women's match was the main feature, the men's the curtain-raiser. Although the women would undoubtedly benefit from a national league, as the men now have, they received the best preparation package of all national players. The squad usually had one week off in every four from the training camp, nine of the squad were paid full-time and the others received compensation so that they did not have to work. The squad has agreed not to discuss contracts, but *FIFA* magazine estimated that the minimum would be over £1,000 per month for players just out of college. The established players receive more and can augment their income by signing sponsorship deals, usually with boot manufacturers. Sponsorship contracts can include annual payments of between £10,000 and £60,000. Michelle Akers told *FIFA* magazine in 1995: 'It's exciting to be paid as a player now. We don't have to bust our butts off the field to survive and train for the US national team in our meagre free time.'[57]

In the preliminary rounds of the competition they beat Denmark 3–0, Sweden 2–1 and drew 0–0 with China. In the semi-final they beat Norway 2–1. In the final against China the USA played well, taking the lead from a goal by Shannon MacMillan in the nineteenth minute, until China's Wen Sun equalised 12 minutes before half-time. The USA's goal-attempts ratio and corners were more than double those of the Chinese in the second half and the winning goal was scored in the sixty-eighth minute by Tiffeny Milbrett. The USA had played 18 games winning 17 and drawing one with China. They had lost only four games in the last three years.

After the Sweden World Cup, April Heinrichs had confidently predicted to me that they would use the experience and put things right for the Olympics. She was also confident about the future of the international game, and hoped that nations like the USA, Norway and Germany would act as an inspiration to others to try and reach higher standards. She said she realised how privileged the USA team was, in respect of resources and opportunities for women, and that more nations should allow greater autonomy to women to play a greater part in running women's football. She felt some men in charge of some of the national teams in the World Cup talked down to 'the girls', even to the media, and that this was unfortunate given that some were over 30 years of age and had been playing internationally for many years.

Coaches and players

The USA's meteoric rise to the top of women's football has been built on three main factors: Title IX gender equity, which has aided the development of an excellent collegiate system; the support and resources provided by the USSF; and the benefit from having outstanding leaders both off and on the pitch.

Anson Dorrance was born in Bombay, India and lived in Ethiopia, Switzerland and Belgium before graduating at UNC in 1974. It was at North Carolina that he started to put into practice his European soccer knowledge when he became UNC's men's soccer coach in 1977, and then the women's UNC Tar Heels' (as they are known) coach in 1979. By 1995, the Tar Heels had compiled an all-time record of 348 victories with just ten draws and ten defeats and between 1982 and 1996 won 13 out of 15 NCAA women's soccer championships. Five different players from the team have been named National Player of the Year a total of nine times and many former players are now coaches. Anson Dorrance was national coach from 1986 to 1994 and is now one of FIFA's women's football technical committee members. In 1996 he published a book entitled *Training Soccer Champions*.[58]

Current national coach Tony DiCicco is an A Licence and Advanced National Diploma coach and acts as the goalkeeping specialist for the National Soccer Coaches' Association of America (NSCAA). He conducts US soccer national licensing camps, and has his own goalkeeping camps nationwide. Tony DiCicco's assistant, Lauren Gregg, is an A Licence coach. She was an assistant coach at UNC from 1983 and a national squad player in 1986. She was named National Soccer Coaches' Association of America 'Coach of the Year' in 1990 and became head coach at the University of Virginia in 1985. She was assistant coach to Anson Dorrance when the USA team captured the China World Cup title and was assistant to Tony DiCicco for the World Cup in 1995 and the Olympic Tournament in 1996. After the Olympics she was appointed a full-time assistant national coach by the USSF with special responsibility for the U20 team. At a symposium called 'The Road to Gold', held at the NCAA Division I Championships in Santa Clara in December 1996, Lauren Gregg explained how the USA had successfully prepared for the Olympics. In essence, she said, they learned how to defend using three in a zonal system, and ensured that they were sufficiently technically skilled defenders to start attacks. They also worked hard to gain and retain possession throughout the team and generally had become more tactically aware, so that every player not only knew her position but others' as well. In training they had worked hard on competitive situations with different one-on-one challenges and players had taken responsibility for their own fitness. It will no longer be a surprise to match commentators, as it was in the Olympic final, to see women delivering crosses into the penalty area with spin, swerve and accuracy.

The USA's most experienced female coach is Jan Smisek, who was in the first national team squad selected 'on paper' in 1982, but was not included when the team actually played its first game in 1985. She is, however, the first woman to gain the USSF A Licence coaching award, and in 1989 was voted 'Coach of the

Year' by the Washington State Youth Soccer Association. Since 1992 she has been Region IV (west coast) Olympic Development Program head coach, which involved her making selections and evaluations of all age-group coaches in the region, and developing the curriculum for both players and coaches. In 1996 she left her full-time post as head coach at Evergreen State College to become one of five new U14 coaching coordinators. She is responsible for Region IV's boys' and girls' development.

She explains that she learned the game as a child, when it was new and there were hardly any soccer coaches:

> When I was about 11 years old my brother taught me soccer. I didn't even know what soccer was until I saw him being taught by a neighbour, and then I gave up softball and volleyball and concentrated on soccer. I started coaching little girls of seven to nine years of age but realised I needed to learn how to coach. In 1975, as soon as I was the required age of 18, I went to a week-long coaching clinic. My parents paid for it as a high-school graduation present. I was the only woman on the course, with 40 men. I was apprehensive at first, but after a few days, I was one of the gang.

Jan Smisek's parents were involved in local soccer, as players and referees, and all her brothers and sisters played too. She says,

> In those days none of the college women had played soccer before, but we were attracted to the game because it was so free and spontaneous and it's characterised by finesse and agility rather than brute strength and skull thickness! My problem was that I always had to start up the teams.

She started up a high-school team and an AYSO little league girls' team and was largely responsible for starting a team at University College of Santa Barbara where she studied PE: "by the time I finished at college there were two teams, whereas in my first year we only had one and played just three matches". Jan Smisek has also set up elite summer soccer camps for girls in Washington state and regularly takes trips to England, where she watches as many professional matches as possible:

> Today's players need to watch the game and become exposed to it on a regular basis and then they will embrace the true passion for it and gain the soccer intelligence

necessary to excel. The American player that studies and analyses the game and goes out and plays outside of coach-organised practice is a rarity. When I tell kids stories about all the little games my best friend and I would play, just the two of us and a soccer ball, they think I'm some kind of weirdo ...

Karen Stanley gained her A Licence coaching award in 1991 when injury ended her playing career. She coached Division I college teams at Notre Dame (Indiana) and University of Southern California before moving on to coach at Santa Rosa in northern California. She serves on the NSCAA's Women's Committee.

Former USA captain April Heinrichs finished her career with 38 goals in 47 matches. She had played four years of collegiate soccer at UNC and then went on to gain the USSF A Licence coaching award. She became head coach at the University of Maryland between 1991 and 1995 before replacing Lauren Gregg at Virginia as head coach. After the Olympics, she was made specifically responsible for the U16 national team.

Several of the USA's top male coaches are from England, including professional ex-players Bobby Howe and Clive Charles from West Ham Utd, who both went to the USA when the North American Soccer League was flourishing in the 1960s and 1970s. Clive Charles has been involved with the national U20 women's team and is also head coach of the men's and women's programmes at the University of Portland in Oregon State. He has coached at the regional and state levels, including the U19 Region IV 'Olympic Development Program' girls' team. Bobby Howe was appointed the USSF national coaching education director in 1996, and explained how his coaching career had been built upon the platform provided by Ron Greenwood, his manager at West Ham. In an article in the USSF's magazine, he said 'Soccer is a game of skill, imagination, reactivity and decision making. Coaching should not stifle but enhance those elements ... All coaches must feel that they have an opportunity on the national coaching staff, regardless of gender or ethnic heritage.'[59]

Another Englishman to make his career in the USA is Trevor Warren, who went to the USA in 1981 to study for a masters degree and played collegiate soccer. He stayed on and is now coach for Lock Haven University's, Pennsylvania, women's and men's programme. He is one of several expatriates who returns to England to scout for talented female football players.

Michelle Akers was born in Seattle, but went to the University of Central Florida in Orlando. She started her international soccer career in 1985 against Denmark and then competed for three seasons in Sweden's national league, with Tyreso, in 1990, 1992 and 1994. Ex-husband Robbie Stahl managed the team and together they took Tyreso to the league championship in 1992. In the same year she scored 43 goals, making her leading scorer, male or female, in the whole country. Up to and including the 1996 Olympic final she had gained 109 caps and scored 92 goals. Michelle has received many awards in football, including the 'Athlete of the Year' by the United States Olympic Committee in 1990 and 1991. She is employed by the USSF and kit sponsors Reebok, for whom she works on promotional activities. She is welcomed as a VIP at top football occasions and was one of the main guests of honour at the men's World Cup Final in the USA in 1994, where she sat with famous ex-player and Brazilian Minister for Sport, Pele. As well as maintaining a demanding physical fitness regime, she also finds time to work as one of the USSF's directors and runs her own soccer camps throughout the USA. Although she is acclaimed internationally, she recognises there is still much to do to improve the opportunities of all women involved in football. She was particularly impressed with the reception she received in Europe, at the inaugural FIFA Women's Football Seminar in Zurich in 1992:

> It was extremely flattering to be recognised and greeted with respect by the many FIFA officials and international dignitaries. I received numerous words of praise about my performance and our team's accomplishments in China. This was a refreshing change compared to the lack of attention and recognition we receive in the United States, even at times from our own federation.[60]

Michelle Akers strikes a balance between the media and sponsors, while taking the opportunity to remind people that there is still a lot of development work to do before the game's full potential is realised. She is currently writing a book *Standing Fast*, due out in 1997.[61]

Colleague Julie Foudy is another veteran of the 1991 China team. She became interested in soccer at the age of seven and joined a local AYSO league. She progressed on to the Olympic Development Program at the age of 13. She played in the Swedish national league for one season in 1994 and now has a professional contract with the USSF.

After playing in her first match against China in 1987, Mia Hamm made her one hundred and twentieth international appearance at the 1996 Olympics aged 25. On the field, the former UNC college star proved herself to be an outstanding athlete and technician and brought her international goal tally to 63. Off the field she is equally outstanding as an ambassador for the game, appearing in major newspapers and magazines and performing on television for CNN and ESPN. She was also the USSF 1996 'Female Athlete of the Year' for the third year in succession. Other leading players are defenders Carla Overbeck, who gained her hundredth cap in the Olympic final, Joy Fawcett, 96 caps, Carin Gabarra, 98 caps, and forwards Tiffeny Milbrett and Shannon MacMillan.

All the leading players are signed up with sponsorship deals. At public occasions, such as the four-day-long NSCAA conventions, the national players have longer queues for autographs than the leading male players and it is common to see posters of the women in action. Despite the fact the American squad is sponsored by Nike, Julie Foudy was in England promoting Reebok's women's boot in 1994. Like other players, she receives a salary in return for wearing the sponsor's kit and appearing at functions and soccer schools.

The 'professionalism' of the USA team was displayed when nine senior players negotiated new contracts with the USSF prior to the Olympics, ignoring the fact that they risked losing their places in the squad. After the Olympic success the USSF confirmed that in the past two years approximately £2.5 to £3 million had been invested in the team. This included full-time pay for the players and £1,600 bonuses to the players' 'pool'.[62] Anne Moses, from the Women's Soccer Foundation, feels that the most important aspect was the symbolic nature of the agreement: 'the USSF and the women's national team players are dependent on each other; neither can reach their fullest potential without the help of the other'.[63]

The remaining challenge for the USSF is to provide a competitive national major league soccer competition for women players. Outside the training camps, the only way for women to prepare for playing at the international level is to join a foreign league, or follow Kristine Lilly's example of playing in men's indoor competitions.

Due to the lack of competitive women's teams in her area, ex-UNC player Kristine Lilly went to play for the Washington Warthogs in the Washington Indoor Soccer League. Her coach is Jim Gabarra, husband of her national team colleague Carin. Kristine explained: 'The indoor game is so fast, it helps my quickness, especially as the guys are always a step ahead in quickness and strength.'[64] Without the possibility of major-league soccer for women in the future, Tiffeny Milbrett and Shannon MacMillan have already gone to play in the Japanese league.

Media

Media coverage of women's soccer in the USA is, compared to that of some European countries, very good. *USA Today* usually carries news of the national team's matches and developments in the women's game, although incredibly the paper ignored their Olympic success. There are numerous publications, such as *Soccer Journal*, the official publication of the National Soccer Coaches' Association of America, as well as commercial magazines such as *Soccer America*. *Soccer America* has been published for over 23 years and although aimed mainly at the male market, it usually has at least one page of women's soccer results and features. *Soccer JR* for girls and boys includes features on women players and coaching tips. The first edition of *Women's Soccer World* appeared in January 1997 and covers all aspects of the women's game around the world.

In view of the large participation rates, the exposure of women's football on television has not been as great as might have been expected. All soccer has to struggle to compete for viewing time with traditional American male games such as American football, baseball and basketball, and women's golf, tennis and basketball receive greater coverage than women's soccer. A few of the top collegiate soccer matches, including the NCAA Championship, have been shown on television in recent years, and the national team has received coverage during important competitions. The problem has been the fact that transmission of women's soccer has been by the cable station ESPN 1, which does not cover the whole of America. Even victory in the Olympic Tournament did not receive nationwide TV coverage, as the television companies were more concerned with the traditional track and field events and basketball.

The Women's Soccer Foundation

The USA has many volunteers working at all levels to improve standards and opportunities and the most successful organisation is the Women's Soccer Foundation, founded in 1989. It is dedicated to strengthening the voice of girls and women in soccer and improving their opportunities as participants and leaders worldwide. It's a non-profit-making organisation which relies on annual contributions and on volunteers to staff projects. It has an information resource, as well as producing an eight-page quarterly newsletter, 'Network', which is concerned with girls' and women's soccer at local, regional, national and international level. There are numerous regular contributors from all over the world. An 'International Leadership' Conference was held in Seattle in December 1993, with delegates from Europe and New Zealand. Meetings were held at the two World Championships in China and Sweden, at which well-known female leaders from different countries shared their experiences. At the Olympics the foundation held a meeting called 'Past Struggles and Future Challenges: an International Look at Women's Soccer Programs'. Guest speakers included Karen Espelund of the Norwegian FA executive, Xanthi Konstaninidou from Greece and Marilyn Childress and Gail Turbyville from Georgia. They were welcomed by Larry Monaco, executive vice-president of US Soccer, who spoke about US Soccer's plans for hosting the 1999 Women's World Cup. The WSF sponsors a World Wide Web homepage on the Internet (http://www.cris.com/~jg198/wsf) with women's soccer information.

WALES

Population: 3 million (1995)
Governing body: The Football Association of Wales (FAW),
Plymouth Chambers, 3 Westgate Street, Cardiff, CF1 1DD.[65]

Landmarks

1973 – First international match v. Republic of Ireland.
1976 – Participated in the first home International Championship.
1978 – Participated in Italian Tournament.
1993 – FAW took responsibility for women's football.
    – Entered European Championships.
    – Formation of new women's Celtic League for inexperienced
players.

Participation and development

Rugby is the national game of Wales and in the past most Welsh
sporting heroes have been rugby players. In the 1920s and 1930s
when women's factory teams were evolving Dick, Kerr Ladies
played in southern Wales against teams from Swansea and Cardiff.
Because of the ban on women using men's football grounds the
matches were played on rugby pitches. On 29 March 1921, 18,000
spectators turned up at the famous Cardiff Arms Park ground to
watch Dick, Kerr Ladies play the local Cardiff women's team.

    The development of a league and club structure has been slow
and over the years most of the serious players have chosen to play
in the English leagues. There are now two senior leagues (Pembroke
and Celtic) and two U16 leagues (Pembroke U16 five-a-side and
South Wales U16 11-a-side). The Welsh Sports Council has funded
two coaching development posts and there are now two Welsh
male coaches, one responsible for North Wales, the other for
South Wales, working under the FAW director of coaching.

Players and the national team

The most successful clubs in Wales are Inter Cardiff and Barry,
which play in the stronger English South-West League, which was
won by Barry in 1996. The Cardiff team has junior sections and
is run by a well-structured committee, some of whom are current
and ex-players. FAW Preliminary Award coach, Michele Adams,

who retired as an international team captain at the end of 1994–95 with 28 caps, is Inter Cardiff's senior team coach. Karen Jones, who is chair of the club, played for Wales in the 1970s and did not retire until 1995. Laura McAllister joined Inter Cardiff in 1993, became captain of the side, and in the same year gained her first Welsh cap. The club has developed young talent but has been unable to keep it. Kathryn Morgan, an international player at 18, signed for rivals Barry, and Georgina Adams, also at the age of 18, decided to combine football with study by going to Pennsylvania's Lock Haven University for the 1996–97 season.[66]

The international team had no support until the FAW took over in 1993. Between 1980 and 1989 only ten internationals were played, all against UK teams. Ex-international England player Sylvia Gore managed the team from 1982 to 1989 but resigned because she was unable to go on supporting the team financially, having already spent £5,000 of her own money. There were no more matches for the international team until 1993, when the secretary and the chief executive, Alun Evans, together with administrator Helen Croft, entered the team into the European Championship with disastrous results.

A manager of a men's team, Lyn Jones took charge of the team during the 1993–94 European Championship campaign. However, with only two training weekends and a friendly match against Iceland, the team was unable to cope with the much higher fitness and overall skill of the other European teams. They twice lost to Germany 12–0, Switzerland 3–2 and 4–2, and Croatia 3–0 and 2–1. After a defeat by the Republic of Ireland in June 1994, Lyn Jones resigned his post and in August Alun Evans also left the FAW. Before his departure Alun appointed me to take over as the new manager in September 1995. From trials, organised by coaching staff at the FAW, I finalised a squad of 16 players to enter a team for the European Championship of 1995–97. The lack of preparation time and general poor state of fitness meant that Wales struggled in the first three games. In the opening game against the Republic of Ireland at Llanelli on 8 October 1995, Wales lost 3–0. In a match against the Faroe Islands, at Bangor on 25 October, Wales were unlucky to lose 1–0 after having 20 shots at goal. This highlighted the problems – there were few players of international standard and some of these were out due to injury. Wales next played Belgium away on 18 November 1995 and lost 2–0. To address the obvious fitness problems I arranged, soon after the first match, for the Welsh Institute of Sports Science to set up a fitness monitoring programme in December and an U25 training day in November. I also located and introduced Welsh players from the English Premier League who had not attended the trials. Often Welsh players who played for English clubs could not get released for Welsh training days and in some cases I found that players did not even know that a Welsh team existed. Despite losing a key defender, who could not be released from work, the return match against the Irish in Dublin proved to be a turning point and the Welsh side scored their first goal for several matches, although they lost 5–1. When they met Scotland in March 1996 the teamwork had improved and their fitness monitoring had been effective and they won 5–1. In the two remaining games Wales lost 3–2 to Scotland on 2 June 1996 but beat the Faroe Islands 1–0 on 5 June. They finished their group in fourth place.

Just before the first Scotland match I found I no longer had the time to oversee the team. The Hampshire FA offered to make my part-time coaching appointment a full-time position but with the proviso that I did not continue as manager of the Welsh side. The FAW was unable to offer me paid employment and I reluctantly resigned. The coach for South Wales subsequently took over my post. Both the South Wales and North Wales coaches have concentrated their work on girls' football, rather than women's, and there is now a national U16 squad. With the total responsibility of girls' and women's football under the FAW, there is an opportunity for a complete development structure which should help raise standards.

9 Blowing the whistle

The 1921 ban not only stopped women's teams from using FA-affiliated pitches but also barred FA officials from officiating. The well-known teams from the early period, such as Dick, Kerr Ladies and Manchester Corinthians, frequently obtained the services of professional players and retired referees, who were only too pleased to help. The presence of famous players gave the spectators a chance to see their Saturday heroes in the unusual role of referee and their presence also provided some backing for the women's sport. During the second boom in women's football in the 1960s, women's teams struggled to overcome the difficulties of the lack of suitable pitches, poor finance and sufficient numbers of volunteers to help organise and officiate; men who were involved as managers would find themselves having to referee their home matches and run the line for the away matches. Once the ban was rescinded, county FAs could be approached to appoint referees but, unfortunately, sometimes there were insufficient referees to cater for both women's and men's matches. This situation could have been alleviated if more women had been allowed to referee FA-affiliated football. The first qualified woman referee, Mrs Pat Dunn from Weymouth, was just one of 29 qualified women referees in 1974. However, these women were not allowed to go on to official county referee lists and could only register with the WFA to referee women's matches. Therefore, the FA were allowing women to train to become officials and then not fully recognising them once they were trained. This situation prevailed until 1975, when the Sex Discrimination Act was introduced, and the FA were forced to accept women refereeing all football matches. There were two major firsts for Women Class I (top scale) referees in the 1980s. In October 1981 Elizabeth Forsdick became the first woman line official for a men's FA Cup tie and in February 1989 Kim George became the first woman to referee a men's FA Cup tie, a preliminary-round match between two non-league men's clubs.[1] The most well-known referee is Dorset FA registered Wendy Toms. She became the first woman to referee a senior men's match when she took charge of the Vauxhall Conference League game between Woking and Telford on 31 August 1996. Then on 26 October 1996 three women officiated a senior men's match for the first time when referee Linda Bailey and referee's assistants Anne Smart and Karen Ford officiated a match between Broomfield Utd and Kent University in a Kent County League match.[2]

It would have seemed ideal for women referees to gain experience by officiating women's matches, especially in view of the dearth of qualified referees for all football games. Instead, young, inexperienced men were frequently appointed to referee women's matches. From the observations of some of the Southampton women's team players, who between 1971 and 1981 appeared in ten national WFA cup finals – and several of whom played at international level – these inexperienced officials would sometimes be quite surprised at the competitiveness of female players, and problems would arise because they adopted a too lenient attitude. England international players had been able to have top male officials for international matches since 1972 but even some of the more experienced referees had a rather paternalistic and avuncular style when refereeing women's games. Naive defenders could often get away with mistimed tackles and left the skilled players feeling unprotected.

The development of organised competitions under the WFA, and closer links with the FA, led to the later stages of the WFA Cup, and Premier League, formed in 1991–92, being officiated by some of the top male FA officials. When the FA took over women's football in 1993, the Referees' Department of the FA appointed match officials for the FA's Challenge Cup and Premier League games.

For county-level matches, referees indicate their availability and therefore can avoid women's or boys' matches. When the FA started making appointments for the women's Premier League matches, there was a recognition that some officials were not keen to officiate women's games and the FA's referees' secretary suggested that, for the 1995–96 season, county FA referees' secretaries compile a list of those who *were* willing to do so. In view of the difficulty in recruiting referees, it is all the more urgent that women are encouraged to become officials. Officials at women's matches do not usually encounter the problems of abusive language and violent behaviour sometimes found at men's and boys' matches. In general, there is less touchline disruption and the purely amateur nature of the women's game means it does not have the intensity associated with the male professional game, with players' and managers' jobs at stake.

John Williams wrote a report in 1994 on issues emerging around the role of the referee, as well as an account of a 'pilot' survey of Class I and Class II referees from Birmingham County FA.[3] In this report Williams alludes to a Granada TV documentary programme *Out of Order* when a top referee, David Elleray, was wired up for sound and many of the comments from the professional players on the pitch had to be bleeped out because of their abusive nature. Williams suggests that the level of violence experienced at matches outside the professional and semi-professional male leagues is perhaps worse and comments: 'The matter of violence and abuse aimed at referees, and the associated difficulties involved in recruiting sufficient numbers of officials to keep pace with the extraordinary growth in the numbers playing the game at this level in recent years, remains critical.'[4] The problem for referees is not only in dealing with the players but also the parents at youth matches who exhibit unruly behaviour. The negative influence of some adults at youth games has become an area of major concern, not only for the FA but also for UEFA and FIFA. At UEFA's Youth Conference, held in Stavanger, Norway in February and March 1995, there was a recognition of the need to address the problem and find ways of bringing about more responsible adult leadership in football.

Given that there are difficulties for officials of male matches, it is perhaps surprising that in my small survey of female referees several women said they preferred refereeing men's and boys' football. Refereeing is demanding, and not particularly financially rewarding, especially compared to the high salaries of some professional players. All football officiating is still an amateur activity, whereby only expenses are paid, plus a small fee, and therefore referees need full-time employment. The poor remuneration, the hazards of being a referee, and bearing in mind that referees have to retire from top-class refereeing at 50, and at 45 for international duties, mean it is almost inevitable that there are recruitment problems. While most local referees are ex-non-league players, few ex-professional players go on to become referees.

There is little historical material relating to women officials and given the belated acceptance of women playing the game, by the FA, it is no wonder that female officials should similarly have been held back. It is still a fairly new occupation for women. In 1980, only 22 county FAs had registered women referees. In 1981 there were eight Class I referees registered and by 1995 this had increased to 20. Even by 1990, there were still two county FAs which were registering their *first* women referees. In 1991 the FA's Referees' Department sent out a survey to find out more about women referees at each county FA, but ten out of the 41 county FAs did not reply and the survey was not completed. My own county of Hampshire is one of the highest trainers of referees and registered their first women in the early 1980s. The total number of registered referees in Hampshire for 1995–96 was: Class I, 402; Class II, 201; and Class III, 1000, making a total of 1603. Out of these 55 were women, only one of whom is Class I and three Class II. For the 1996–97 season only 35 of these women registered and the total number of men and women referees registered is 1347, 256 down on the previous season.

Williams found, in his 1994 study of 463 referees in the West Midlands, that only 0.4 per cent of the respondents were women. In his opinion, women find it difficult to take up officiating because married women, in particular, tend to adopt weekend child-care, and other domestic responsibilities, which limits their leisure time. In the study, 43 per cent of the respondents thought women should be encouraged to take up refereeing and 30 per cent said they would encourage their daughter to take it up. However, 24 per cent disagreed with women becoming referees and 41 per cent disagreed with their daughter taking it up.[5]

In 1995, the FA's strategy document, 'Women and Football', details a successful pilot scheme of 'women-only' courses for the training of match officials, set up by the FA's Referees Department and Coaching and Education Department, along with the county FAs. It is hoped that this will become general practice. Williams feels that progress in encouraging women referees has been and will continue to be slow even though forward-looking county FAs will be starting up their own 'women-only' refereeing courses, and considering other ways of attracting more female recruits. He believes county FAs need to examine the extent to which their image and activities operate, consciously or otherwise, to exclude or discourage women from involvement in the game as match officials. His views concur with those of Lord Justice Taylor, as expressed in the 'Hillsborough Stadium Disaster Report', 1990, that the presence of women in the football environment will help 'socialise' the male. Taylor, of course, referred to their presence on the terraces as spectators, helping to ameliorate poor crowd behaviour, while Williams sees female referees helping in the general development of young players. He also recognises the need for more female role models at the higher level of the game. At present, there is little chance of potential female referees being encouraged by seeing others work. Williams laments that fact that the FA's document 'The Blueprint for the Future of Football', published in June 1991, mentioned the need for a research and development programme to collect and analyse data concerning refereeing but there were no funds allocated to pursue such a programme. Such research might have thrown some light on the lack of female officials and their needs.

There are serious issues relating to female officials that need investigation, such as: overcoming some the residual prejudice that creates barriers for women; the need for more women trainers; and the allocation of mentors to provide experience and support through the early years. Other aspects to be considered are more general, such as: access to leisure time for officiating; being able to keep fit; access to transport; and overcoming financial constraints. Less serious, but all the same an issue, is the need for female changing facilities.

International comparison

In recent years FIFA has started to address the problems of female officials. In 1996, FIFA decided to rename the position of linesman as 'referee's assistant', which not only overcomes the gender bias in terminology but also, in their opinion, reflects the greater responsibility that linespersons have in a match – and it is a term that has been adopted by all concerned. Developments in certain countries, such as Sweden and Norway, have significantly advanced the interests and opportunities of women referees. Sweden set up a ten-year plan in collaboration with other Scandinavian countries, aimed at guaranteeing instruction and training, in order to produce a sufficient number of women referees. The first match to be refereed by a woman, with FIFA's authorisation, was between Sweden and Norway in 1985, and it also included two female referee's assistants. The return fixture also had three female officials. Nevertheless, it has not been easy – even in the Scandinavian countries – for women to gain access to the male domain of officiating. According to Lars-Ake Bjorck, a member of FIFA's referees' committee: 'Opposition was considerable, even in their own ranks, as they frequently expressed more confidence in male referees as opposed to female.'[6] The problem, he felt, was that: 'Instruction and training for referees was geared towards male referees, that is to say, the related programmes at the time were conceived by men for men. No wonder, then, that women couldn't succeed!'[7] In 1989, FIFA organised, in conjunction with Norway, a course of instruction specifically for women referees and this opened the door to an international refereeing career. One of the participants was Ingrid Jonsson, who was a referee's assistant at the FIFA Women's World Cup Final in China in 1991 and refereed the FIFA Women's World Cup Final in Sweden in 1995. She set up special courses and training programmes for women referees and, to date, Sweden has approximately 1,000 women referees, largely because of her initiative.

Bente Skogvang, an ex-international Norwegian player, has been Norway's leading female official since 1986, and has also played a key role in encouraging more females into officiating. Since 1980, Bente has found little difficulty in combining playing at the top level and refereeing, and only in 1989 did she decide to concentrate more on her refereeing role. She decided to play for the 'old girls' league – a predominantly recreational league, for 28-year-old players and over. She became the first female to referee a Norwegian FA Women's Cup Final in 1986. A year later, she refereed her first international match and in 1995 she was placed on FIFA's list of international female officials. She was a referee in the 1995 World Cup in Sweden, and officiated at the Atlanta Olympic Women's Football tournament final in 1996. In Norway she is one of 11 female referees at the highest grade and she can referee level 2 and 3 senior men's matches and level 1 and 2 female matches. The 11 female referees also include another FIFA referee and four FIFA referee's assistants. Despite Bente's achievements as a referee, and as a referee inspector and instructor, she discloses that she has found, even in Norway, that it has been difficult to break into the male-dominated refereeing world: "We still don't have the same status as male referees, and we have to follow 'the male rules'. We also have to be better than men if we want to referee at the same level as they do in men's games.

Because, since 1986, I have been the number-one female referee, I have broken through many, many, barriers."

Sonia Denoncourt is from Quebec, and is presently considered, along with Ingrid Jonsson and Bente Skogvang, one of the top female referees in the world. She has achieved some notable 'firsts': first woman on FIFA's list, first Canadian woman to officiate as a referee's assistant in a professional men's premier division match; first to referee a men's game in the professional North American Soccer League; and first woman referee to gain the 'Referee of the Year Award' in Canada in 1995. Sonia has a BEd in PE and a masters degree in sports administration. While studying she became involved in participating in basketball, football and ice hockey, and captained most of the teams in which she played. This meant: "I had to deal with referees all the time, and I always respected them even if I thought they were wrong!" Sonia qualified as a referee at the age of 14 and since the age of 16 has become seriously involved in officiating. She says she really loves refereeing, and decided at 14 to make the choice between refereeing and playing:

> I loved the challenge of the game. I like the enormous ability that a referee must have to be successful. We need a lot of concentration, physical fitness, ability to read the game, and know the intentions of the player. We have to be strong, and have a good personality, as well as a good knowledge of the laws of the game, and be able to apply fair play, protect the players – and every game is a different challenge.

She says that it is a great advantage to have played the game and to understand everyone's role in the team, but admits she owes much to the support of Dino Soupliotis, a former FIFA referee and now a FIFA instructor, who took her seriously and decided to help her get to the top:

> He follows my career and progress and is the most influential person in my success now. He is a sort of 'soccer-dad'. He acts as my father and is always on my back, pushing me to work, train and referee as much as possible. Soccer must be the first activity all the time, even before work, family or anything else.

She certainly doesn't referee for the remuneration and, in 18 years of refereeing, feels she has probably spent more money than she has gained. She does get paid all her expenses for food, lodging and travel, and she was pleased to say that FIFA look after their referees very well. Sonia believes the most difficult obstacle for women referees is having to deal with the gender factor:

> I am a woman in a man's world, so far, and have to be a lot better than the majority of men to be able to perform and have my chance to referee a big game. It is the same in society with any other non-traditional business or role ... The difficulties for women to become referees are enormous. In general, refereeing is demanding anyway, but we have also to fight against the fact that we are a minority so there are insufficient role models as referees, coaches and administrators. Women also have the problem of having to build a family, pregnancy, and the lack of money in women's sports, compared to men's.

Sonia feels that it is easier to make progress in more egalitarian countries like Sweden, Denmark and Norway, and more recently Canada, because women are encouraged and because there are "men and women with political power who have pushed the women's referee programmes to develop more women referees".

Sonia was a guest speaker at the FIFA Symposium in Prague in November 1995 and addressed some gender issues in refereeing. She reminded her audience that, generally speaking, women's football is similar to men's football, the main difference being in physical strength and power, but that differences should not be used as barriers to women's football development. The barriers have been, and still are, more to do with social and cultural constraints peculiar to each country. She said with specific reference to refereeing:

> Psychologically and behaviourally, men and women may react differently, but two people of the same gender may also react differently, and therefore there should be no difference between the sexes and especially no discrimination ... If the same physical performance and refereeing skills are required from men and women, shouldn't the latter also be able to perform at international level? The discomfort lies mainly in accepting a social change and seeing a woman in a role traditionally reserved for men. But are there any valid reasons why a woman cannot accomplish the same task?

Certainly Sonia has wholeheartedly accepted the responsibility of being an international role model, and it is hoped that other female referees can learn from her.

FIFA competitions

FIFA organised the first women's world tournament in Quangzouo, China, in 1988 – a competition that was seen as an unofficial 'World Cup'. FIFA went on to organise the inaugural Women's World Cup, again in China, in 1991, and for the first time six female officials were appointed. All of these acted as referee's assistants, except for Claudia Vasconcelos Guedes of Brazil, who refereed the game played for third place, and became the first women to referee a FIFA competition.

In 1994 FIFA's referees' committee introduced an official list for international women referees and referee's assistants, with 26 referees and 31 referee's assistants, and agreed that the 1995 final of the Women's World Cup in Sweden would be refereed by a woman. Six male and six female referees, as well six of each gender who acted as referee's assistants, officiated at the 26 matches. The opening match was refereed by Sonia Denoncourt, together with two female referee's assistants. Ingrid Jonsson of Sweden became the first woman to referee an official FIFA championship final, and two women ran the line – Gitte Holm of Denmark and Maria Del Socorro of Mexico. For the Atlanta Olympics FIFA appointed eight female referees out of a total of 16. There is also the possibility that a female referee and referee's assistant will be appointed for the next men's World Cup in France in 1998. FIFA's register of international referees in 1996 lists a total of 40 women referees and 45 female referee's assistants. The following countries have two international women referees: Denmark, Germany, Italy, Norway, Sweden, Trinidad and Tobago. Brazil has four. England, Scotland, Northern Ireland, the Republic of Ireland and Wales have none.

Recruitment and training in England

According to Lars-Ake Bjorck, the biggest difference between a good referee and an excellent one is in the number of national league and international matches he or she referees and, therefore, it is important that more women gain this type of experience.

It may also be encouraging for women to know that evidence has suggested that they generally obtain better fitness results than their male colleagues. This is tested on the Cooper 12-minute run – a recognised way of assessing basic aerobic fitness.

The FA referees' department has total responsibility for the training of all referee instructors through national courses held each year to produce FA-licensed instructors. Area advisers are appointed to liaise and support referee instructors as required through elected county FA training officers. Within each county there should be local training officers, responsible for the training and recruitment of referees for local youth and adult leagues.

In Hampshire, referees are mostly recruited from youth leagues, where clubs are encouraged to provide at least two qualified people when they register their club. Hampshire trained approximately 300 referees in 1995, about half of whom were recruited from youth leagues. Women are not specifically targeted but an article in the local newspaper's 'women's page' about a newly-qualified woman referee did create some interest. The FA encourages training of referees by offering an incentive payment to county FAs of £2 for each newly-qualified referee and a further £5 retention bonus if the referee registers for a third season. The incentive and bonus payments are paid into the county FA's account to be used in any way they wish.

Referees' courses are organised at county level. In Hampshire the course lasts for 20 hours and the cost, for the trainee, varies between £7 and 15, depending on which branch of the Referees' Association the applicant applies to. The fee includes the provision of all instruction material and books, examination and registration costs. The course lasts for ten weeks, including a final oral and written examination to demonstrate knowledge and application of the laws of Association Football. Newly-qualified referees who are 16 years of age or over are issued with a certificate of registration as a Class III referee. Successful candidates over 14 years and under 16 years are registered as Class III (Youth) referees and officiate only in youth competitions. Assessors watch and report on the performance of the referees during matches and, in this way, referees are considered for promotion to the next class. Also each club rates the referee's performance after each game. Promotion committees decide on the suitability of referees for advancement from the recommendations of assessors and club marking. If the referee is receiving several less than satisfactory assessments, he or she will be assigned a mentor. It usually takes two or three years to get promotion. Normally, newly-qualified referees control only junior games. Once a referee becomes Class I, he or she would progress, for example, in Hampshire through to matches in the following order: Hampshire League, Wessex, Southern, Conference, Football League, Premier League, FIFA international. Each time they would first run the line and then be appointed referee. All referees have to register each season with the county FA within whose area they reside. In Hampshire it costs £8 to register and this includes insurance cover during, and travelling to and from, the match. The FA have recommended for the 1997–98 season a standard national fee of £7 for all classifications. Although professional and semi-professional league referees have to retire at the age of 50 for domestic competitions, there is no age limit for refereeing in local leagues. Referees can register with other county associations on payment of a further registration fee.

The FA recommends that every referee should join the local branch of the Referees' Association. There are over 300 branches of this association throughout England, Wales and Northern Ireland, and their basic function is to look after the interests of the referee. The local branches hold regular meetings where newly-qualified referees can meet experienced referees who can assist with problems. These meetings can take the form of instructional evenings, as well as social gatherings. The FA issues a booklet, 'Advice for Newly Qualified Referees', which includes information on match procedures, physical fitness and training, assessment and promotion, as well as advice on report writing, and a check-list for self-criticism.

Refereeing in England

Many of the women referees I questioned during the course of writing this book came from a footballing and sporting background, either as players themselves or because they had close male friends, or relatives, involved as referees, players and managers. These men encouraged the women's involvement in the first place, and have subsequently supported them. This acceptance and support seems vital in helping the women cope with officiating in a male environment – especially in dealing with the offputting verbal abuse of players and spectators. It is apparent that most women prefer the perceived higher standard, and higher status, of male adult games, and enjoy male youth games.

While women's football does not have the same level of abuse from the players or spectators, it is mostly seen by these officials as low-status, of a poor standard, and, basically not likely to lead to their own promotion.[8]

Jill (aged 32) qualified as a referee in 1988, began as a referee's assistant, and progressed to Class II. She wants to progress further but has to look after the children on Saturdays while her husband plays, so she is content for the time being officiating at the lower-standard Sunday games and U18 boys' youth matches. She said she enjoyed refereeing all matches but finds women's football more difficult to follow because the standard is not as high and therefore the flow of the game is unpredictable. She is very strict about foul or abusive language and will not tolerate it from men or women players. Men sometimes challenge her authority but, on the other hand, she believes that many of them are more careful about using abusive language in front of a woman.

Nina (aged 16) qualified in 1995. She likes watching football but laments some of the bad behaviour of players. In one of her matches, she had to send two players off, and then had to abandon the game because some of the other players started fighting. She said, in general, the boys' teams are enjoyable to referee but some of them give you 'a lot of mouth' and this could be unsettling.

Sarah (aged 23) qualified at the beginning of the 1993–94 season. She hopes to progress to Class I. She said she finds it difficult juggling her time between running a team and refereeing other matches – this could be as many as one or two midweek and two or three on Sundays. Her preference is to referee 14-year-old boys and above, as she becomes impatient with younger boys, but dislikes the presence of abusive parents at youth matches. She finds the main problem in refereeing is the foul and abusive language from men, but thinks they are less intimidating than the parents at youth matches. She finds that the women's game flows less well than men's or boys'.

Carol (aged 28) became a qualified referee in 1995, and obtained a coaching certificate, having given up playing football due to a back injury. Carol says she loves football but also finds time for volleyball, swimming and cycling. Her boyfriend is also a referee. She referees every week, usually Saturday afternoons in a men's league, and enjoys refereeing adults more than boys because adult football is more challenging. Her main problems come from abusive parents at boys' youth matches, although she finds that men question decisions and complain quite a lot – a lot more than women. Carol admits to being stricter with women.

Jean (aged 25) qualified in 1994, having been persuaded to take the course by her father. Although she found the training and exam relatively easy, after watching some matches she realised she would be incapable of actually officiating at a match because of her lack of knowledge of playing. Not feeling confident, she didn't think she could handle the abuse referees received. She regrets that she was not offered the opportunity to referee women's matches, with which she would have been more comfortable.

Sandra (aged 33) admits to loving the game, particularly as refereeing allows her to be involved without having to play. She referees on Saturdays and Sundays for two or three weekends per month, or when her responsibility to her young family allows. She hopes to progress and works hard at her fitness. She has found the county FA training officers supportive but feels information could be more accessible. The worst problems for her are people who complain about her decisions, and she regrets that male referees don't always take women's football seriously.

Vera (aged 34) is another woman who plays football but has also found time to referee. She has been Class I since 1988 and attends her local Referees' Association functions. She became involved in officiating to learn more about the laws of the game while she was still playing. She prefers to referee men's football because the standard is higher. She finds that boys tend to listen more whereas women players tend to be friendly but their game is more 'difficult to read'.

Sheila Parker (aged 49) qualified at a Lancashire County FA training course in 1984, and started refereeing because she wanted to remain involved with football after retiring from her illustrious career as the first England captain and a player for some of the finest women's clubs. She is now able to concentrate fully on refereeing but when she first started officiating she admits she sometimes watched the game instead. At one England women's friendly match, she forgot she was refereeing, and when the players broke away to warm up, she joined them, until she suddenly realised she should be calling up the captains to start the match! She currently officiates youth football matches because a back problem prevents her from being mobile enough to referee men's football. She admitted that she sometimes found the high level of verbal abuse from parents at youth matches very off-putting. The support of the Chorley Referees' Association is important to her and she says, 'it's like being in a family', and when all the changes occurred in the laws of the game in the 1995–96 season it was useful to her to be able to refer to the association for help. Lancashire FA has a few other women referees, including one 18-year-old, who has never played football. Sheila believes it's important to have played. She was sure that the poor attitude of players has become worse and that many of the problems stem from seeing professionals behave badly on TV, and not being properly disciplined. Another problem is male referees who treat women players with greater leniency, particularly when they refuse to penalise handball. She says, "They feel women players are only protecting their face or chests, and can't see that some are actually gaining the advantage by using their hands."

Obviously, the exclusion of women for so long from the traditional male football culture has made it difficult for women to become involved, even in the necessary service of refereeing, which is in desperate need of recruits. While county FAs, such as Hampshire, should be commended for leading the way in encouraging more women to train for refereeing, there remain areas that need addressing. We need better promotion of courses, more women training officers, and more 'women-only' courses. Once qualified, women referees may need extra support, as Sheila Parker illustrated. The question of abusive players and supporters is of concern to all administrators, but there needs to be a special awareness that it must be offputting to some women – especially the less experienced. As the women's game continues to expand, serious consideration of these issues is required to attract more women into refereeing. The FA referees' secretary suggested to me that another way by which women referees can gain more experience is to attend international courses of instruction, run by the FA and FIFA, every two years, at Lilleshall National Sports Centre. Such courses give referees the opportunity to meet and learn from the top officials in the world. Perhaps the FA should consider launching a recruitment campaign targeting women ex-players, as there are many who wish to continue their involvement with the game beyond their playing days. Football authorities have been emphasising 'Fair Play' codes of practice by players. It must be hoped too that there will be more emphasis on fair play for those women aspiring to be officials and those trying to progress up the career ladder. It is encouraging to recall

Sonia Denoncourt's concluding remarks at the FIFA Symposium, when she said:

> More national associations are registering female players and female leagues (188 national associations out of 191 affiliated to FIFA), the media are giving women's football greater attention, and football is the team sport that is the most practised by women worldwide – the figures speak for themselves.

10 Support from the stands

The Sir Norman Chester Centre for Football Research fact sheet, 'The History of Female Football Fans', refers to evidence of women being permitted free entrance to some professional club grounds in the late nineteenth century until the privilege was abolished at Preston in 1885, 'after an Easter Monday game at which some two thousand women and girls were alleged to have been present'.[1] At the 1927 Cup Final, the press noted that 'a remarkable feature was the women who had accompanied their husbands and sweethearts' to the game.[2] And, according to research, the time between the two world wars saw Brentford FC gain so much female support that they became known as the 'ladies' team'.[3] In *Football and Its Fans*, Rogan Taylor recounts the role female fans played in the 1930s and 1950s organising charity matches and fundraising for clubs – including 'beauty contests' which were staged to encourage more support, presumably from men.[4]

Little interest was taken in football fans until violence and safety standards at matches focused attention upon them. The three most significant events involving English fans were: the riot at the Heysel Stadium in Belgium in 1985, which led to the death of 39 of Liverpool and Juventus supporters; the fire at Bradford City's ground in 1985; and the 95 fans crushed to death at Sheffield Wednesday's Hillsborough ground in April 1989. The Popplewell Report (1986) was the first piece of major research on the subject of fans.[5] Popplewell commissioned research for his enquiry from the University of Surrey and it involved interviews with 1,000 football attenders – none of those interviewed was female.[6] Ignorance of the existence of female fans at the grounds of professional football clubs was widespread. When the secretary of the FA, Ted Croker – renowned for his dislike of women playing football – launched the FA's 'Friends of Football' campaign in 1986, according to Williams and Woodhouse, it focused:

on the 'family' and highlighted young boys who play football, fathers who take their sons to matches, and mothers who, dutifully, wash the dirty football kit. The campaign was scrapped almost instantaneously ... contra to the FA's ideas about the 'proper' role of women as football's backroom staff, women spectators on average probably made up between 10–15 per cent of football crowds in the 1980s.[7]

Attitudes towards women's involvement in football slowly began to change as a result of the Heysel tragedy in 1985. Debates within government and football circles began to focus on the need of attracting a new kind of football supporter and, in particular, on the importance of bringing 'families' into the game. Lord Justice Taylor's report, following the Hillsborough disaster in 1989, recommended that women could play an important role in 'civilising' potentially volatile male football crowds.[8] Opportunities opened up for voluntary or part-time women workers to be employed with 'family enclosures', creches, and in the growing commercial activities of clubs. A small number of clubs, including Arsenal and Millwall, involved women in the Professional Footballers' Association (PFA)/Football League community programmes. Arsenal even took steps to include women on their Youth Training scheme staff.

In the aftermath of Heysel, two supporters, Rogan Taylor and Peter Garrett, set up the Football Supporters' Association (FSA). The main aims were: to improve the image of the game; to improve the standard of services provided for fans; and to achieve representation for fans at every level of the game. Jackie Woodhouse's survey of women spectators via the membership lists of the FSA was the first actually to elicit the views of women. The findings indicated that there was considerable and predictable role conflict between their identities as women and as football fans. Woodhouse found that female fans do identify damaging forms of sexism within the sport and that: 'The majority of respondents were in favour of the greater involvement of women as administrators, officials and so on in the game, due to the belief that this would be to the benefit of all fans concerned.'[9] However, some female fans express caution about making changes to 'feminise' male football and possibly call into question their status as 'real' fans. The main platform upon which Lord Justice Taylor built his recommendations was for grounds to be all-seater. They would be safer and would encourage more women and families to come to matches. Woodhouse found that less than one in five of the sample (18.3 per cent of the 285 respondents) agreed that all-seaters will be safer. She says,

> for some female fans at least, neither family areas nor seats are what they find attractive or exciting about football attendance. They favour the home terraces [the standing area at English grounds which is historically used by the most partisan and vociferous home fans] and do so probably for reasons which are similar to those put forward by many male fans with similar preferences.[10]

The theory behind the building of all-seater stadia was the assumption that seated spectators will behave in a more civilised manner and the attraction of women and children would create a family atmosphere, similar to the baseball and football stadia in the USA. In particular, it was thought the presence of women would have a calming and civilising influence on men. Subsequently, critics of this policy felt that the 'feminising' of football stadia, along with the increase in corporate entertainment in hospitality boxes, deprived grounds of their traditional atmosphere which was a male haven for lively behaviour – areas that have become famous at some large stadia, such as Liverpool's 'Kop' end and Manchester United's Stretford end. While in Woodhouse's survey '47.7 per cent occasionally experienced or witnessed behaviour deemed to be offensive, and 16.1 per cent said this happened regularly, over a third of the sample (36.1 per cent) said this was hardly ever the case'.[11] She also found that 'for some women it is clear that the "masculine" atmosphere is part of their enjoyment of the occasion'.[12] The research accepted that more women attending matches would improve the general atmosphere and behaviour of the crowds, but there was substantial doubt in the minds of many female fans about the desirability of this situation. The main concern was

> that this should not become defined as part of their 'role or responsibility' at football. Why should they have to 'risk unpopularity', it is argued, when all they want to do is watch the game? ... Many women then, may not actually wish to be a part of facilitating a significant change in the atmosphere of games, especially if, as some of them seemed to suspect, the aim is simply to attract more females to

matches to change the behaviour of men, rather than to attract genuine female fans to the game.[13]

It is the shifting of responsibility of collective male violence on to women.

Woodhouse's survey also found that 73 per cent felt that the football authorities and clubs could do more to attract female spectators to football and identified a wide variety of improvements which clubs could make. The lack of female toilets was identified by six out of ten respondents. There is a need for a greater variety of refreshments, rather than the ubiquitous fast-food and chocolate bars, a need for more club creches and active campaigning to combat racism, sexism and hooliganism. Also mentioned was the need for the clubs to acknowledge that female fans exist and have a role to play in the club other than as tea-ladies or club shop workers. The third most popular improvement the women suggested is that male attitudes towards women at all levels of the game need to be challenged and altered before any real progress can be made:

> Many female fans feel that the answer to encouraging more women to attend matches lies in an attack on the very roots of the game's culture, a culture which some see as a microcosm of gender relations in society as a whole.[14]

One female supporter from Middlesbrough is quoted as saying, 'The chaps are on the inside and understand how things ought to be, the lads are on the pitch and terraces, and women don't come into the equation at all.'[15] Although only 9.1 per cent of the sample had actually played football, and only 25.6 per cent had been to watch a women's match, several identified the need to increase the opportunities for girls to play football at school as a means of enouraging more women into the game, as players and spectators. Their suggestions also included that the FA should change their ruling which prevented mixed competitive football in schools (which did not come into effect until 1991 for the under-eleven-year-olds). Another popular idea by 64.4 per cent of the survey was for more men's League clubs to adopt women's teams. At the time of survey approximately 30 male clubs had established women's teams.

Undoubtedly the majority of the respondents felt that in the present male-dominated game, many men are either ignorant of, or chose to ignore, the views of female fans. A small proportion of respondents (10.2 per cent) were opposed to a greater role for women, preferring to see it remain run by men, for men. Woodhouse sees this as 'acquiescence' to a dominant male culture by a few, while others were concerned 'for equality of opportunity for females rather than for tokenism or some sort of quota system designed to "artificially" increase levels of female involvement in football'.[16]

When England's men's team won the 1966 World Cup, it is estimated that of the 93,000 crowd at Wembley, only 1 per cent were women. The *Daily Telegraph* quoted figures from the British Market Research Bureau which showed that between 1989 and 1994 the number of women who paid to watch at least one game had risen by 25 per cent to 1,041 million in 1994. England's dramatic semi-final defeat in the World Cup 1990 by Germany was watched by 25 million viewers in Britain alone, and 48 per cent were women.[17] The FA Premier League Fan Survey 1994–95, which involved replies from 15,170 Premier League fans, and included 1,924 female fans (12.8 per cent of the whole sample) suggests that female fans are highly committed. Almost seven out of ten female fans were season ticket holders (67.5 per cent), which was slightly higher than the rate for men (66.7 per cent). Also three-quarters of the women attend at least one away match and 4.6 per cent attend all, compared to 3.1 per cent of men. Over a quarter who started watching regularly since the change to all-seater stadia are women, which meant there were twice as many 'new' female fans. Female fans are generally younger than their male counterparts, with almost half being 30 years of age or younger, and 84.4 per cent of female fans watch football in a mixed group. The majority of women felt that the FA Premier League had been 'good' for women's football and they particularly liked the increased comfort and safety, although they were less happy with the widening gulf between the large and small clubs and the increased greed in the game. A larger percentage of women (55.5 per cent) felt that their own club is 'much more important' than the national team, compared to 47.7 per cent of men.[18]

In a *Guardian* article Laura Thompson highlighted the influence of the World Cup and the more welcoming environment of stadia since the Taylor Report, in attracting women to the grounds. She says: 'They [women] account for around one in eight of all supporters. And, of those who have started regularly attending Premier League games since the advent of all-seater stadia ... women represent one in four.'[19] She also acknowledges the powerful influence of advertising and commercialism and the fact that clubs have become aware of the new female market. The FA survey found that 20.6 per cent of women spent more than men (averaging £100 per season) on club merchandise.[20] While many men wear replica club shirts and leisure wear, much of the money women spend could be largely accounted for by purchases for their children. Another interesting finding from the FA survey was that less fashionable clubs were more frequently watched by women with the attendances at Sheffield Wednesday and Norwich accounting for 17 per cent of females.[21] Thompson suggests: 'These women are not there to make a feminist point, but because it is where they want to be. Their respect for the game is absolute and the last thing they would want to do is to force a change upon its essentially male nature.'[22] This accords with Woodhouse's findings to the extent that 10.2 per cent of her sample thought the game should be for men and that attempts to 'feminise' football went against the 'masculine' edge that they found attractive. It seems what women do not want is the sole responsibility for changing male behaviour.

Fans of the women's game

The two World Cup competitions for women's football in 1991 and 1995 attracted attendances of 510,000 and 112,213 respectively for the 26 matches. The two finals attracted 63,000 and 17,158 respectively.[23] Although the Swedish World Cup attracted fewer, the expected number was exceeded by ten per cent and all tickets were purchased, whereas in China many were complimentary. In China the novelty factor of women playing football probably encouraged more fans to attend, borne out to some degree by the fact that around 4,000 locals watched one of Germany's pre-match training sessions. The USA's national team achieves the largest regular following (around 6,000 for a top game), often resulting in a 'sell-out' at their college grounds. As part of the pre-Olympic Tournament build-up in 1996, the USA beat China 1–0 in Washington with 6,091 spectators, a game which also had live TV coverage. They attracted the highest home attendance of all, 8,975 when they lost to Norway at Jacksonville Municipal Stadium in Florida. However, the Olympic Final between the USA and China broke the record for a women's match with 76,489 at Sanford Stadium in Athens, Georgia on 1

August 1996. In Germany national team games attract around 3,000 to 4,000 and they achieved an incredible 22,000 when they defeated Norway in the European Championship final in Osnabruck in July 1989. Important international matches in Scandinavia and Italy attract nearly 10,000. There were 8,500 watching Norway win the European Championship against Sweden in Oslo in 1987 and 8,000 saw them defeat Italy in the 1993 final in Cesena.

Although Dick, Kerr Ladies' and Manchester Corinthians' games regularly drew significant crowds, British fans have not been attracted to the women's game in the huge numbers that watched matches prior to the 1921 ban. Approximately 2,000 to 3,000 fans now attend women's FA Cup Finals and international matches but the 1978 England v. Belgium attendance record of 5,471 at Southampton is still the modern record for the largest crowd for a women's football match not part of another event. The potentially crowd-pulling UEFA championship tie between England and Italy at Sunderland FC, in November 1995, attracted only 1,722 spectators, although 2,024 attended the one-sided 5–0 defeat of Croatia in the same month, at Charlton Athletic's ground in London. The 1996 UK Living FA Women's Challenge Cup Final attracted 2,122 to Millwall's London ground. Premier League matches normally expect around 100 to 200 spectators and these will usually contain more male than female fans.

Over the years the women's game has attracted the consistent and loyal support of many male fans. Some even say they prefer women's football to men's because it has a slower pace, reminiscent of the men's game before it became so professional and commercialised. Typical of the these male supporters is Julian Lillington, who has been following the women's game since the early 1990s. Sporting an England women's team shirt given to him by a player after he'd loyally travelled around Sweden, supporting the team, he told me, "I read about the Orient women's team in Leyton Orient's programme and started to watch women's matches instead of men's. Women show more commitment – they run their socks off. Men know they're going to get paid, but women do it for the love of it." Julian managed to get himself a press pass for the World Cup in Sweden on the back of his connections with the Orient fanzine and watched ten matches altogether. His press pass gained him access to the players and he was photographed on the pitch with Norway's captain, Gro Espeseth, just after she received the World Cup. He explained that he'd learnt to put up with the 'leg pulling' from his mates: "It's a great way to meet people and I enjoyed the World Cup. England did their best." He said he was looking forward to a new season of England reaching the European championship finals of 1997. Sadly for Julian, and for England, they didn't.

Today, there is more recognition of the potential in women as football fans and participants through men's football clubs. Changes have brought a more 'civilised' climate inside the grounds, and the growing attention to the female market has resulted in several professional men's clubs allowing women's teams to take their name and use the club's training facilities, transport and kit. However, if those involved in men's football, from professional down to local amateur level, are seriously concerned about developing more opportunities for women, what's required is a better understanding of their needs. By including females at all stages, whether as fans, players, administrators or directors, the game will not have to rely on advertising campaigns, commercially-driven exercises, or 'knee jerk' reactions to tragedies, to accommodate women's interest in football. Enjoyable as it may have been for women fans to sing the Euro '96 song, 'We're in this together', it is now up to the authorities to demonstrate that it wasn't just rhetoric.

11 'Goals and gals don't really mix' – the English media

'It's like a dog walking on its hind legs. It is not well done, but it is surprising to see it done at all.' Although Dr Johnson was referring to a woman preaching, it encapsulates the English print media's view of women's football and was used by Brian Glanville in a *Sunday Times* report of his observations on England's third official international match, when they defeated Scotland 8–0 at Nuneaton in June 1973.[1] Glanville's article conveyed the usual surprise that women can kick, dribble, head a ball, or even play football at all. As far back as 1922, the *New York Times* and *Washington Post* printed serious reports about Dick, Kerr Ladies' matches against men's teams in the USA.[2] Seventy-five years on, the marginalisation of women's football is still far greater in Britain than in many other countries, particularly the USA, Scandinavia, Germany and Italy.[3]

The print media in England have played an important role in how the women's game is perceived and media images continue to fluctuate from positive straight reporting to negative and biased carping. In general, men have controlled women's football and, concomitantly, media messages about the game have been distilled through male journalists; the era of women's sports journalists is relatively new. Reports of games have, on the whole, been patronising and condescending, representative of a rather insidious and implicit need for women's football to have the approval of men. This approval ranges from male administrators, managers, coaches and professional players; women have had little chance to be anything other than volunteer secretaries of clubs or leagues and rarely has their opinion, or the opinion of the players, been sought. Women's football has followed the trend in other sports of increasing its female participation, but has seen no equivalent growth in the proportion of women in influential and decision-making positions. With some notable exceptions, the media have managed to mirror this, thereby helping to reinforce some of the more hostile and prejudiced perceptions that have surrounded the game.

In the past even seriously-intentioned reports about the footballers usually included comments on the players' marital status, and whether they had children. Even today reports are written from 'the novelty of women playing football' perspective and their appearance, rather than their football ability, is usually observed. This is because, as Jennifer Hargreaves points out:

> Sportswomen are treated ambivalently – on the one hand they are newsworthy for their athletic efforts and successes, but because sport still poses a threat to popular ideas about femininity, readers are assured in various ways that they remain 'real' women. Similar procedures occur on television. The audience is reassured that *despite* their involvement in sport, they are still real women, an assertion backed up by reference to family, husbands, and children (the implication being that sport is a mere diversion) (original emphasis).[4]

Despite the globalisation of women's football and attendant media coverage, especially of European, World and Olympic championships, there are only a few media role models with the stature of Michelle Akers and Carolina Morace. In England, the current vogue has been for journalists to compare England players, such as Debbie Bampton, with male counterparts – 'Ooh-aah Can-to-na' becoming 'ooh, aah, Deb-or-rah'.[5] When Steffi Graff plays at the Wimbledon tennis championships, a reporter would be ridiculed for trying to assess her skills in comparison with those of Boris Becker. Sadly, this is not the case in football and these incorrect, commonly-held assumptions about 'women wishing to compete' with male players or to be compared to them, still persist.

Another perpetual problem is the use of inaccurate information about the women's game, which has come about through the lack of proper record-keeping. In the early days, the WFA had a volunteer press officer but after a few years the position was not maintained. Later the WFA used the services of a public-relations company, Scott and Jones, and they published a bulletin for the National League. By 1992 both the bulletin and the use of the company's services had become victims of the WFA's 'financial constraints'. When WFA records were handed to the FA, in 1993, they were incomplete and lacking basic information such as players' international appearances. Without accurate documentation it is impossible to learn from the past and the lack of knowledge has only served to encourage each generation of journalists to treat the women's game as a novelty or inadvertently provide incorrect and confusing information. Here are three typical instances. An England v. Italy match programme, for a game on 1 November 1995, credits Debbie Bampton with having played 'more than 70 times for her country'. In the roll call she is credited only with 13 caps gained since the FA took over the team in 1993. Pete Davies of the *Mail on Sunday* quotes BBC reporter Clive Tilsley saying, after England's defeat by Germany in 1994, 'Well, we've only been going for two years, haven't we?'[6] England had started their international team ten years before Germany. Liverpool's goalkeeper, Rachel Brown, supposedly became, at 15 years of age, the youngest player in a Cup Final in 1996. This appeared to be a media breakthrough as it appeared on the sports pages of *The Times*.[7] This statistic is incorrect because two Southampton players were younger: full-back Karen Buchanan was 14 when she played in the inaugural Cup Final in 1971; and Sharon Roberts was 13 when she played in Southampton's defeat of QPR in the 1978 final.

All publicity is good publicity?

Newspaper reports on women's matches did not change much from the 1920s to the 1950s. Always of equal importance to recounting the score, and sometimes vague information on how the goals were scored and by whom, was the obligatory reassurance that the team contained normal, married women, who were merely playing football as a means to an end – raising money for charity. Newspaper and magazine articles about Dick, Kerr Ladies bear out Jennifer Hargreaves's point about labelling girls as 'tomboys' when they play football.[8] The *Daily Dispatch* report in June 1946 of Jean Seymour's match for Preston (Dick, Kerr Ladies) says,

> Scorning dolls and girlish toys, Jean Gollin [Seymour] ... has always been a tomboy whose idea of a good time has been to play football with boys. Now aged 16 she has made her

debut as the youngest member of the famous Preston Ladies football team and scored a goal in her first game.[9]

It says nothing about her football ability. The *Northern Daily Post* even captured a wonderful photo of Jean heading the ball into a goal, of which any centre-forward would have been proud, and yet the newspaper merely calls it 'Practice at Preston'.[10] The national newspaper, the *Daily Sketch*, also used the photograph and reported her debut in a stereotypical manner by saying, 'She [Jean] always did prefer to play football even when as a child other girls of her age played with dolls.'[11] Another report of a Dick, Kerr Ladies' match, by the *Herald* in 1946, doesn't even record their opponents or the results. Instead, the short report, accompanied by a photo of Connie Lynch shooting for goal, and another of Frances Foulkes drinking a cup of tea, highlights the fact there is only one married member of the team, with the caption reading 'Twenty-one misses and a missus'. The report says, 'Wot, no lemons! Not for 22-year-old Frances Foulkes, the only Mrs of the 22 stalwarts who clashed at Glossop yesterday.'[12]

Matters peripheral to football would also figure in newspaper reports. These included the charitable cause for which the match was played, the guest of honour – who was invariably the mayor or mayoress – the civic reception attended, and the spectators. In its report of the Dick, Kerr Ladies' match against a combined English and French XI in 1947 the local newspaper in Hyde, Cheshire, includes a reference to the crowd of 5,000 containing a 'large proportion of women round the touch-line, and they were not slow to shout encouragement to both sides'.[13] However, some reports did compliment the skill of the players. A report on Dick, Kerr Ladies in the *Lancashire Evening Post*, of their 5–2 victory away to Weymouth says, 'The play of the visitors for the first 20 minutes was nothing short of sparkling. With graceful ease they swung the ball from one to another. Expert footwork and deft touches brought applause from all round the ground.'[14]

By the 1960s, with the setting up of autonomous, unofficial leagues, formal competitions had started to occur and there were new major competitions such as the Deal Tournament and the Butlin's Cup. These gave the press an opportunity to observe good matches but the game fell prey to the least desirable type of media coverage that sought to mock women's attempts to play. Typical at this time were photos of 'show biz' personalities, and professional male players, 'playing' against 'model girl' teams in aid of charity. Worse were photos of women 'defending' free-kicks with their hands protecting the vulnerable parts of their upper body – I've yet to witness this happening in a real women's game.

When the Southampton League started in 1966, matches were reported by the local paper with the usual comments about the players' appearance, information about charity matches and about guests of honour. *Goal* magazine provided Southampton with its first taste of national recognition with a team photo and the caption 'These Saints are real swingers.' It then managed to mix the twin ingredients of acknowledging the team's footballing feats, while reminding readers that women players should not be taken as seriously as their male counterparts. It recorded the fact that the team had scored 100 goals in 12 matches, but then made the inevitable connection with the Saints' men's team: 'Perhaps the style won't be that of Terry Paine, Ron Davies, John McGrath and Gerry Gurr. But there should be plenty to watch to keep the fans happy!'[15]

The contradictory attitude in the press to women's football is illustrated by the reporting in the *Daily Mirror* at the time of the Butlin's Cup competition in 1969. They provided a serious report of Southampton's 13–0 rout of Beecham Belles and included a photo of me scoring my tenth goal of the game.[16] Then the *Daily Mirror* was the perpetrator of one of the most damaging incidents in press coverage – the 'Joan Tench' affair. As the Mirror Group of Newspapers had sponsored the competition they wished to publicise the final between Fodens and Westthorn at Willesden Sports stadium, and to do so they contrived a photograph of Fodens' Joan Tench going up to head the ball and then finding her shorts around her knees. The caption read 'Soccer girl Joan loses her shorts in a Cup Final leap' and the opening sentence of the accompanying article said, 'This fine display of football skill has just turned into something of a let-down for inside-left Joan Tench. Joan may have lost her shorts, but she certainly hasn't lost face.'[17] This incident led to the WFA terminating their association with the competition the following year.

The press could not resist from indulging in this kind of 'humour'. When the FA Council were considering the lifting of the 1921 ban in 1969, sports editor of the *Daily Express*, John Morgan, reported it in the following manner:

> There was some formal tut-tutting over possible problems like ... What do we do about referees? (well, they couldn't

be women, could they?). What do we do about disciplinary measures? (well, can you imagine the disciplinary commission having to adjudicate on 'Who pinched Ethel's bra?').

He completes the article by imagining a manager of a team called the Aston Villa Amazons needing a new centre-forward: 'Does he go for a Twiggy-type [the pencil-thin model of the time] who can bang 'em in with both feet? Or does he go for Sabrina, that means 42–24–39, who can pull 'em in by the thousands? *Very interesting* ... and welcome' (original emphasis).[18]

By the early 1970s women were agitating for greater equality and this was reflected to some extent in the sports reporting. Also UEFA's instruction in 1971 that national associations take greater control of women's football may have prompted more awareness from the media that the game was being taken seriously in Europe. Sue Freeman of the *Daily Express* took up some of the issues relating to women's football by contrasting my experiences of playing in England and Italy. She welcomed the FA's lifting of the ban and expressed the hope that my transfer to Italy would mean that: 'British men will start taking women footballers more seriously.' But she also warned that some representatives of the FA would still not consider it a suitable game for women because of inherent prejudice: 'So, what it really boils down to is the old masculine argument that men like women to look like women – and they often don't covered in smudges, kicking a football about.'[19]

The attitude in the English press contrasted greatly with the positive images about women's football to be found in the Italian press, which treated the women's game with respect. Rome's *Corriere dello Sport* had regular reports on the women's National League matches, the international team, and general articles about women's football issues including reaction to UEFA directives. The comprehensive and informed coverage women's football received from *Corriere dello Sport*'s Gianni Bezzi was better than anything consistently found in Britain today.

The Italian press covered the story of my proposed transfer well, and I was interviewed by the Milan-based monthly news magazine *L'Europea*, which included three full-page colour action photographs.[20] All the English tabloids exaggerated my transfer, emphasising the 'professional' deal by suggesting I would be earning as much as £100 a week, and living a life of glamorous luxury in Rome. Harry Miller's report in the *Daily Mirror* was typical:

> Britain's first girl export to the land of lira and lavish living made her debut for Real Torino over the weekend but didn't really enjoy it. Even Denis Law, Jimmy Greaves and Joe Baker [British professional players who had all played in Italy several years earlier] took many stormy months and matches to come to that conclusion ... We wouldn't bet on it but right now the odds look against Sue making a similar mistake to Law, Greaves, and Baker, who were lured to Italy by big lira offers.[21]

Not only was this report inaccurate, the exaggerated claims it made about my earnings could have jeopardised my playing future in England.

Serious competition

The press and television had an ideal opportunity to observe women's football properly in the first WFA Cup Final in May 1971 between Southampton and Stewarton and Thistle. Unfortunately a photographer from the local *Echo* insisted on a pre-Cup Final photo of Lesley Lloyd putting on her shirt and captain's armband, and managed to include a glimpse of her bra, which did not go down well with Lesley or her husband, Graham.[22] Furthermore, on the day of the Cup Final, our manager was troubled by a reporter looking for a 'story' about lesbians in the team. The reporter was disappointed when he found that most of the team had husbands and boyfriends who were at the match supporting them, as they had all season.

Surprisingly perhaps, it was the male football magazines that took the first WFA Cup Final seriously. *Goal* magazine had two pages of photos of Southampton's victory, and *Striker* magazine, despite the headline 'Girls will be boys', carried photos of the team with the Cup and information on the game's development in England and Italy. The reporter Bob Dawbarn admitted that until this match he had been sceptical about women's football: 'There are those who think that girls charging around a muddy football pitch is in some way rather disgusting. I must admit I had a few doubts myself. But that was before I saw the real stuff ... and I was impressed.' He went on to say he found the final: 'entertaining and often good football and the standard of heading was far higher than you would see in almost any male park football ... movements were built up with real artistry and many of them finished with really hard shots'.[23]

The establishment of an international team in 1972 provided the media with an opportunity to observe the best players in England and Europe. Pre-match publicity and match reports of the games were in some cases straightforward. However, there was still trivialisation and it was around this time I had direct experience of how manipulative the press could be. After I'd returned from playing in Italy a reporter from *Titbits* magazine telephoned and asked for my opinions on playing football, especially about any problems concerned with having a male manager. I certainly didn't give the reporter any reason to print the kind of 'story' that emerged some weeks later. He obtained a photograph of me and juxtaposed it with one of a man surrounded by adoring women in provocative poses, masquerading as footballers in a changing room with their manager. The article suggested that women's football was becoming a scenario in which players and managers had more on their mind than football. This was a memorable and unpleasant lesson in the print media's ability wilfully to exploit individuals for their own ends.

It was particularly disheartening that Brian Glanville, who had previously been so positive about women's football, cast his doubts about it in his report in the *Sunday Times* on England's third international, headlined 'Goals and gals don't really mix'. He used blatant chauvinistic comments about the players' technical inadequacies, and appearance, saying, 'A couple of English players ... both blonde, used their heads efficiently, but in general the only adequate word to characterise proceedings was scrappy.' There is little comment about the actual match, and instead he goes off at a tangent, making disparaging comments: 'One's chief doubt about women's football is the same one has about Women's Lib itself; the most insidious triumph of the male-dominated society is that it has lured women into pursuing masculine goals.' He concludes by saying that he doubted if anyone paying to see a women's football match for the first time would be induced to pay again and that it has 'never taken wing largely for physiological reasons ... Without it [physical strength] the ball cannot be kicked crisply and cleanly, and the consequence is an infinity of inchoate play in no man's land.'[24]

Despite Glanville's sceptical attitude, some reporters, such as David Wright of *Goal* magazine, felt the game had turned a corner for women's football. In an article headlined 'Men only? Don't you believe it ... the game now being played by the fair sex isn't a joke', he gives an extremely positive report about England and the game's progress both here and abroad.[25] The disparity in the descriptions of the same match between Glanville and Wright highlights the difficulties women's football had in being taken seriously. In the same article in *Goal* magazine, John Adams, England's manager at this time, said, 'Women's football will, in the next 15 months, become the fastest-growing sport of all in terms of participation.' This observation took 20 years to come true.

Recent years

Press coverage has improved. The *Sunday Times* provided outstanding promotion when the England team won the 'Sports Team of the Year' award after their success in the 1988 'Little World Cup' in Italy and Andrew Longmore had written some very good articles in *The Times*. Nevertheless, Jeff Powell's article for the *Daily Mail* in 1996, where he berates FIFA's general secretary Joseph S. Blatter for saying that 'by 2010 women's football will be as important as the men's', illustrates that women's football still has some way to go in terms of press acceptability. Powell is clearly worried:

> I'm not totally unaware that some of the lasses have been strapping on the shinpads and getting stuck into each other for a few years now. Nor do I subscribe to the prejudice rife in many a hidebound bastion of the game that these girls may not be the most feline of creatures. It's just that I don't want them getting too big for their boots, nor for their size ten dresses. It's just that suddenly, in football, they're everywhere.[26]

The press also continue to emphasise the personal aspects of a woman footballer's life. In 1996 the *Islington Gazette* reported Marieanne Spacey's pregnancy with the headline 'Their striker's in the club!' and manager Vic Akers uttered the hackneyed: 'Pregnancies are something that most football managers don't have to think about.'[27]

In the last 20 years we have seen the emergence of a few more women sports journalists. In a survey (carried out for this book in 1996) of 63 national and regional newspapers, there were 550 full-time male sports reporters, not including freelance contributors, and 20 full-time female reporters, including women sub-editors who also did reporting. There were approximately 43 freelance women sports writers and sometimes women feature writers were brought in to cover special events. In nearly all the papers, the women sports reporters covered sport in general and were not necessarily designated to cover women's sports. There were a few women with specialist subjects such as football, rugby, motor racing, athletics, gymnastics and showjumping. Most sports desks said they would welcome more contributions from women. They said they would send either a man or a woman to report on women's football but the lack of women reporters inevitably meant it was a male reporter. Most regional newspapers said they did cover women's football, especially if the local team had reached a high position in the local or national leagues. Some also cover girls' football in schools. National newspapers tend to cover major events only, such as the Women's World Cup Final. The *Daily Star* newspaper has sponsored Arsenal's women's team for several years and reports regularly on their matches and other National League results.

All the quality papers have women feature writers. For example the *Telegraph* has Sue Mott and Sarah Edworthy, plus a number of other women covering specific sports, and the *Sunday Telegraph* has Julie Welch. Julie Welch, who was writing for the *Sunday Times* in the 1980s, was one of the first female reporters of men's football. Olivia Blair writes on football for the *Independent* and Amy Lindsey is a football journalist for the *Observer*. Sally Jones, the *Observer*'s tennis reporter, has also covered football and in 1994 she noted that: 'One of the top three showcase games of the women's soccer season [the League Cup Final] is turning out to be one of the best-kept secrets of the year.' She went on to provide good pre-match information on the final, based on an interview with Marieanne Spacey.[28] Clearly, it would help improve the print media's attitude if we had more women reporting and more women commenting on the women's game.

Television

TV, on the whole, though slow to pick up on women's football, has been favourable in its coverage. The first TV reports of the WFA

Cup Final results were in the 1970s. They were announced on the BBC's Sunday-evening news. It was the BBC, too, who televised recorded highlights of Southampton's 2–1 defeat of QPR in the 1976 Cup Final. Highlights of the repeat team final the following year, at Dulwich Hamlet, were shown prior to BBC's live coverage of the men's Cup Final a week later. Unfortunately, this breakthrough into TV was not sustained in the ensuing years and it wasn't until 1989 that Channel Four started to provide regular and excellent coverage of women's football, including the WFA Cup competition and some England matches. This was presented by Hazel Irvine, who had become one of the first television reporters of men's football in Scotland. Sadly, Channel Four pulled out from covering the 1992–93 season and Sky TV has taken up where Channel Four left off. Through their *UK Living* programme, they sponsor the competition and televise the final live. Eleanor Oldroyd presented the broadcast of the 1996 UK Living Women's FA Cup Final between Croydon and Liverpool, watched by one million viewers. Eleanor teamed up with the BBC's John Helm and Sue Law to provide the commentary. Sue Law (an ex-player for Millwall, Bromley and England) was able to provide a welcome and informed opinion on the game. Some players, who viewed the 1996 coverage of the final, said they preferred the Channel Four format that also included highlights of the later rounds of the competition. Additionally, they wished to edit out the general advertisement for Reebok sports gear that was clearly aimed at a male rather than a female audience. It's surprising that neither Reebok, nor Adidas (with their 'Equipment Real' women's boot), thought to promote their products specifically to women.

Documentary programmes about women's football have been few and far between. Southern Television's *Nice one Sue ...* in 1978 was the first and the best yet produced. In January 1987 the BBC broadcast a documentary, *Home and Away*, about the 'drain' of talented women players abroad. It featured Kerry Davis and Debbie Bampton, who according to the programme had both gone to Italy to seek a higher standard of game, and reputedly earned £150 per week. Inevitably, without any serious football research, the programme gave the impression that this was a new phenomenon and failed to mention that it had happened in the 1970s with myself and a number of other players.

On 3 January 1995, the BBC televised a documentary film by Paul Pierrot about the Doncaster Belles, *The Belles*, that unfortunately concentrated more on the off-the-field activities than on the actual football played. It wasn't surprising, therefore, as Pete Davies records in his book about the team, that they received a letter from the FA's chief executive, Graham Kelly, warning them not to repeat what in the FA's opinion had been 'regrettable in its content and timing, unacceptable for its language and behaviour, and a disincentive to parents and teachers'.[29] Some of the Doncaster players told me, after their game with Everton in November 1995, that they thought any unpalatable parts would be edited out. The Doncaster Belles, with several international players, have become the team to which others aspire, and certainly many associated with the game were dismayed that all the positive images emanating from the media in recent years had been undermined. The BBC's Pat Gregory, who also sits on the FA's women's committee, said that as far as she knew, it wasn't the producer's intention to show women's football in a bad light. She added,

> The BBC might have concentrated a bit more on the football rather than the celebration ... but that doesn't take away the fact that Doncaster were extremely naive in the way they behaved, knowing that the cameras were there ... There was an opportunity to portray the club as a serious football club and you come away after months of filming with an impression that is embarrassing – it's really very sad and disappointing.

Not long after the programme was transmitted, Doncaster's Gill Coultard, who had recounted the story of an England player head-butting another, lost the England captaincy.

Fanzines and other publications

From 1978 the WFA distributed a regular official magazine called *Women's Football*, which conveyed information to the clubs, but it finished around the early 1990s. *Born Kicking* was the first women's football fanzine to be produced, by Jane Purdon in Newcastle, in the late 1980s and early 1990s. Its aim was to give a voice to women's football at the grassroots level and it raised issues such as the FA's role in the women's game. *Sunday Kicks*, a bi-monthly, first published in 1992 by Wilf Frith, was again an alternative to the official opinion. *Sunday Kicks* lasted until July 1996, with 15 editions. Wilf Frith now contributes to *On the Ball*, a women's monthly football magazine, launched in October 1996 by Andy Mullen and Joanne Smith. Tommy Malcolm produces a Scottish women's football fanzine, *Kick Off,* which he started in April 1995 and this follows the *Sunday Kicks'* format, although the standard of printing and reproduction is not as high.

To date there have been few books published on women's football in England and most of these have been mentioned, such as Gail Newsham's and David Williamson's on Dick, Kerr Ladies and Pete Davies's on the Doncaster Belles. Karren Brady, managing director of Birmingham City, has written two: her biography *Brady Plays the Blues* (published by Pavillion in 1995) and *United* (published by LittleBrown in 1996). Leicester University's Sir Norman Chester Centre for Football Research publishes occasional research papers. Since the FA's takeover of the WFA, *FA News* includes two or three pages of women's football news, particularly on the England team and the UK Living FA Women's Cup matches as does *F.C.*, the FA's bi-monthly magazine for football clubs and players.

Children's football publications

It wasn't just the playing of women's football that enjoyed its heyday in the 1920s, but it was the time that probably the first football book for girls was written. It was called *Bess of Blacktown – A Mill Lass Footer Yarn,* and it turned the real-life drama of the munitions factory women into what was described at the time as 'a thrilling drama ... centred on one group of mill girls in the north of England'.[30]

There were numerous football magazines for boys and men, reproducing images of the top male professional players. The *Tiger* comic, which started in 1952, featured a fictitious football star called 'Roy of the Rovers', which later became a complete football comic under this name, and Roy became the hero of many football-worshipping children, myself included. Hargreaves comments on how it hasn't changed:

> The hidden ideology is very powerful. In Britain, most popular weeklies are produced for 'all-boy' or 'all-girl' readerships and there is far less attention given to female sports than to male ones. The process starts early: in comics for young boys, sports, and in particular football, have a very high profile. Football is treated as an adventure, a way of

being 'macho' and 'one of the boys' in a 'separate' world of masculinity. Girls are never portrayed as playing football ... In marked contrast, in girls' comics sports have a low profile: some attention is given to 'feminine-appropriate sports' but they are seldom treated as a focus. They seldom portray girls' athleticism and love of sports. If there is an article on a minority sport like football it will be included as an occasional feature, highlighting its non-conventional aspect and marginalising the sport.[31]

Getting the media 'on-side'

The Sports Council's consultation document, 'Women and Sport', acknowledges the important role of the media in influencing people's perceptions and attitudes: 'The message clearly given by national newspapers and television is that sport is for men, and women play little part in the British sporting scene.' Its findings were that only 0.5 per cent to 5 per cent of total sports space in the national newspapers is devoted to women's sport and male football, horse racing and cricket predominate. Furthermore, the document said that traditional female team games such as hockey and netball, which most girls play at school, receive minimal coverage, and confirmed that women's football still struggles to get any regular media coverage. Over the years, it has tended to attract attention only for its novelty value.[32]

Jennifer Hargreaves also examined ways in which ideologies of sporting femininity and images of sexuality are reproduced in the media and act as a material force on women's participation in sports. In focusing on the under-representation of women's sports in the press and on television and radio, she says:

We receive a very limited and partial view because attention is given almost exclusively to top-level, competitive and 'feminine-appropriate' events, or to the sporting feats or aspects of the lives of sportswomen that are deemed to be unusual, spectacular, controversial or newsworthy ... in all countries in the West, men's competitive sports and idealized images of masculinity are promoted systematically in the sports media; in comparison, women's sports are marginalized and trivialized.[33]

The promotion of the women's game is now the responsibility of the FA's Public Affairs Department. Their professional expertise has provided a higher profile for the international team with quality presentation, such as the provision of a media kit for the Sweden World Cup. In conjunction with the sponsors, increased media coverage was also apparent for the latter stages of the UK Living FA Women's Cup and they produced a glossy pack containing a promotional video. The FA also spent £500,000 on an advertising campaign to woo women spectators to Euro '96. Recently the FA have produced a short overview of women's football in England containing some basic historical 'facts', participation figures, and a description of the structure of the leagues. They plan to provide several more information sheets on specific aspects of the women's game such as on its history, domestic competitions, and international play.

Perhaps the FA can persuade the media at large that they have a crucial role to play in promoting the women's game. One hopes that there will be a growing number of well-informed men and women able to convey positive messages about the sport. The indications are that the media responds well to women's football when it is staged and performed at a 'professional' level and backed up with accurate and current information. Robert Philip, for example, in the *Daily Telegraph*, was full of praise for the inaugural Olympic final in Georgia. He says,

> Baron de Coubertin ... Ron Atkinson ... misogynists everywhere ... can you hear me? Women's football is absolutely fabulous ... In a game of breathtaking skills (and quite refreshingly, in this cynical age, precious few fouls), America's triumph will serve as a massive boost for the game in this country where football has become by far the most popular college sport among middle-class females.[34]

He does, of course, in time-honoured tradition, compare the female stars to famous male players; Akers is 'the Pele of the women's game' and Mia Hamm 'the emerging Maradona [possessing] the elegance and balance of a ballerina and the kick of a mule', but the article is as positive as any ever written. Even Brian Glanville may have to admit, one day, that goals and gals really do mix after all.

12 'Boys *and* girls come out to play ...'

As well as the media's influence on women's football, there has to be some acknowledgement of other powerful socialisation agencies, such as family, peer groups and schools and their effect on attitudes to women's sports. Hargreaves highlights research that suggests that the behaviour of parents and other adults towards children differs according to the sex of the child.[1] In reference to women playing football it seems that paternal interest with a positive attitude and practical support can be instrumental in enabling girls and women to play and succeed. Many women football players in Britain have acknowledged the support of fathers as well as husbands and boyfriends, who have encouraged and helped them overcome the social stigma attached to playing a 'man's' game.

Margaret Thornborough, player (and later assistant manager) for Dick, Kerr Ladies in the 1930s, tells of how she contemplated giving up playing when she married, but her husband wanted her to stay on as he enjoyed following her around the country watching her matches. England's first captain, Sheila Parker, also received her main support from husband Malcolm, whose enthusiasm even led Sheila to say, "he was too supportive on some occasions", alluding to the fact that he wouldn't miss any one of her games. Three players from the original Southampton team married boyfriends who supported them during their successes of the late 1960s and early 1970s. One of those boyfriends, Malcolm, husband of Southampton full-back Pat Judd, illustrated his undying pride in his wife's football achievements when, in May 1996, he contacted the local *Daily Echo* and invited the paper to the club's twenty-fifth anniversary celebration of winning the first WFA Cup Final on 9 May 1971.[2]

Two of England's top players, Marieanne Spacey and Debbie Bampton, like many other women, admit that they owe much of their early progress to the support of their fathers. It was Debbie's father who went out and found her a team to play in when she was 11 years old and he has closely followed her career ever since. Many women who played in the first women's football league in Southampton in 1966 also owed much to their fathers, such as Daryll Holloway (Norman Holloway, Southampton manager) and Sandra Holt (Harry Holt, first Southampton League secretary) during a time when private, and public, support and approval were especially significant. Today, no woman player speaks more highly of her parents' early encouragement than the USA's star player, Michelle Akers, who frequently mentions their support and guidance in her public speeches.

Development and education

Girls in England are still channelled into stereotypical behaviour in sport, both at home and in school, which is reinforced through magazines and TV programmes. It is less of a problem in countries such as Germany, Norway, Sweden and the USA, which provide opportunities for girls to learn all games at a young age and therefore counteract any negative influences. Current England player, Karen Farley, can recall not being allowed to play football at her school in Ashford, Kent and eventually moving to Sweden to ensure her football career would develop. She says in an interview with Andrew Longmore in *The Times*: 'Here, my club in Stockholm has girls' teams at under seven, under nine, and under 11 and that would be the same in every town.' Andrew Longmore comments that in terms of her game 'she displays a physical self-confidence that marks her out from most of the England team'.[3]

The Theresa Bennett case in 1978 helped improve opportunities for primary-school-aged girls to play football. Twelve-year-old Theresa was banned by the FA from playing football with boys in a local league. In a court case, *Theresa Bennett v. the FA*, the FA's decision was initially overturned on the grounds that it had failed to provide her with recreation facilities, but the FA won on appeal under Section 44 of the Sex Discrimination Act (1975). Hargreaves believes the appeal by the FA was won because 'the judgment hinged on outmoded biological beliefs, that women have many other qualities superior to those of men but they have not got the strength and stamina to run, kick, tackle and so forth'. She indicates the fallacy of the argument by explaining that it meant that females, because of their physiques, should not be allowed to play against males, ignoring the fact that girls were often bigger and stronger than boys in the 5–11 age category.[4] The affair provoked considerable sympathy from the media for Theresa, and many other girls who were enthusiastic about playing football. Eventually the problem was overcome, when in 1991, the ban on girls playing mixed competitive football under 11 years of age was rescinded and the English Schools Football Association (ESFA) was charged with the responsibility of developing girls' as well as boys' football in schools.

The government's National Curriculum (1991) for schools requires that at primary-school age (for children 5–11 years – divided for National Curriculum purposes into Key Stage 1 for 5–7 and Key Stage 2 for 7–11 years) children play 'invasion games' of which football is one. The problem for girls is that they have fewer out-of-school opportunities to play football than boys. Boys' socialisation experience outside the school, and their tendency to practise games more at home and in the playgrounds, means they come to PE lessons more physically competent than girls. Therefore girls, even at this early age, may not experience equal opportunity. By the time children leave primary school, they will probably have started to play in single-sex teams, boys playing rugby, football and cricket, and girls playing netball, hockey and rounders (a summer game almost exclusively found in schools). Until recently, girls played these games only at school and football was not available. Furthermore, Hargreaves's research showed that primary-aged girls and boys often have sex-linked attitudes and abilities in sports and PE which are linked to their experiences outside school.[5]

Training the teachers

Even though, since the late nineteenth century, the playing of competitive games has been greatly emphasised in British schools, the training of primary-school teachers has not provided much instruction in football teaching. The problem has been exacerbated because the majority of primary-school teachers are female, with little or no background experience in the activity. Fortunately things are improving as a result of the government's 'Sport: Raising the Game – Document 6', which was produced in response to the prime minister's concern at falling standards in school sport and to the decline in the performances of English national sports teams.[6] The Sports Council, through its National Junior Sports Programme (NJSP), took on a central role in developing and implementing many of the policy proposals. The main objective of these proposals is developing sports excellence, especially in young people, through the use of Lottery sports funding. The NJSP provides a framework within which schools, local authorities, governing bodies of sports, sports clubs and youth organisations could work together to provide quality sport for the 4–18 age group in a planned and coordinated way. At the heart of the NJSP is the TOP Programme, jointly developed by the English Sports Council and the Youth Sport Trust. The BT TOP Sport scheme introduces several sports to 7–11-year- olds (Key Stage 2) by providing a bag of basic equipment for each game, including coaching cards and training, to aid primary-school teachers' delivery of the activity according to the demands of the National Curriculum. TOP Play (core skills and fun activities for 4–9-year-olds) and BT TOP Sport were introduced into 2,000 primary schools in April 1996 but did not include football. The FA has since become involved and BT TOP Sport football will begin in April 1997. The FA selected ten Advanced Licence coaches (I am the only woman Advanced Licence coach at present and was selected) to receive training from the Youth Sport Trust in delivering TOP Sport football. The idea is to pass on the training down to other coaches throughout the country. TOP Sport football is also a key part of the FA Teaching Certificate – Key Stage 1 and 2. The FA, in conjunction with the Physical Education Association of the UK, specially designed the Football Curriculum Guide, as the resource for this award and the FA Teaching Certificate – Key Stage 3 and 4 (years 11–16). Therefore, girls as well as boys will receive a better introduction to football and will be better equipped to develop their skills. This will particularly help girls involved in other Sports Council initiatives aimed at raising standards. One of these initiatives is the Sports Council schools' project carried out in conjunction with the Hampshire FA and with Berkshire & Buckingham FA. The Sports Council supports the two County FAs in providing trained, qualified coaches for primary schools' extra-curricular football coaching to girls and boys and development centres into which the young can progress. The initiative can also provide support for teachers in curriculum time, as well as help in finding 'exit routes' for the pupils into development-minded local clubs. Ajax of Amsterdam provides the ideal youth football development model which British clubs could learn from. Ajax staff carefully plan a boy's development from eight years of age into adulthood, and even involve the support of parents.

In 1995 the BBC produced six football videos for schools called *Sportsbank: Soccer*. The video and teachers' notes provided primary-school teachers with much-needed resources on basic football coaching as well as information on diet, fitness and sociological aspects of the sport.[7] The producer invited me to participate because she wanted children to see a female, as well as a male coach, teaching the game. A male professional player gave the fitness information and Arsenal's Marieanne Spacey and I spoke about the developmental needs of the game. The producer of *Sportsbank* had identified and filled a large void in schoolchildren's football development by being the first to provide material specifically aimed at primary teachers inexperienced in teaching football. Others have provided similar video material, such as the Adidas-backed *Schools' Football Initiative* video and guide, and the PFA have also produced a video pack.

Prior to 1993, the WFA used to organise an U16 11-a-side Cup competition for clubs and now the FA organises an indoor five-a-side competition. In 1995, the FA launched a pilot scheme in conjunction with ten county FAs to initiate small-sided local youth girls' leagues. This led, in Hampshire for example, to two local authority sports development officers taking the main responsibility for targeting girls, and with the assistance of the County Youth FA, two leagues were started. The FA started to fund the establishment of girls' small-sided leagues in 1996 and by the end of the year they estimated that there were 7,500 girls playing in 44 leagues with more leagues in the pipeline.[8] FA funding of these leagues has meant that the work carried out to establish them can be sustained with the necessary funding for venues, equipment, and training for volunteers in coaching, refereeing and first aid.

Since the ESFA started to take responsibility for schoolgirl football in 1991, they have been proactive in its development by introducing four competitions: the ESFA Adidas Predator, six-a-side and seven-a-side competitions (both with finals at Wembley Stadium), the ESFA Wagon Wheels five-a-side indoor competition, that started in 1996 (played at Aston Villa's Leisure Centre) and the Vimto Trophy. Since 1993 they have run an U16 individual schools' competition which took place in 1996 at Notts County's ground.

The FA is encouraging county youth sections and boys' football teams to develop girls' sections, but the problem is that generally, boys' team managers are fathers of one of the team, and it can be difficult for them to find time to organise a girls' team or find people to fulfil the girls' team manager's role. As Karen Espelund made clear at the UEFA Youth Conference in 1995, it is the responsibility for national and regional federations to give training and opportunities to former women players to fulfil girls' and women's development roles.[9]

Those county FAs, such as Hampshire, and other agencies which have been involved in local girls' football development, have shown admirable commitment, but as I found in a small research project for the Sports Council, the fundamental requirement is someone to coordinate it within a clearly defined, well-resourced structure in which not only participants are identified, but leaders found, trained and channelled into roles. The success of the Southampton secondary-school league illustrated this. As part of my Hants FA development role, I took on overall coordination between the external agencies, the local ESFA, education authority, and local authority sports development officer, but relied on two teachers to coordinate the schools' involvement. The Southampton district ESFA representative, Alan Fredericks, drew on his local knowledge of the junior schools to organise a girls' league, which for the 1996–97 season totalled 14 Southampton schools. Anne Harding, a Southampton Saints player for over 20 years, and holder of the FA Preliminary Licence award, coordinated the secondary-school league. Most of the secondary teachers were women PE teachers, keen to develop football, but it was Anne Harding's knowledge of girls' and women's football and overall impetus that was the key to its success. She was appointed in September 1996 as assistant Hants FA County Coaching Representative (girls and women) but her appointment, like others throughout the country, is voluntary. Full-time paid posts are necessary to allow effective development work. Fortunately for girls in Southampton, there are several experienced players who, along with parents of current players, work voluntarily to help in local development initiatives. Other women like Sylvia Gore and Jean Seymour also work voluntarily in developing women's football and many more could be involved through adequate training and funding. With local knowledge of girls' and women's football, they can coordinate all the local agencies and ensure that the expertise and resources are effectively directed according to actual local needs. Brighton and Hove Albion's Julie Hemsley has been appointed to take responsibility for girls' and women's football development in the Sussex area. Funds for the post are being provided by four groups: the FA, Sussex FA, Brighton and Hove Albion's Community Scheme and the Sports Council. It will be interesting to see whether this will become a model replicated throughout the country.

In the community

The FA held exploratory meetings with clubs and the county FAs in 1996 regarding their plans to rationalise the league structure, including bringing the ten regional feeder leagues to the Premier League into a more coherent pyramid system on the lines of boys' and men's football. The county FAs will then play a larger part. This should accommodate not only a better competition structure, but improved administration and communication within women's football and between men's and women's football, at least at the local level. Who will establish the leadership roles, and how, is as yet unclear.

The reaction of football authorities to disturbances at grounds in the 1980s was one of the reasons for the birth of the PFA 'Football and Community' scheme in 1986. One of its aims was to create better liaison with the community, especially children and schools. The schemes are operated by clubs through the Footballers' Further Education and Vocational Training Society (FFE and VTS) with the support of the PFA. Approximately 88 professional clubs are involved in schemes, plus a small number of semi-professional clubs and some FA county associations. The 1991–93 Football and the Community Development Programme Business and Action Plan had a target of 75,000 girls to be included 'through coaching and other football involvement' to be achieved by the end of 1993. Figures provided by the PFA in 1995 reveal that in fact 200,000 girls were involved in the scheme activities in total. Nearly 30 per cent of the total national activities of the scheme now involve girls. Increasingly, community projects provide opportunities for girls and women to play football at different levels on a structured development basis, in U12, U14, U16 and women's teams, in accordance with FA age banding recommendations. The message to girls is that professional clubs have begun to recognise and include them and it can only help in breaking down some of the barriers that have excluded them in the past.

Southampton FC, like most professional clubs, runs thriving courses that include visits from professional players. However, while talented boys can move into a club's Centre of Excellence, Millwall was, until 1996, the only club that had a centre for girls. There are 141 centres, catering for 9576 boys, in the country. Leeds United started one in November 1996. The Millwall centre is overseen by Millwall Lionesses and England player Lou Waller, who is one of the few female community officers. The FA requires Advanced Licence coaches at these centres and therefore Lou, who is a Preliminary Licence coach, has to employ a male Advanced Licence coach for the girls. Lou works at the club alongside Jim Hicks, who manages the Lionesses. Sue Law has the club to thank for her development into an England player. In the 'Millwall and the Community' booklet written by Chris Lightbrown in the early 1990s, Chris quotes Sue when she was with the Lionesses:

> I spend £20 a week travelling from Peacehaven to train and play with the Lionesses ... I needed the best possible training and play to secure my England place. No one else in women's football had developed a whole structure of coaches, and youth and reserve sides, let alone things like the physiotherapy we get from Millwall's physio. Millwall have done the work for women's football that the FA should have done in this country.

Southampton's director of football, Lawrie McMenemy, allows me to run popular 'girls-only' courses, with all the same benefits as the boys' courses. Talented girls can play for the Southampton Saints girls' team, but if their full potential is to be realised, they too need development centres. Preston North End is another club that offers girls opportunities that their famous predecessors, Dick, Kerr Ladies, could only dream of. There are weekly coaching sessions for schoolgirl teams and for the 1996–97 season, in conjunction with the Lancashire FA, a Girls' Football League was formed with 29 girls' teams in the U12 and U14 divisions. Preston North End women's team has also been entered into the Fourth Division of the North-West Women's Regional League. The next challenge will be for other clubs to offer the same Youth Training Schemes (YTS) to young women as they offer to teenage boys to prepare them for a football career. To date, only Arsenal have allowed women to join the YTS scheme (which was funded by Islington Council for approximately two years in the early 1990s but no longer continues), although they can, of course, offer them the opportunity to play for their Arsenal women's team only in the strictly non-professional women's Premier League.

Comparisons with schoolboy development

Girls in England now need a structure similar to that provided for the boys (or the girls in Scandinavia) in which they can progress. The ESFA provides a full range of representative opportunities for boys, from local school and district, right through to England from U15, U16 and U18. Many of England's top international players have developed through these international schoolboy teams – such as Bobby Charlton and ex-national coach Terry Venables. Every year one of England's schoolboy international matches is played at Wembley national stadium (with around 30,000 spectators) and programmes are printed comparable to those of the full professional England team. A publication 'Football in Schools' was circulated for ten years by the ESFA, but funding stopped in 1994, and now they produce a newsletter. Local newspapers cover schoolboy football comprehensively, with the weekend sports pages providing results, league tables and articles. Girls' football hardly warrants a mention, unless the team has won a competition or has been started as part of an initiative by the local authority or club. There are still no representative teams at any age level, apart from the senior England team.

When the FA took charge of women's football in 1993 they brought in two-year age banding in girls' football, in line with the boys' football (whereby girls' youth teams operate as U16, U14 and so on, and only at age 14 can they play for an adult team), but there are problems with this. Boys' and men's football has a strong and lucrative semi-professional and professional career structure which encourages boys to progress through the different levels of development. There is not the same incentive for girls to move up to join adult players with whom they are not familiar. One of the reasons why many girls play is for the social and recreational experience, and this is reinforced by the fact that there is hardly any girls' 'representative' football beyond a few league representative team selections. Therefore, at 14, girls prefer to remain with their peers in a youth team. Some are content to stay playing football at the recreational level but the potential international players need a proper structure, access to quality coaching and training, and competition experience. With no clear development path it is difficult for players to make the big leap from club to international standard and with no professional pay incentives it becomes hard for any recreational player to devote an extraordinary amount of spare time, regardless of how much they love it, to football.

Women's football at university level

The first university competition was a five-a-side one held at Nottingham in 1980 with 14 teams. It was won by Loughborough. Since then it has been won by Loughborough on six more occasions and by the following only once: Salford, East Anglia, Bangor (Wales), Exeter, Leicester, Leeds, Manchester, Marjon (Plymouth). An 11-a-side tournament was started in the 1988–89 season with 16 teams, with Loughborough beating Exeter in the final. Loughborough won this competition on three more occasions, and the other winners were Birmingham and Bedford. For the 1994–95 season university sport was restructured and the British Universities Sports Association (BUSA) became responsible for its organisation. As university sports programmes do not usually have large budgets one of the aims of the restructuring was to reduce travelling costs to a minimum. As a result, block fixtures operate alongside other sports in seven divisions in England. By 1995–96 the number of university teams playing in the 11-a-side tournament had risen to 89 teams in England, seven in Scotland and eight in Wales. The women's teams rely on volunteers to organise everything. Dr Colin Aldis is a volunteer who has played a large part in university women's football by starting the English university representative team in 1989. Trials take place to select squads for inter-divisional tournaments and from these matches, an English universities' national team is selected to play against Scottish and Welsh universities' teams. The 1996 Home International Tournament at Liverpool University was won by England, who defeated both Scotland and Wales by 7–1. Northern Ireland universities were not represented because of a lack of players. Several England international players have come through the universities system, such as Sian Williams

(Loughborough and now Arsenal) and the two Liverpool players Clare Taylor (Hull) and Becky Easton (Salford).

BUSA caters for about 50 sports at approximately 150 universities. Men's 11-a-side football has been in existence since 1921 and they have been represented as Great Britain (GB) in the World Student Games. Unfortunately, problems of funding, and difficulties regarding the issue of full 'representation' in a Great Britain team, were not resolved and a women's squad did not enter the first ever World Student Games tournament for women's football, held in Hamilton, Canada in 1993. The final, in which China beat the USA, was watched by 5,000 spectators. Russia was third and Chinese Taipei fourth. The other teams involved in order of final placing were Canada, Japan, Ontario (included to facilitate the competition's structure) and Australia. The USA team contained several of their 1991 World Cup-winning players such as Julie Foudy, Kristine Lilly and Mia Hamm. The fact that the leading nations, USA and China, participated in the tournament, represents another opportunity, and another level, at which British women's football could develop.

The problem for student sport is that it is poorly funded. Representative football teams have to look to various sources for help, such as the governing body, the Sports Council, the Football Trust and sponsorship. This means that a replication of the USA university scholarship system, which helps develop their talented women players – as it does China's – is unlikely to occur in the immediate future. An example of the funding some universities in the US receive is shown by the budget of the University of Connecticut in 1995, which was £142,000, although as much as 80 per cent was spent on the men's teams. South Carolina had a budget of £191,000 and coach Sue Kelly was hired at a full-time salary of £26,000. College teams and coaches in England can only dream of resources at this level – unless, of course, they make the dream a reality. Coaches and managers in the USA are wise to the pool of student soccer talent in Britain, and Trevor Warren, coach of Lockhaven University, recently recruited a talented young student, Georgina Adams, who was playing for the Welsh club, Inter Cardiff. In the USA, of course, the downside is that there is not yet a strong club structure for women to join when they leave college soccer.

Participation figures from the FA for the 1996–97 season show that there are 693 women's teams and 704 girls' teams with approximately 14,000 and 10,000 players respectively. Coaching awards gained by women were improving. In 1995, 251 gained the Preliminary award Class III, 476 gained the FA Teaching Certificate and 1,001 the FA Leaders award.

In wider British society, there is still much to be done to increase sporting opportunities for girls and women in general. Studies in 1995 by the Sports Council for Wales into the extent and nature of sporting disadvantage suffered by female participants had two major conclusions:

> whether it be in families, in schools, or in sporting provision in communities, girls are systematically disadvantaged in terms of sporting opportunities when compared to boys; that although the situation is changing in some respects, the long standing, general association of sporting endeavour with masculinity, rather than femininity persists.[10]

13 Future fixtures?

The struggle for women to play football in England has been long and tortuous. In 1996 two anniversaries passed. It was 75 years since the FA banned women's football and 30 years since the renaissance of the game in this country. In the Sweden World Cup report, João Havelange, president of FIFA, wrote about women's football's impressive debut in the inaugural FIFA World Cup in China and his pleasure in seeing, in the Sweden World Cup, the good examples women had set for players of both sexes in the spirit of fair play and dedication to offensive [attacking] football.[1] In *FIFA* magazine, general secretary Joseph S. Blatter discussed the momentum gained in women's football since the 1991 World Cup and, with over 100 of FIFA's 1991 affiliated associations regularly organising women's competitions, he made the encouraging statement that 'the future of football is feminine'.[2] Joseph S. Blatter joins a chorus of men in the modern era in England, from Norman Holloway and Arthur Hobbs to entrepreneurs, and many of England women's team managers, who have seen football as a sport that women can play with benefits to all.

UEFA's recommendation in 1971, that national associations take control of the women's game, provided the impetus for nations like Sweden, Norway and Germany to embrace the spirit of the request and truly develop the sport. Here, the response to UEFA's recommendation by the FA, and other agencies, was lukewarm and it took a huge effort and sacrifice on the part of individuals, like Flo Bilton, Arthur Hobbs and the FA secretary Denis Follows, to secure basic opportunities for women and propel developments forward. Although UEFA were slow to implement a European competition, this was put in place by 1982 and followed by FIFA's inaugural World Cup in 1991. These competitions have done much to enhance the growth of women's football around the world.

Theresa Bennett's challenge of the FA was important in that it highlighted the fundamental need for better playing opportunities at school. In the past ten years the situation has improved and since 1993 the FA have been more proactive in rationalising the women's leagues, providing better preparation for the England team, improved promotion of the UK Living FA Cup, and development forums for Premier League clubs. Other football authorities have helped too, such as the ESFA, PFA and Football Trust, and the Sports Council have helped finance locally developed girls' leagues. However, in spite of the new initiatives, the problem remains in this country that women's football is still essentially defined by men. In the first issue of *Women's World Soccer*, publisher and editor Roger Rogers commented on the attitude in England towards women's football:

> Unfortunately there has always been a poor attitude by many Englishmen toward women's sports and soccer in particular. It exists at all levels but particularly may be found in the upper echelons, including the ruling body of the English FA, who threw women out of their organisation for 50 years ... It has a distinct similarity to mad cow disease in that it is caused by years of ingesting contaminated material. In this case they have been fed the idea that only men can play and teach football because of their mental and physical superiority over women.[3]

An example of the prevailing attitude is summed up with the attempts to give the game more exposure by using women's matches as curtain-raisers. Women's Premier League clubs Wembley and Arsenal played in an exhibition game preceding the England v. Croatia men's match at Wembley Stadium on 24 April 1996. Wembley also played a six-a-side exhibition match prior to the England v. Netherlands Euro '96 game at Wembley in June. Was the motive for staging these matches merely to entertain the fans, and prevent crowd disorder, or to promote women's football? Should we not have progressed from seeking to gain acceptability and legitimacy, as the WFA did when the Central Council for Physical Recreation put forward the idea of Southampton and Manchester Corinthians teams playing promotional exhibition matches at the Wembley Pool in the early 1970s? Since 1985 the DFB of Germany has scheduled women's cup finals prior to the men's finals at the Berlin Stadium, thereby providing a *real* opportunity to promote the women's game. In England, when Newcastle and Manchester United opened the men's 1996–97 season, in August, with their Charity Shield match at Wembley, two regional league women's clubs with the same name as the men's teams but with little or no connection to them, played a curtain-raiser exhibition game. The partisan spectators were entertained but it was almost as though this was offered as a diversion before the business of a serious men's game commenced. Why couldn't Premier League and UK Living FA Women's Cup winners, Croydon, and League runners-up Doncaster Belles, have played?

As we approach the twenty-first century, there is less discrimination on grounds of gender, but as we have seen, in some countries women's opportunities in sport, and in football in particular, are not equal to men's. Crucially, Norway, Sweden, Germany and the USA have trusted women as leaders of their game. Here, it is particularly difficult for women to obtain genuine leadership roles and therefore to be involved in making decisions about their own sport. In the USA women have been strong in pressing for their rights to play and develop their game. Not only did the national team renegotiate their contracts but they also successfully lobbied to reinstate the women's U19 programme which had been suspended because of budget constraints. Compared to more enlightened nations, we in Britain are still striving for fundamental and basic rights. The game remains, to a large extent, the most junior extension of the man's game – a recreational pastime in which football is a reason to socialise and not to improve standards of play or performance. It's therefore not surprising that players are not sufficiently fit or tactically and technically proficient. The pioneers in the past enjoyed their game and probably survived because of the camaraderie it provoked, but their pride, passion and necessary determination seemed to encourage them to take responsibility for being fit and skilful, perhaps in the same way as some of the great men players did in the past, such as Tom Finney and Bobby Charlton, who as boys practised their football skills in the street. This echoes Jan Smisek's feelings that women would be better players if they discovered some of the passion for the game the former players had.

Today, opportunities to play have increased but it still remains difficult in this country for women collectively and individually to achieve high standards in all aspects of the game. Too much time has been wasted. Visionary leadership is needed to ensure that we coordinate all the agencies which have the expertise and power to make effective and swift progress. It is vital that we harness the experience and knowledge of as many ex-players as possible in coaching, refereeing and administration and, most importantly, fund training opportunities.

At least now there are role models in the women's game such as FIFA and UEFA administrators Karen Espelund and Hannelore Ratzeburg, coaches Tine Theune-Meyer and Gunilla Paijkull, referees of international standing such as Sonia Denoncourt, Ingrid Jonsson, Claudia Vasconcelos Guedes and Bente Skogvang. There's been a significant lack in the body of knowledge about women's football. Over the years the women's game has been sustained through the voluntary efforts of players, referees, coaches, administrators and supporters, both here and abroad. In recognising the achievements of those who have contributed to its progress, I hope it will give inspiration to women footballers to reach their potential and that football will become, before too long, *their* game.

Notes

Foreword

1. J. Hargreaves, *Sporting Females*, Routledge, London, 1994.
2. D. Whitson and D. McIntosh, 'Gender and power: explanations of gender inequalities in Canadian sport organisations', *International Review for the Sociology of Sport*, vol. 24, no. 2, Sage, London, pp. 137–50.
3. S. Scraton, *Shaping up to Womanhood: Gender and Girls' Physical Education*, Open University Press, Milton Keynes, 1992.
4. A. Flintoff, 'One of the Boys? An Ethnographic Study of Gender Relations, Co-education and Initial Teacher Education in Physical Education', unpublished PhD thesis, Open University, 1992.
5. This research is a qualitative cross-national project investigating the meaning of sport in the lives of women in different European countries. Interviews have been conducted with women who participate in football, tennis and gymnastics at recreational and top level in England, Germany, Norway and Spain. The project coordinators are Professor Sheila Scraton (England), Professor Kari Fasting (Norway), Professor Gertrud Pfister (Germany) and Dr Ana Bunuel (Spain).
6. L. Robinson, 'Images of women athletes: a content analysis of the British media', *Working Papers in Sport and Society*, University of Warwick, Coventry, 1993.

1 Invading the pitch

1. Information supplied by the FA.
2. Jennifer Hargreaves, *Sporting Females*, Routledge, London, 1994, p. 43.
3. Ibid., p. 145.
4. Ibid., p. 30.
5. D.J. Williamson, *Belles of the Ball*, R & D Associates, Devon, 1991, p. 5.
6. Gail Newsham, *In a League of their own!*, Pride of Place, Chorley, 1994.
7. Sue Mott, 'Belles of the Ball' in *On the Line*, BBC Television, 1989.
8. Gail Newsham, op. cit., p. 19.

 9. Ibid., p. 20.
10. Ibid., p. 23.
11. John Williams and Jackie Woodhouse, 'Can play, will play? Women and football in Britain' in J. Williams and S. Wagg (eds), *British Football and Social Change: Getting into Europe*, Leicester University Press, Leicester, 1991, p. 91.
12. Gail Newsham, op. cit., p. 45.
13. Ibid., p. 55.
14. Ibid., p. 61.
15. Ibid., p. 63.
16. Ibid., p. 116.
17. Ibid., p. 58.
18. Williams and Woodhouse, op. cit., p. 93.
19. Gail Newsham, op. cit., p. 60.
20. Quoted ibid., p. 63.
21. Ibid., p. 64.
22. Ibid., p. 135.
23. Ibid., p. 82.
24. D.J. Williamson, op. cit., p. 82.
25. Ibid., p. 83.
26. Williams and Woodhouse, op. cit., p. 93.
27. Tom Finney, in Gail Newsham, op. cit., Foreword.
28. Gail Newsham, op. cit., p. 76.
29. Ibid., p. 96.
30. Ibid., p. 112.
31. Williams and Woodhouse, op. cit., p. 94.
32. D.J. Williamson, op. cit., p. 87.

2 Post-war players and clubs

1. Taken from a local newspaper, Prescot, Lancashire (cutting from Sylvia Gore's scrapbook).
2. Cutting from Jean Seymour's scrapbook, undated.
3. Taken from a programme for the British Legion Memorial Building Fund (Hyde Branch) charity match on 25 June 1947.
4. Cutting from Jean Seymour's scrapbook, undated.
5. 'Women and Football, A Strategy Document'. An undated document published by the FA in 1995, p. 28.

3 Southampton – from local league to Italy

1. Cutting from Sue Lopez's archive material, *Southern Evening Echo*, approximately December, 1966.
2. *Southern Evening Echo*, 15 July 1966.
3. The *Southern Evening Echo*, 21 October 1966, gave the results and League positions for the first time.

4. T. Hart, *Book of Football*, Marshall Cavendish, London, 1972, p. 592.

5 Women's Football Association, 1969–1993

1. The provisional title is *Legs Eleven* and is due to be published in 1997 (publisher as yet unknown).
2. From notes provided by David Marlowe to assist my research, 10 March 1996.
3. Ibid.
4. John Morgan, *Daily Express*, 2 December 1969.
5. Detailed in a letter from Arthur Hobbs to the Scottish FA, 15 August 1970, where Arthur Hobbs says Denis Follows wrote to him on 21 January 1970.
6. Minutes of WFA meeting, 1 August 1970.
7. Minutes of WFA meeting, 12 December 1970.
8. Ibid.
9. Ibid.
10. John Williams and Jackie Woodhouse, 'Can play, will play? Women and football in Britain', in J. Williams and S. Wagg (eds), *British Football and Social Change: Getting into Europe*, Leicester University Press, Leicester, 1991.
11. Ibid., p. 102.
12. Ibid., p. 102.
13. Richard Faulkner's resignation letter to WFA officials, 7 October 1991.
14. 'Distaff cuts', *Sunday Times*, 9 December 1992.
15. Louise Taylor, 'Women find a place on the pitch', *The Times*, 12 November 1992.
16. The team was: Debbie Bampton (Arsenal), Sammy Britton (Bronte), Gail Boreman, Gill Coultard (captain), Tracey Davidson, Karen Walker (all Doncaster Belles), Kerry Davis (Knowsley), Sue Law (Bromley, now Croydon), Marieanne Spacey (Wimbledon, now Arsenal), Clare Taylor (Knowsley, now Liverpool), Lou Waller (Millwall Lionesses).
17. Clive White, 'Women's football: once banned by the FA, the code will soon be back in the fold', *Independent*, 19 March 1993.

6 The WFA Cup and Southampton's golden years

1. T. Hart, *Book of Football*, Marshall Cavendish, London, 1972, p. 591.
2. Wessex Women's Football League AGM Minutes, secretary's report, 3 July 1972.
3. Peter Batt, 'Dates have the order of the boot', *Sun*, 17 April 1973.
4. Frank Keating, 'Bridge of thighs', *Guardian*, 16 May 1977.
5. Letter to *Southern Evening Echo*, 16 May 1979.

6. Sue Buckett, 'Soton girls do it by pride', *Southern Evening Echo*, 5 May 1979.
7. John Williams and Jackie Woodhouse, 'Can play, will play? Women and football in Britain', in J. Williams and S. Wagg (eds), *British Football and Social Change: Getting into Europe*, Leicester University Press, Leicester, p. 99.
8. See Pete Davies, *I Lost My Heart to the Belles*, Heinemann, 1966, for more information on the Doncaster Belles.

7 The England team

1. John Adams quoted in, D. Wright, 'Men Only?', *Goal*, 18 August 1973.
2. R. Yallop, 'C'mon – you lovely lads', *Guardian*, 7 November 1974. He explained how the game in England depended on club subscriptions from the players. He mentioned a £1,400 grant from the Sports Council, and sponsorship of about £400 from Mitre – for their association with the national knock-out cup. It seemed some of this money may have been used to provide England players with proper uniform tracksuits, as this was the last international in which we wore own multi-coloured gear.
3. Jimmy Hill, 'Take a tip Revie – it's time to follow the girls!', *News of the World*, 10 November 1974.
4. The Scotland match was Southampton player Pat Chapman's first game, and she went on to gain a total of 32 caps before retiring from international football in 1984, with a European Championship runners-up medal.
5. John Morgan, 'You can call me a ladies' man', *Daily Express*, 16 November 1977.
6. A Premier League match, 28 March 1993, between Arsenal and the Doncaster Belles, played at Highbury, attracted a crowd of 18,193. The game was played before a men's veterans' match between Arsenal and Spurs and was a testimonial to the boxer, Michael Watson.
7. Kate Battersby, 'Mohr earns Germany first-leg advantage', *Daily Telegraph*, 2 December 1994.
8. The UEFA finals will be held jointly in Sweden and Norway in June 1997 with teams from Norway, Sweden, Germany, Denmark, Italy, Spain, France and Russia.
9. The FA coaching course structure changed in August 1996 and candidates' fees for the longer and more comprehensive UEFA 'B' Part 1 Certificate course, which replaces the old-style Preliminary Licence award, are more expensive but include instruction material which previously had to be purchased separately. The course also includes sports science modules such as fitness and nutrition. Candidates' fees for the Preliminary course were usually in the region of £50, whereas its replacement, the FA Certificate Award, costs in the region of £95.

The Advanced Licence still costs in the region of £620. Mini-soccer and FA initiatives, such as local girls' leagues, will of course benefit girls' football development. Although local girls' leagues are attracting financial support from the FA, there needs to be a comprehensive, well-funded development structure from grassroots to elite international level, including more women qualified in coaching, refereeing and first aid.

10. All Olympic representation is made by a Great Britain team, and not individually from England, Northern Ireland, Scotland and Wales. Therefore, if the four nations had combined to form a GB women's football team for the inaugural Olympic Women's Football Tournament, a precedent for GB teams would have been made and this would have had ramifications for other international football competitions, and could have endangered the existence of the English, Welsh, Scottish and Irish teams.

8 Lessons from foreign fields

1. Information for this chapter was supplied by: USA-based Women's Soccer Foundation quarterly publication, *Network*, with special assistance from Ruth Callard and Ann Moses; FIFA publications such as World Cup reports of 1991 and 1995; *Storia del Calcio Femminile (1968–1973)*, Roma 1974; Rainer Hennies (Germany), Thorsten Frennstedt (Sweden) and Joop de Graaf (the Netherlands), as well as Wilf Frith (former editor of *Sunday Kicks*, now news editor of *On the Ball*) and Colin Aldis. All of these people not only helped with information about their own countries but with material on other nations as well. Getting information on some national teams has been difficult. Certain individuals directly involved with their associations provided most of the information in their section, such as Inger Marie Vingdal and Bente Skogvang (Norway), Keld Gantzhorn (Denmark), Maureen McGonigle (Scotland), Helen Croft and Michele Adams (Wales), Niamh O'Donoghue (Republic of Ireland) and Chris Unwin (Northern Ireland).

2. *Women's Soccer World*, Jan/Feb 1997. *Women's Soccer World* is published six times a year by Women's Soccer World Inc, 1728 Mulberry Street, Montgomery, Alabama, 36106, USA.

3. Participants are: Professors Sheila Scraton (Leeds Metropolitan University), Gertrude Pfister (Frei University, Berlin), Kari Fasting (Norwegian University of Sport, Oslo) and Dr Ana Bunuel (Institute of Sport, Madrid). The project is funded by the four universities at which the authors work, as well as the International Olympic Commission and other sports organisations.

4. *FIFA Directory*, 1996.

5. Andrew Longmore, *The Times*, 9 June 1995, from Swedish press reports.

6. *Women's Soccer World*, Jan/Feb 1997, op. cit.

7. FIFA Report, 'Women's World Cup China', 1991.
8. Ibid.
9. Ibid.
10. FIFA Report, 'Women's World Cup Sweden', 1995
11. *Sunday Kicks*, June/July 1996.
12. Information supplied by Keld Gantzhorn, ex-coach of the Danish national women's team.
13. Information in this section generously supplied by German football journalist Rainer Hennies.
14. *Niedersachsen Fussball*, February 1970. *Niedersachsen Fussball* was the official magazine of Neidersachsen FA; today it is called *Fussball Journal*.
15. Eberhard Wittig, 'Damen-Fussball im Mommsenstadion', *Tagesspiegel*, 12 October 1957.
16. 'Endspiel England – Deutschland', *Tagesspiegel*, 3 November 1957.
17. *Niedersachsen Fussball*, May 1970.
18. H. Ratzeburg and H. Biese, *Frauen Fussball Maisterschaftern*, Agon Sportverlag, Kassel, 1995.
19. *FIFA* magazine, Zurich, June 1996, pp. 16–19.
20. Ibid.
21. Ibid.
22. Ibid.
23. Ibid.
24. *Niedersachsen Fussball*, undated.
25. Information supplied by Rainer Hennies.
26. Walter Seite, 'Women's football positive development! Adequate media acceptance?', *Der Sportjournalist*, July 1995.
27. Ibid.
28. Sources: early material on Italian league from B. Migliardi, *Storia del Calcio Femminile (1968–1973)*, Stab. Tipolitografico Edigraf, Roma, 1974; and my own archive material. The international information regarding pre-official European Championship matches obtained from my own archives and Martin Reagan, the England manager during this time. Official World Cup material from FIFA 'Women's World Cup China', 1991, Rainer Hennies and Joop de Graaf.
29. She was the third highest capped player behind Norway's Heidi Store, with 145 and Pia Sundhage, with 146.
30. 1993 European Championship programme.
31. Thorsten Frennstedt of *Nya Mal* Women's Football Magazine. *Nya Mal* can be obtained from Alegardsg 159, 43150 Molndal, Sweden.
32. *dieda*, August 1993, p. 59.
33. Information supplied by Joop de Graaf, a supporter of women's football in the Netherlands.
34. Information supplied by Lesley Boomer, executive officer, Women's Soccer Association of New Zealand.
35. Information supplied by Chris Unwin, vice-president of the NIFWA.

36. Information supplied by Inger Marie Vingdal, including Norway's *Media Guide* for the 1995 Sweden World Championships; and Bente Skogvang of the Norwegian FA.

37. The golden goal rule means that the team which after full and extra time, breaks the deadlock of a draw with a goal, immediately wins the game.

38. Pete Davies, *I Lost My Heart to the Belles*, Heinemann, London, 1996, p. 324.

39. Transcript of a speech by Karen Espelund at the fourth UEFA Youth Conference, Stavanger, Norway, 17 February 1995.

40. Information supplied by Niamh O'Donoghue, president of the Ladies' Football Association of Ireland.

41. Information supplied by Maureen McGonigle, executive administrator, Scottish Women's FA.

42. Doug Gillon, 'From Stewarton to the San Siro and Rose still gets a kick from playing', the *Herald*, 29 November 1992.

43. The *Scotsman*, 'Brown boost for women', 30 November 1992.

44. Thorsten Frennstedt, *Nya Mal*, interview 18 June 1995.

45. *Nya Mal*, no. 3, 1995, p. 63.

46. John Williams and Jackie Woodhouse, 'Can play, will play? Women and football in Britain' in J. Williams and S. Wagg (eds), *British Football and Social Change: Getting into Europe*, Leicester University Press, 1991, p. 100.

47. Most information in this section was kindly provided by the Women's Soccer Foundation (WSF) Network Publications, and WSF Directors, Ann Moses and Ruth Callard; April Heinrichs, USSF coach; Jan Smisek, USSF coach; Trevor Warren, head coach, Lock Haven University, PA; *US Soccer Media Guide* 1994 and 1995; the *Keeper's Line*, Issue 109, July/August, 1996.

48. According to research by the Soccer Industry Council of America.

49. Figures provided by the National Federation of State High Schools Association (NFSHSA) *1994–95 Handbook*.

50. According to research by the Soccer Industry Council of America.

51. NFSHSA *1994–95 Handbook*.

52. Information supplied by Ruth Callard and Ann Moses, Women's Soccer Foundation, February 1995.

53. Vinny Gill, 'Men coaching women – definitely worthwhile', *Soccer* magazine, March 1995. *Soccer* magazine can be obtained from 5211 S. Washington Avenue, Titusville, Florida, 32780.

54. *USA Today*, August 1994.

55. Vinny Gill, op. cit.

56. FIFA Report, 'Women's World Cup China' 1991.

57 'The future of football is feminine', *FIFA* magazine, May 1995.

58. Anson Dorrance, *Training Soccer Champions*, JTC Sports Inc., Apex, North Carolina, 1996.

59. Bobby Howe, 'Howe's philosophy' US *Soccer* magazine, Winter, 1996, p. 11.

60. Michelle Akers, 'An encouraging visit to FIFA headquarters', *Soccer International*, January 1993, pp. 14–15.
61. Michelle Akers, *Standing Fast*, due to be published in 1997, Integrated Resources, Bloomington, Indiana.
62. Mike Woitalla, 'Under tremendous pressure, DiCicco proves himself' *Soccer America*, 19 August 1996. Available from Berling Communications Inc., 1235 10th Street, Berkeley, California 94710–1508.
63. Ann Moses, *Network*, March–May 1996.
64. Marcus Schneider, 'Kristine Lilly – a lady amongst the men', *FIFA magazine*, April 1996.
65. Information supplied by Helen Croft, administrator, FAW.
66. Information supplied by Michele Adams, manager, Inter Cardiff.

9 Blowing the whistle

1. John Williams and Jackie Woodhouse, 'Can play will play? Women and football in Britain' in J. Williams and S. Wagg (eds), British Football and Social Change: Getting into Europe, Leicester University Press, Leicester, 1991, p. 105.
2. *On the Ball*, no. 2, December 1996.
3. John Williams, 'Lords of truth? Football refereeing for the 1990s, local findings and international trends', Sir Norman Chester Centre for Football Research, Leicester University, Leicester, 1994.
4. Ibid., p. 3.
5. Ibid., pp. 51–2.
6. FIFA Report, 'Women's World Cup Sweden', 1995.
7. Ibid.
8. With the exception of Sheila Parker, all the referees mentioned in this chapter have pseudonyms for the sake of anonymity.

10 Support from the stands

1. Sir Norman Chester Centre for Football Research, 'A History of Female Football Fans, no. 9, December 1995, p. 1.
2. Ibid., p. 2.
3. E. Dunning, P. Murphy and J. Williams, *The Roots of Football Hooliganism*, Routledge, 1988, p. 101.
4. R. Taylor, *Football and Its Fans*, Leicester University Press, 1992.
5. O. Popplewell, *Crowd Safety and Control at Sports Grounds: Final Report*, London, HMSO, 1986.
6. D. Canter, M. Comber, and D. Uzzell, *Football in Its Place*, Routledge, London, 1989.
7. John Williams and Jackie Woodhouse, 'Can play, will play? Women and Football in Britain', in J. Williams and S. Wagg (eds), *British*

Football and Social Change: Getting into Europe, Leicester University Press, Leicester, 1991, p. 103.

8. Jackie Woodhouse, *A National Survey of Female Fans*, Sir Norman Chester Centre for Football Research, 1991, p. 4.
9. Ibid., p. 4.
10. Ibid., p. 24.
11. Ibid., p. 26.
12. Ibid., p. 23.
13. Ibid., p. 23.
14. John Williams and Jackie Woodhouse, op. cit., p. 104.
15. Jackie Woodhouse, op. cit., p. 32.
16. Ibid., p. 38.
17. J.B. Kelly, 'Women to the fore in what was once a man's world', *Daily Telegraph*, 18 June 1994.
18. FA Premier League Fan Survey 1994/5, Sir Norman Chester Centre for Football Research, Leicester, pp. 15–16.
19. L. Thompson, 'A match made in heaven', *Guardian*, 21 September 1995.
20. FA Premier League Fan Survey, op. cit., Figure 6.
21. FA Premier League Fan Survey, op. cit., Figure 19.
22. L. Thompson, 1995, op. cit.
23. FIFA's Women's World Cup Reports, China 1991 and Sweden 1995.

11 'Goals and gals don't really mix' – the English media

1. Brian Glanville, 'Goals and gals don't really mix', *Sunday Times*, 24 June 1973. Dr Johnson's original comment was: 'A woman's preaching is like a dog's walking on his hinder legs. It is not done well but you are suprised to find it done at all.' Boswell, *Life*, vol. 1.
2. D.J. Williamson, *Belles of the Ball*, R & D Associates, Devon, 1991, p. 91.
3. Details of media coverage in these countries are included in the information about them in Chapter 8.
4. J. Hargreaves, *Sporting Females*, Routledge, London, 1994, p. 164.
5. Mike Ward, 'Ooh, aah, Deborah', *Today*, 3 June 1995.
6. Pete Davies, 'Sweet F.A.', *Mail on Sunday*, 16 July 1995.
7. Sarah Forde, 'Record breaker Brown finds secret of catching them young', *The Times*, 26 April 1996.
8. J. Hargreaves, op cit., p. 164.
9. *Daily Dispatch*, June 1946, cutting from Jean Seymours scrapbook, no precise date.
10. 'Practice at Preston', *Northern Daily Post*, April 1946, cutting from Jean Seymour's scrapbook, no precise date.
11. *Daily Sketch*, May 1946, cutting from Jean Seymour's scrapbook, no precise date.

12. The *Herald*, May 1946, cutting from Jean Seymour's scrapbook, no precise date.
13. Hyde local newspaper, 22 July 1947.
14. *Lancashire Evening Post*, 13 June 1946.
15. 'These Saints are real swingers', *Goal*, 21 June 1969.
16. 'Goal No. 10 ... for new Soccer star called Sue', *Daily Mirror*, 8 September 1969.
17. 'Soccer girl Joan loses her shorts in a Cup Final leap', *Daily Mirror*, 20 October 1969.
18. John Morgan, 'FA say O.K. to the girls', *Daily Express*, 2 December, 1969.
19. Sue Freeman, 'Up for transfer – a girl who lives for kicks', *Daily Express*, 21 March 1970.
20. Guido Gerosa, 'La Ragazza Centravanti', *L'Europea*, 27 November 1969.
21. Harry Miller, 'Sue will not be trapped into joining lira bunnies', *Daily Mirror*, 18 November 1969.
22. 'So what Arsenal! We won too!!', *Southampton Evening Echo*, 10 May 1971.
23. Bob Dawbarn, 'Girls will be boys', *Striker*, 18 September 1971.
24. Brian Glanville, 'Goals and gals don't really mix', *Sunday Times*, 24 June 1973.
25. David Wright, 'Men only? Don't you believe it ... the game now being played by the fair sex isn't a joke', *Goal*, 18 August 1973.
26. Jeff Powell, 'Sorry ladies, you can't win a man's game', *Daily Mail*, 30 January 1996.
27. Janine Derbyshire, 'Gunners are as sick as parrots ... their striker's in the club', *Islington Gazette*, 2 May 1996.
28. Sally Jones, 'Sweet FA from on high for a grand finale', *Observer*, 13 November 1994.
29. P. Davies, *I Lost My Heart to the Belles*, Heinemann, London, 1996, p. 205.
30. D.J. Williamson, op. cit., p. 93.
31. J. Hargreaves, op. cit., p. 149.
32. Sports Council, 'Women and Sport – A Consultation Document', Sports Council, London, 1992.
33. J. Hargeaves, op. cit., p. 193.
34. Robert Philip, 'Ailing Akers fights back to land blow for women's game', *Daily Telegraph*, 3 August 1996.

12 'Boys *and* girls come out to play ...'

1. J. Hargreaves, *Sporting Females*, Routledge, London, 1994.
2. Patricia Thompson, 'Looking back to the soccer glory years', *Daily Echo*, 10 May 1996.
3. Andrew Longmore, 'Farley's gamble paying rich dividend', *The Times*, 12 June 1995.

4. J. Hargreaves, op. cit., p. 153.
5. Ibid., p. 176.
6. *Raising the Game*, HMSO, London, 1995.
7. Sportsbank: Soccer, BBC Education, 1995. Information about the video and teachers' notes (ISBN 1 86000 009 6) available from BBC Education Information, White City, London W12 7TS.
8. *FA Magazine*, for football clubs and players, 'Girls come out to Play', issue 20, December 1996/January 1997, pp. 4–5.
9. Karen Espelund, UEFA Youth Conference, February 1995.
10. 'Changing the Rules: Women, girls and sport', Sports Council for Wales, Cardiff, December, 1995, p. 22.

13 Future fixtures?

1. FIFA Report, 'Women's World Cup Sweden', 1995, p. 4.
2. *FIFA* magazine, no. 34, May 1995, p. 5.
3. Roger Rogers, *Women's World Soccer*, Jan/Feb 1997.

Bibliography

Butler, B., *The Official History of the FA*, Queen Anne Press, Harpenden, 1991.

Canter, D., Comber, M. and Uzzell, D., *Football in Its Place*, Routledge, London, 1989.

Davies, P., *I Lost My Heart to the Belles*, Heinemann, London, 1996.

Dorrance, A., *Training Soccer Champions*, JTC Sports Inc., Apex, North Carolina, 1996.

Dunning, E., Murphy, P. and Williams, J., *The Roots of Football Hooliganism*, Routledge, London, 1988.

FIFA, 'Women's World Cup China', Zurich, 1991.

— 'Women's World Cup Sweden', Zurich, 1995.

Flintoff, A., 'One of the Boys? An Ethnographic Study of Gender Relations, Co-education and Initial Teacher Education in Physical Education', unpublished PhD thesis, Open University, 1992.

Football Association, 'The Blueprint for the Future of Football', London, 1981.

— 'Woman and Football', an undated strategy document available in 1995.

Green, E., Hebron, S. and Woodward, D., 'Leisure and Gender: A study of Sheffield women's leisure experience', in Sports Council consultation document, 'Women in Sport', Sports Council, London, 1987.

Hargreaves, J., *Sporting Females*, Routledge, London, 1994.

Hart, T., *Book of Football*, Marshall Cavendish, London, 1972.

HMSO, *Raising the Game*, London, 1995.

Migliardi, B., *Storia del Calcio Femminile (1968–1973)*, Stab. Tipolitografico Edigraf, Roma, 1974.

Newsham, G., *In a League of their own!*, Pride of Place, Chorley, 1994.

Popplewell, O., *Crowd Safety and Control at Sports Grounds: Final Report*, HMSO, London, 1986.

Ratzeburg, H. and Biese, H., *Frauen Fussball Maisterschaftern*, Agon Sportverlag, Kassel, 1995.

Robinson, L., 'Images of women athletes: a content analysis of the British media', Working Papers in Sport and Society, University of Warwick, Coventry, 1993.

— 'Women and Sport: Policy and Frameworks for Action', Sports Council, London, 1993.

Scraton, S., 'Images of femininity and the teaching of girls' Physical Education' in Evans, J. (ed), *Physical Education, Sport and Schooling*, Falmer Press, Lewes, 1986.

— 'Boys muscle in where angels fear to tread: girls' sub-cultures and PE' in Horne, J., Jary, D. and Tomlinson, A. (eds), *Sport, Leisure and Social Relations*, Routledge and Kegan Paul, London, 1987.

— *Shaping Up to Womanhood: Gender and Girls' Physical Education*, Open University Press, Milton Keynes, 1992.

Sir Norman Chester Centre for Football Research, Fact Sheet no. 5, 'Women's Football', Sir Norman Chester Centre for Football Research, Leicester, 1995.

— Fact Sheet no. 9, 'A History of Female Football Fans', 1995.

Sports Council, 'Women and Sport – A Consultation Document', Sports Council, London, 1992.

— 'Women and Sport, Policy and Frameworks for Action', Sports Council, London, 1993.

Sports Council for Wales, Changing the Rules: Women, girls and sport, Sports Council for Wales, Cardiff, 1995.

Taylor, R. *Football and Its Fans*, Leicester University Press, Leicester, 1992.

Whannel, G. *Fields in Vision: Television Sports and Cultural Transformation*, Routledge, London, 1992.

Whitson, D. and McIntosh, D. 'Gender and power: explanations of gender inequalties in Canadian sport organisations', *International Review for the Sociology of Sport*, Vol. 24, no. 2, Sage, London.

Williams, J. 'Lords of truth?: football refereeing for the 1990s, local findings and international trends', Sir Norman Chester Centre for Football Research, Leicester, 1994.

Williams, J. and Woodhouse J., 'Can play, will play? Women and football in Britain', in Williams, J. and Wagg, S. (eds) *British Football and Social Change: Getting into Europe*, Leicester University Press, Leicester, 1991.

Williamson, D.J., *Belles of the Ball*, R & D Associates, Devon, 1991.

Woodhouse, J., *A National Survey of Female Football Fans*, Sir Norman Chester Centre for Football Research, Leicester, 1991.

Key dates

1863   FA organise men's football in England.

1888   First professional men's league in England.

1895   Nettie Honeyball organises first women's match, between teams from the north and south of England.

1917   Dick, Kerr Ladies play at Preston FC's Deepdale ground, before 10,000 spectators, and raise £600 for charity.

1920   Dick, Kerr Ladies draw 1–1 in Paris against French XI.
    – Boxing Day, Dick, Kerr Ladies beat St Helens 4–0 at Everton's Goodison Park in front of 22,000 spectators, with 10,000 locked outside the ground.

1921   150 women's teams in England.
    – 5 December, FA ban women's football, refusing them use of affiliated grounds and deem football unsuitable for women.
    – 10 December, Ladies' FA formed with 60 clubs.

1922   Dick, Kerr Ladies play men's teams in the USA.

1949   Manchester Corinthians formed.

1955   Dutch Ladies' Soccer Association formed.
    – The Dutch FA, Koninklijke Nederlandsche Voetbalbond (KNVB) ban women from using grounds affiliated to the KNVB.
    – West Germany ban women from using grounds affiliated to the Deutscher Fussball-Bund (DFB).

1956   West Germany beat the Netherlands 2–1 in Essen, in front of 18,000 spectators.

1957   Manchester Corinthians beat West Germany 4–1 in the final of a four-nation tournament (including the Netherlands and Austria) at the Berlin Stadium.

1965   Dick, Kerr Ladies disband through lack of players, having played 828 games, winning 758, drawing 46 and losing 24. They had raised £175,000 for charity.

1966   Southampton League formed with seven clubs; the first league in England since the 1921 ban.
    – December, Southampton XI beat a Portsmouth XI, 5–0.

1967   Inaugural Deal Tournament organised by Arthur Hobbs.

1968   Unofficial Federation for Italian women's football FICF, formed in Viareggio.
    – First Italian championship – won by Genoa.
    – First Italian international v. Czechoslovakia.

1969   Deal International Tournament with teams from Czechoslovakia and Scotland.
  – Fodens (England) beat Hooverettes (Scotland) in final of Butlin's Cup.
  – November, English Women's FA formed (WFA) with 49 clubs.
  – November, first Italian tournament – Italy beat Denmark in the final.

1970   German FA (DFB) rescind ban and give official recognition to women's football.
  – WFA inaugural AGM, with seven affiliated leagues.
  – FA rescind ban on women's football and consider recognition of the WFA.
  – Southampton beat Hooverettes in the final of Deal International Tournament.
  – Italy stage unofficial 'World Cup' tournament, Denmark beat Italy in the final.

1971   West Germany has 1,110 teams.
  – Dutch FA (KNVB) take control of women's football.
  – May, inaugural WFA Cup competition, Southampton beat Stewarton and Thistle in the final.
  – June, UEFA Conference passes a motion requesting that all national associations take control of women's football.
  – November, FA recognises WFA as governing body of women's football in England.
  – Sue Lopez becomes first English woman to play as a semi-professional in Italian national league (for Roma).
  – Unofficial 'World Cup' in Mexico, Denmark beat Mexico in the final.

1972   First official England match, beating Scotland 3–2 in Greenock.
  – Two Italian federations unite with 46 clubs in four regional championships.

1973   Danish FA organises competitions for women's teams.
  – England has 298 clubs.
  – The Netherlands play first international match v. England.
  – Sweden play first international match v. Finland.

1974   First women's championship in Germany.
  – Denmark play first official international v. Sweden.
  – Denmark win the first Nordic countries championship.
  – First women FA Preliminary coaches (five).

1975   Sweden beat England 2–0 – England's first defeat since team started in 1972.
  – New Zealand defeats Thailand 3–1 in first Asian Confederation Cup Final.
  – Washington state in US forms a women's over-30 league.
  – Mexican player Esther Mora Soto, aged 16, plays semi-professionally in Italy.

1976   England has 300 clubs, 25 leagues.
  – Norwegian FA officially organise women's football.

1977   Hannelore Ratzeburg represents women's football on German FA committee.
1978   Norway's first official international match, v. Sweden.
        – Swedish FA take control of women's football.
1979   Italian Tournament with 12 teams, Denmark beat Italy 2–0 in the final.
        – November, England play Belgium at the Dell, Southampton, winning 3–0, with a record gate of 5,471, the first match to be played on a First Division ground since 1921.
1980   Germany has 2,457 teams.
        – Japan has 52 teams and 919 players.
        – Linda Whitehead appointed as first professional English WFA administrator.
1981   First German Cup Final, won by Bergisch Gladbach against TuS Worrstadt, 5–0.
1982   First German international match, v. Switzerland.
1983   FIFA instruct national governing bodies to take greater responsibility for women's football.
        – FA affiliates the Women's FA.
1984   Inaugural UEFA Championship finals – Sweden and England tie 1–1 on aggregate and Sweden win 4–3 on penalties.
1985   England win Italian Tournament.
        – Germany has 2,543 women's teams and 950 U14 girls' teams.
        – First women's Cup Final played at Berlin Olympic Stadium before men's Cup Final, FSV Frankfurt beat Duisburg.
        – FIFA consent to three Swedish women officiating Norway v. Sweden friendly international.
        – USA play first international, v. Italy in Jesolo, Italy.
        – Jan Smisek becomes first woman to obtain USSF National A Coaching licence.
1986   Italian FA incorporates FICGCF completely.
        – Sweden has first U16 international, v. Norway.
        – Chinese national team tours Europe.
        – Bente Skogvang becomes first woman to referee a Norwegian women's Cup Final.
        – George Mason College become champions in the NCAA Division 1 tournament in the US.
        – Canada plays first official international, v. USA in Minneapolis, Minnesota.
        – Norwegian delegation suggest a women's world cup at FIFA annual congress in Mexico City.
1987   Inaugural England U21 team started, play four matches and become defunct.
        – National League organised in Norway.
1988   FIFA's first invitational tournament in Guangzhou, China PR, won by Norway.
        – First Brazilian international match, v. Spain.

– Gunilla Paijkull becomes the first woman to coach a national team (Sweden).

– Tina Theune-Meyer becomes first woman to gain German FA Coaching Degree.

– Michelle Akers receives annual endorsement from UMBRO USA.

– Greek FA recognises women's football.

1989   Germany beat Norway in UEFA final – with 22,000 spectators at Osnabruck.

– Women's Soccer Foundation founded in Seattle, Washington.

– WFA Cup Final televised live by Channel Four with almost three million viewers.

1990   Sweden starts U20 international team.

– Germany introduces a north and south national league.

– Germany starts an U19 team.

– Marina Sbardella is appointed president of Italian Women's Football.

– Sue Lopez gains FA Advanced Licence coaching award.

1991   USA beat Norway 2–1 in inaugural FIFA World Cup in China.

– Claudia de Vasconcelos Guedes (Brazil) becomes first woman to referee a FIFA competition match in the play-off for third and fourth positions.

– Germany win UEFA championship beating Norway 3–1.

– Germany has 3,109 teams, including GDR teams, and 475,658 women and 45,371 U16 players.

– Hannelore Ratzeburg of the German FA serves on FIFA women's football committee.

– Nigeria forms a national team.

– Trinidad and Tobago play their first international in Haiti as part of CONCACAF qualifying tournament.

– Japan has National League with ten teams, and has 573 teams and 11,992 players.

– English Premier League starts with 9,000 players.

1992   Inaugural FIFA Seminar on women's football in Zurich.

– First FIFA women referees and referee's assistant list with 26 referees and 31 referee's assistants.

– USA start U16 and U20 national teams.

– Inaugural FA conference on women's football at Lilleshall Sports Centre.

– November, last England team under the auspices of the WFA lose 3–0 to Italy at Rotherham in UEFA quarter-final match.

1993   FA take over full control of women's football in England.

– China wins World Student tournament in Canada.

– FA of Wales take responsibility for women's football.

– Women's Soccer Foundation 'Links to Leadership' conference in Seattle.

1994   Norway has 2,383 teams plus U10 mixed teams and 28 years plus teams and 55,000 players – 40,000 are under 17.

– Ireland introduces U16 and U20 teams.

1995   Norway beat Germany 2–0 in World Cup Final in Sweden –
       17,158 spectators, refereed by Ingrid Jonsson of Sweden, who
       becomes the first woman to referee the final of a FIFA
       competition.
       – Germany beat Sweden 3–2 in UEFA Championship final.
       – Germany has 1,847 women's teams and 2,568 U16 teams and
       490,923 women players, 121,921 U16 players.
       – Sweden has 158,000 players including 120,000 U15 girls, and
       approximately 1,300 teams.
       – Hannelore Ratzeburg (Germany), Linda Grant (South Africa),
       Josephine King (New Zealand), and Marina Sbardella (Italy),
       serve on FIFA's women's football committee.
1996   Gunilla Paijkull (Sweden) becomes first woman to be appointed
       by the FIFA executive committee to a coaches' instructors' panel.
       – Karen Espelund (UEFA women's committee member) becomes
       vice-president of the Norwegian FA with responsibility for elite
       football for men and women.
       – Football becomes the most popular sport for females in Norway.
       – USA beats China 2–1 in the inaugural Olympic tournament,
       in front of 76,489 spectators.
       – Bente Skogvang referees the Olympic final.
       – Tina Theune-Meyer takes charge of German national team upon
       retirement of Gero Bisanz.
       – Marika Domanski-Lyfors takes charge of the Swedish national
       team.
       – Pia Sundhage retires after Olympic tournament with a world
       record of 146 caps and becomes Swedish coach for U20 team.
       – Anna Signeul becomes Swedish coach for U16 team.
1997   Lauren Gregg becomes first woman in the USA to be appointed
       full-time national coach, responsible for the U20 team, as well
       as assistant coach of the women's team.
       – April Heinrichs takes responsibility for USA U16 team.

Results

English competitions

Deal International Women's Tournament

1967	Dover GPO
1968	Manchester Corinthians
1969	Manchester Corinthians
1970	Southampton
1971	Stewarton and Thistle

WFA Cup

1971	Southampton
1972	Southampton
1973	Southampton
1974	Fodens
1975	Southampton
1976	Southampton
1977	QPR
1978	Southampton
1979	Southampton
1980	St Helens
1981	Southampton
1982	Lowestoft
1983	Doncaster Belles
1984	Howbury Grange
1985	Friends of Fulham
1986	Norwich
1987	Doncaster Belles
1988	Doncaster Belles
1989	Leasowe Pacific
1990	Doncaster Belles
1991	Millwall Lionesses
1992	Doncaster Belles

FA Cup

1993	Arsenal
1994	Doncaster Belles
1995	Arsenal
1996	Croydon

National Premier League

1992	Doncaster Belles
1993	Arsenal
1994	Doncaster Belles
1995	Arsenal
1996	Croydon

International competitions

UEFA Championship

1984	Sweden
1987	Norway
1989	Germany
1991	Germany
1993	Norway
1995	Germany

FIFA World Cup

1988	(unoffical) Norway
1991	USA
1995	Norway

Olympic Tournament 1996

USA

Most-capped players*

Pia Sundhage	146 Retired Sweden
Heidi Store	145 Active Norway
Carolina Morace	138 Active Italy
Kristine Lilly	121 Active USA
Mia Hamm	120 Active USA
Carin Gabarra	118 Active USA
Elisabeth Leidinge	112 Retired Sweden
Linda Medalen	111 Active Norway

Lena Videkull	111 Retired Sweden
Sylvia Neid	111 Retired Germany
Elisabetta Vignotto	110 Retired Italy
Gunn Nyborg	110 Retired Norway
Michelle Akers	109 Active USA
Heidi Mohr	104 Active Germany
Joy Fawcett	101 Active USA
Carla Overbeck	101 Active USA

* Information from *Women's Soccer World*, January/February 1997

Organisations

AYSO – American Youth Soccer Organisation
BUSA – British Universities Sports Association
CONCACAF – Confederation of North and Central America and Caribbean Federations
CONMEBOL – Federations Confederación Sud Americana de Fútbol
DFB – Deutscher Fussball-Bund
ESFA – English Schools Football Association
FA – Football Association
FAI – Football Association of Ireland
FAW – Football Association of Wales
FFE and VTS – Footballers' Further Education and Vocational Training Society
FIFA – Fédération Internationale de Football Association
FIGC – Federazione Italiana Giuoco Calcio
FSA – Football Supporters' Association
IFA – Irish Football Association Ltd
KNVB – Koninklijke Nederlandsche Voetbalbond
LFAI – Ladies' Football Association of Ireland
NAIA – National Association of Intercollegiate Athletics
NCAA – National Collegiate Athletic Association
NCF – National Coaching Foundation
NIWFA – Northern Ireland Women's Football Association
NJSP – National Junior Sports Programme
NSCAA – National Soccer Coaches' Association of America
PFA – Professional Footballers' Association
SAY – Soccer Association for Youth
SFA – Scottish Football Association
SNZ – Soccer New Zealand
SWFA – Scottish Women's Football Association
UEFA – Union of European Football Associations
USSF – United States Soccer Federation
USYSA – United States Youth Soccer Association
WFA – Women's Football Association
WSANZ – Women's Soccer Association of New Zealand
WSF – Women's Soccer Foundation
YTS – Youth Training Scheme

Useful addresses

For information on participation and refereeing in England contact your local county FA or the FA at Lancaster Gate (address below). The FA's Technical Department (formerly the Coaching and Education Department) is at Potters Bar and can be contacted for the following information: coaching and development of women's football; fact sheets on women's football; forming a club and advice on how to apply for financial assistance for initiatives in developing locally-based, youth female leagues. Most professional men's clubs, some semi-professional clubs and local authorities run holiday coaching schemes for girls as well as boys and should be contacted direct. County FAs and clubs also run mini-soccer centres. The Association of Football Coaches and Teachers (AFCAT) is an independent association for men and women involved in football at all levels, dedicated to improving coaching standards.

The FA, 16 Lancaster Gate, London W2 3LW. Tel: 0171 262 4542.

The FA, Technical Department, 9 Wyllyotts Place, Potters Bar, Herts, EN6 2JD. Tel: 01707 651840, Fax: 01707 644190.

Other useful addresses are:

AFCAT, Cathedral Chambers, Great George Street, Leeds, LS2 8BD. Tel: 0113 244 4566, Fax: 0113 244 3996.

The English Schools Football Association, 4a Eastgate Street, Stafford, ST16 2NQ.

FIFA, FIFA House, 11 Hitziweg, PO Box 85, 8030, Zurich, Switzerland.

The Football Trust, Walkden House, 10 Melton Streeet, London, NW1 2EJ.

The Professional Footballers' Association, 2 Oxford Court, Bishopsgate, off Lower Mosely Street, Manchester, M2 3WQ.

The Sir Norman Chester Centre for Football Research, University of Leicester, University Road, Leicester, LE1 7RH.

The Sports Council, 16 Upper Woburn Place, London WC1H OQP.

UEFA, PO Box, Chemin de la Redoute 54, 1260, Nyon, Switzerland.

Women's Soccer Foundation, 608 NE 63rd Street, Seattle, WA 98115–6545, USA.

Women's Sports Foundation, Wesley House, 4 Wild Court, London, WC2 4AU.

Index

Index by Judith Lavender